CONQUEST OF THE SIERRA

CONQUEST OF THE SIERRA

Spaniards and Indians in Colonial Oaxaca

By John K. Chance

University of Oklahoma Press : Norman and London

By John K. Chance

Race and Class in Colonial Oaxaca (Stanford, 1978)
Indice del Archivo del Juzgado de Villa Alta, Oaxaca: Epoca colonial (Nashville, 1978)
(with Douglas Butterworth) *Latin American Urbanization* (Cambridge, England, 1981)
Razas y clases de la Oaxaca colonial (Mexico City, 1982)
Conquest of the Sierra: Spaniards and Indians in Colonial Oaxaca (Norman, 1989)

Library of Congress Cataloging-in-Publication Data

Chance, John K.
    Conquest of the Sierra : Spaniards and Indians in Colonial Oaxaca
/ by John K. Chance. — 1st ed.
      p.   cm.
    Bibliography: p.
    Includes index.
    ISBN 0-8061-2222-6 (alk. paper)
    1. Indians of Mexico—Mexico—San Ildefonso Villa Alta Region—
History. 2. Zapotec Indians—History. 3. San Ildefonso Villa Alta
(Mexico)—History. I. Title.
F1219.1.011C44   1989
972'.74—dc20   89-40213

The paper in this book meets the guidelines for permanence and durability of the Committee on Production Guidelines for Book Longevity of the Council on Library Resources, Inc. ∞

For Julia

CONTENTS

TABLES

MAPS

PREFACE

MESOAMERICAN ETHNOHISTORY has made considerable strides in recent years. New and better sources, increased utilization of local archival data, and more sophisticated theory have forged a distinctive field of study inspired in equal measure by the disciplines of anthropology and history. One of the most important things we have learned from current research on the history of Indian Mesoamerica is a healthy respect for diversity—in culture, social structure, and economy, among other spheres. Even within regions that were once treated as culturally homogeneous—such as the Valley of Mexico—it is becoming increasingly clear that patterns or structures characteristic of one community may not apply to others located just a short distance away. Furthermore, the more we learn about social stratification and the nonelite populations in these societies in the pre-Hispanic and colonial periods, the more impressed we become with the social and cultural differences that separated the strata of nobles and commoners. Such considerations call into question many of the facile generalizations once made about "Aztec society," "the highland Maya," or "Zapotec culture," to mention just a few examples.[1]

Even greater uncertainty surrounds the lesser known, less developed societies of southern Mexico that were—and still are—peripheral to the major power and population centers. The inhabitants of places like northern and southern Oaxaca, Guerrero, or the Sierra de Puebla too often get lost in the rush as scholars flock to the more advanced, better documented, and more glamorous regions like the Valley of Mexico, the Puebla-Tlaxcala region, Tarascan Michoacán, the Mixteca Alta, or the Valley of Oaxaca.[2] Not surprisingly, when one of the "backwater" groups is given extensive scrutiny, it usually is found to differ from its more powerful neighbors in many important respects.

A fascination with the core societies of Mesoamerica has led ethnohistorians largely to ignore the periphery. If we are to remedy this situation, it is most profitable to assume, in the absence of concrete information, that the peripheral areas and peoples were *unlike* their central counterparts. As Eva Hunt suggested in her study of the late pre-Hispanic and early colonial Cuicatecs of Oaxaca: "Historically then, the provincial Cuicatec stood in relation to the Mexica [Aztecs] as the antiquated rural elites of Latin America stand to twentieth-century Washington and New York."[3]

The Cuicatecs were also a provincial people in relation to the Valley Zapotecs and Mixtecs of Oaxaca, differing from their neighbors in degrees of social complexity and stratification, levels of wealth, and concepts of property ownership. Still other regions of Oaxaca, particularly the northern and southern mountains, were home to other peripheral ethnolinguistic groups such as the Mazatecs, Chatinos, Triques, and Chontal, to mention but a few (see map 1). This book deals with five such groups that inhabit a large portion of the mountains of northeast Oaxaca. Three of these peoples speak languages of the Zapotec family—Cajonos, Nexitzo, and Bixanos Zapotec—while the other two, the eastern Chinantecs and highland Mixes, speak distinct languages of their own. In the Mesoamerican scheme of things, all of these peoples were (and still are) relatively poor and geographically isolated, produced few craft items for exchange, and participated little in the interregional trading networks run by such core powers as Tenochtitlan (the Aztec capital) and the various states in the Valley of Oaxaca. During the colonial period, the focus of this study, these five groups composed nearly the entire population of the Alcaldía Mayor (political district) of Villa Alta, the largest of twenty-one such jurisdictions that carved up what is now the modern state of Oaxaca. This book is thus about life on the outskirts of colonial southern Mexico, and the reader seeking accounts of the glories of high civilization and the riches reaped by the conquering Spaniards will not find them here. The peoples of the Villa Alta region were among the least advanced in Post-Classic Oaxaca, and though a few Spanish merchants and political officials did amass considerable fortunes for their trading activities there, Villa Alta remained a remote outpost that attracted few peninsular or creole colonists. It is one of the principal arguments of this book that we can learn much about Mexico, its people, and the periphery of preindustrial world capitalism by shifting our focus to precisely these sorts of regions.

This book, therefore, attempts a regional ethnohistory from the time of the Conquest until Independence in the early nineteenth century, a period of three hundred years. Though there were never many of them, the Spaniards of Villa Alta and others in Antequera (now the city of Oaxaca) and Mexico City considerably influenced the course of events and cannot be ignored. Political officials, merchants, and priests were the principal Spanish actors and their actions had direct, if sometimes paradoxical, effects on the Indian population. Until recently, studies of Indian societies in colonial Mexico tended to stress the cataclysmic events and institutions of the sixteenth century.[4] Much current work, however, pays more attention to the eighteenth century and suggests that late colonial Indian society was much more than a simple outgrowth or pale reflection of earlier years. Eric Van Young notes two important trends in late colonial Mexican Indian society: increasing internal social differentiation and the continuing resilience of corporate, land-holding peasant villages.[5] Both of these characteristics apply to northern Oaxaca, and a major theme of this book (especially in chapter 5) is to demonstrate how the resilience of Indian communal structures and status differentiation in the eighteenth century benefited Spaniards and Indians alike.

This study also seeks to contribute to the growing literature on regional differences in colonial Mesoamerica. Just as the Indian societies differed more among themselves than we have sometimes thought, the Spanish colonial policies, practices, and populations imposed in different regions were far from uniform. To take but one example, we now know that the colonial *hacienda*, once treated as a monolithic institution, in fact varied considerably in size and structure and in the impact it had on indigenous populations. William Taylor's detailed study in the Valley of Oaxaca has shown that Indian villages and *caciques* (native rulers) in that region were able to hold onto their lands and titles despite the attempts of local *hacendados* to control them.[6]

This book covers a different sort of region, one that lay adjacent to the Valley of Oaxaca but contained virtually no haciendas, few mines, and a numerically insignificant Spanish population. In the rugged Sierra Zapoteca, Indian labor was exploited primarily by Spanish political officials acting on behalf of urban merchants. Trade was the all-important colonial enterprise, and for the Indians it meant forced production of two key commodities: cotton textiles and cochineal dyestuff. The Spanish administration and politics surrounding the commerce in these items in Villa Alta and other parts of Oaxaca has been laid bare by Brian Hamnett in his *Politics and Trade in Southern Mexico, 1750–1821*. My own research has benefited greatly from Hamnett's study, and here I hope to flesh out the other side of the story: the social and political consequences for local Indians and Spaniards of this particular mode of colonial extraction. The picture that unfolds in the following chapters does not fit the established molds constructed for other parts of Oaxaca, though parts of it may apply to other peripheral Sierra regions of New Spain. In any case, amidst the growing variety of colonial strategies and indigenous adaptations it would serve no useful purpose to designate some regions as "typical" and others as "atypical." A balanced understanding of colonial Mexico can be achieved only through study of as many regional variants as possible—both core and peripheral—and the factors and mechanisms that combined to create and maintain them.

A primary goal of this study is to assess the impact of Spanish trading practices on the internal social organization of Indian communities. If the conclusions are to have comparative value, the relevant variables must be defined precisely, and in the present case this means coming to grips with a capitalist market system and an essentially noncapitalist mode of production. The Spanish-controlled market in cotton textiles and cochineal dye extended to both national and international levels, involving much of northern Oaxaca in the world market or, as Immanuel Wallerstein would put it, the capitalist world-system.[7] Yet the mechanisms employed to induce the Indian peasants to weave the textiles and cultivate the cochineal were based not on market principles or on wage labor, but on force. This amounts, I will argue, to a very special kind of integration into the capitalist world economy, one that was by no means unique to the Sierra Zapoteca of Oaxaca but that seems to have persisted vigorously there considerably longer than in other parts of New Spain. As I hope to show, this had very real consequences for local village life.

This book is conceived as an historical ethnography of both colonizers and colonized. But since the Spanish population, the subject of chapter 2, never amounted to more than a few hundred people and inhabited only one of the district's 110 communities, the emphasis throughout is on the Indians and their participation in a distinctive regional form of colonialism. Chapter 1 provides the setting and discusses what little is known about the area before Spanish contact. Chapter 2 deals with the Conquest, the founding of the Spanish town of Villa Alta, and its history to the early years of the nineteenth century. Population trends and settlement patterns in the Indian communities are the subject of chapter 3. Population counts and estimates are given on a village-by-village basis for several intervals between 1548 and 1970, and this is the only chapter which goes beyond the confines of the colonial period. While this procedure may seem anomalous, the ready availability of census figures for the nineteenth and twentieth centuries and the valuable perspective they provide on the colonial counts makes them too important to ignore. Chapter 4 describes the economy of the region with an emphasis on trade and marketing, while chapter 5 focuses on the sociopolitical organization of Indian communities, in particular of political office holding and social stratification. Missionization by Dominican friars and secular priests, together with the persistence of indigenous religious beliefs and practices, are treated in chapter 6. Chapter 7, the Conclusion, attempts to pull all the strands of the argument together and place this case study within a broader comparative perspective.

Most of the sources used are unpublished documents from various archives in Mexico and Spain. These are cited in full in the Notes and discussed at length in the Bibliographical Essay. One note on orthography: colonial spelling of names of places and ethnic groups varied considerably, so I have employed the most widely accepted modern spellings whenever possible. Communities that exist today are in most cases identified using the spellings found in the 1970 Mexican National Census.

John K. Chance

Tempe, Arizona

ACKNOWLEDGMENTS

I WISH TO THANK a number of people and institutions that helped me in the writing of this book. My archival research in Mexico and Spain was made possible by a grant from the National Science Foundation and three summer faculty research grants from Lawrence University. A sabbatical leave from the University of Denver in the spring of 1984 provided me with time to write.

In Mexico, Hugo Manuel Félix García and Benito Bautista Cabrera kindly granted me access to the Archivo del Juzgado in Villa Alta. I also received help and support from Manuel Esparza, then director of the Centro Regional de Oaxaca of the Instituto Nacional de Antropología e Historia, and Félix Villanueva, staff photographer at the Centro. Luis Castañeda Guzmán graciously made available his collection of documents, and Father Antonio Villalobos permitted me to study in the parish archive in Villa Alta. I also owe much to the staffs of the Archivo General de la Nación in Mexico City and the Archivo General de Indias in Seville.

Among the many friends and colleagues who gave me useful comments and suggestions at various points are Luis Castañeda Guzmán, Nancy Farriss, Bernardo García Martínez, Laura Nader, John Paddock, Philip C. Parnell, Rodolfo Pastor, María de los Angeles Romero, William B. Taylor, Cecil R. Welte, and Joseph W. Whitecotton. I am especially indebted to Woodrow Borah for his comments on an earlier version of chapter 3 and to Roger Reeck for sharing with me his unpublished paper on "The Languages of the Sierra Zapoteca" and for providing me with the base map of linguistic areas of Oaxaca (see map 1). Special thanks also go to Ronald Spores, whose wise counsel and support are deeply appreciated. Sharon Stiffler typed the manuscript and Shearon D. Vaughn drew the maps. My wife, Julia Hernández de Chance, worked with me in the archives in Seville and Villa Alta and has helped with this project in more ways than she comprehends.

J.K.C.

CONQUEST OF THE SIERRA

CHAPTER 1

INTRODUCTION

THE STATE OF OAXACA encompasses some of the most rugged, mountainous terrain in southern Mexico. The eastern and western cordilleras of the Mexican plateau come together in Oaxaca, forming a seemingly endless series of ridges dotted with a few high valleys. Populating the region's slopes, canyons, and valleys are members of fifteen major linguistic groups (see map 1), and these in turn are marked by numerous dialectical variations. Oaxaca has long been known for its high degree of ethnic and linguistic diversity, though many groups, such as the Triques, Amusgos, Chatinos, and Huaves, among others, have always been restricted in territory and population. Two large linguistic groups have long dominated the region: the Mixtec speakers, who inhabit most of the western portion of Oaxaca, and the Zapotec speakers, who are numerically predominant in the east. The central Valley of Oaxaca, home of the state's capital city, has been the major power center of the entire region since well before the time of Christ.

Mainly Zapotec until the centuries before contact, when portions of it came under Mixtec influence, the Valley of Oaxaca gave rise to the most developed forms of indigenous sociopolitical organization in ancient Oaxaca. Urban society with a full-fledged state organization reached its full flowering in the mountaintop Zapotec city of Monte Albán. This metropolis dominated the Valley and surrounding regions and is noted for its highly developed monumental architecture, bas-relief carving, a stela-altar complex, calendrics, and hieroglyphic writing. All these elements were to continue in the Valley until the time of Spanish contact, but Monte Albán was abandoned about 1000 A.D. and replaced by a series of small city- or town-states involved in shifting and unstable alliances. Warfare among these states became increasingly common; by 1521 Mixtecs had long occupied many towns in the central part of the Valley, and a small number of Aztecs had also arrived (perhaps around 1486), subjecting Valley Zapotecs and Mixtecs alike to tribute and bringing them nominally into the area of dominion of the Triple Alliance.

The Valley of Oaxaca is by far the most studied region of the state archaeologically, historically, and ethnographically. Much of what is known about Zapotec culture is based on sources and research pertaining to this core

3

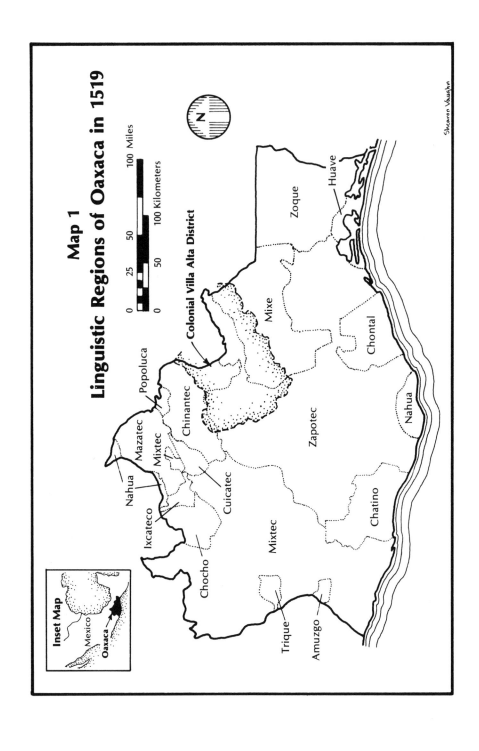

Map 1
Linguistic Regions of Oaxaca in 1519

area.[1] The periphery has attracted much less attention; the southern Zapotecs, for example, are very little known, as are most of Oaxaca's smaller
ethnolinguistic groups. As one turns to works on colonial history and ethnohistory, the picture is much the same.[2] Studies done in the Valley have
predominated and by default have come to represent the Oaxaca region as a
whole in the minds of many scholars.[3] (Research on the Mixteca runs a close
second.) By focusing on the Villa Alta district of northern Oaxaca with its
large mountain Zapotec, Chinantec, and Mixe populations, this study will
emphasize the distinctiveness of colonial society in the Sierra from the Valley
and other regions.

The steep slopes and deep canyons of the Sierra Zapoteca stand in stark
contrast to the flat alluvial plain of the Valley of Oaxaca. Just as the Spaniards of the sixteenth century found many of the native trails too difficult for
their horses and pack trains, most of the Sierra's roads today are negotiable
only by certain types of trucks and a hardy flock of buses. Many towns can
still be reached only by foot or on horseback. The area encompassed by the
colonial Alcaldía Mayor of Villa Alta (see maps 2 and 3) today consists of the
modern Distritos of Villa Alta and Choapan, the adjacent western part of
the Distrito Mixe, and a large eastern portion of the Distrito de Ixtlán. This
territory stretches from the top of the Sierra Madre down into the gulf
coastal plains, and the colonial district also included a small part of what is
now Veracruz.[4] Most, but not all, of this country is mountainous. There is
wide variation in elevation and ecology, ranging from the 3,396-meter peak
of Mount Zempoaltépetl in the Mixe zone to the *tierra caliente* (hot country)
of the Río de la Lana, which separates Oaxaca and Veracruz. In climate and
vegetation the region is like neither the plateau nor the coastal areas; on the
whole it is more humid and warmer than the dry central highlands (including the Valley of Oaxaca). Like much of southern Mexico, it receives most
of its rainfall between May and October.

It is difficult to contrast precisely the geographies of colonial Villa Alta's
five ethnolinguistic groups for there are large differences in altitude and mi-
croclimates in all zones. In general, however, the Mixes and the Cajonos
and Nexitzo Zapotecs occupy the most mountainous southern and western
parts of the territory. Composed of a series of high mountain chains separated only by deep canyons and narrow ravines, these zones form the most
rugged part of Oaxaca. Much of this territory is forested. Rivers that tra-
verse the area flow toward the lowlands of Veracruz and form part of the
Papaloapan drainage system.

The semiarid Cajonos Zapotec zone is by far the driest of the district, and
as one travels north toward the town of Villa Alta or toward the Nexitzo
zone the volume of rainfall increases considerably. The Nexitzo-speaking region, also known as the Rincón, or "Corner," is generally humid and temperate. The inhabitants say they are "cornered" by mountains to the south,

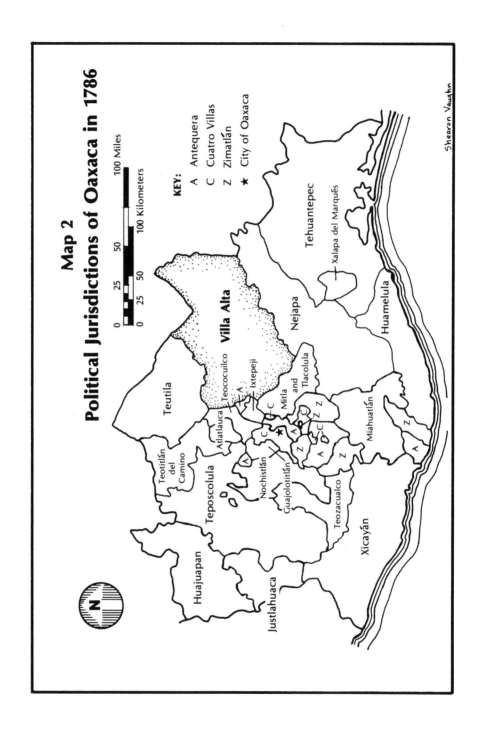

Map 2

Political Jurisdictions of Oaxaca in 1786

KEY:

A   Antequera
C   Cuatro Villas
Z   Zimatlán
★   City of Oaxaca

100 Miles
0   25   50   100 Kilometers
0   25   50

Teutila

Villa Alta

Teococuilco
Ixtepeji

Teocuilco

Nejapa

Tehuantepec

Xalapa del Marqués

Huamelula

Atlatlauca

Mitla
and
Tlacolula

Miahuatlán

Teotitlán
del
Camino

Nochistlán

Guajolotitlán

Teposcolula

Teozacualco

Xicayán

Huajuapan

Justlahuaca

Shearon Vaughn

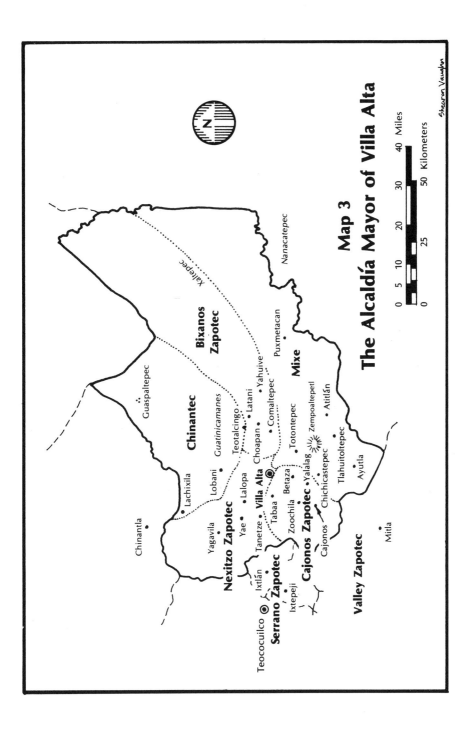

N

Chinantla

Lachixila

Lobani

Yagavila
Yae • • Lalopa
Tanetze • • Villa Alta
Zoochila • Tabaa
Betaza

Nexitzo Zapotec

Cajonos
Chichicastepec

Cajonos Zapotec • Yalalag

Teococuilco ◉ Ixtlán
Ixtepeji
Serrano Zapotec

Valley Zapotec

Mitla

Guaspaltepec

Chinantec

Guatinicamanes

Teotalcingo •
Choapan • • Latani
• Comaltepec
• Yahuive
Puxmetacan
Totontepec
Zempoaltepetl
• Atitlán
Tlahuiltoltepec
Ayutla

Mixe

Bixanos
Zapotec

Xallepec

Nanacatepec

Shearon Vaughn

Map 3
The Alcaldía Mayor of Villa Alta

0   5 10   20   30   40 Miles

0   25   50 Kilometers

east, and west.[5] The heart of the region lies between the Río del Rincón to the west and the Río Cajonos to the east, both of which join in the north to flow down to Veracruz and the Gulf of Mexico. Compared with the Rincón and Cajonos zones, the Mixe highlands are a little higher, more rugged, more heavily forested, and wetter. Pine forests, oak rain forests, and cloud forests are common, with many elevations of three thousand to thirty-four hundred meters. During the wet season, between May and October, it sometimes rains continuously for two weeks at a time. March and April are the only really dry months, though rarely is there a clear day.[6]

The Bixanos Zapotec zone and that part of the Chinantec area that lies within the Villa Alta district, while still mountainous, are considerably lower in elevation than the southern portions of the jurisdiction. Lower still is the large northeastern territory, which has been sparsely inhabited since the late sixteenth century. The Bixanos town of Choapan lies at only six hundred meters elevation and Comaltepec at eight hundred, in contrast to settlements in the other ethnic zones that generally hover close to two thousand meters. The Bixanos climate tends toward hot and humid with a nine-month rainy season that leaves March, April, and May as the only dry months. A number of rivers and streams cut through this region, though their waters are little exploited to expand the limited amount of tillable land.[7]

Despite its considerable diversity, the entire district was recognized as a meaningful unit by the Spaniards in the sixteenth century. Before the jurisdiction of Nejapa split off from that of Villa Alta in 1570, the entire territory was known to the colonists as Las Zapotecas. Why and how the boundaries were drawn between different political jurisdictions in the Sierra remains obscure, but the conquerors seem to have been guided by the distribution of native languages as well as by externally imposed political and economic considerations.

Linguists differ over the number of Zapotec languages that may be distinguished, the estimates ranging from nine to more than forty. Whatever the number, these languages differ from one another as much as the various Romance languages. Four Zapotec language areas are commonly distinguished in the northern, mountainous part of the state of Oaxaca. Serrano Zapotec is spoken in the Sierra Juárez, in the Distrito de Ixtlán, which in colonial times was carved up by the jurisdictions of Antequera, Ixtepeji, and Teococuilco. Speakers in the remaining three northern Zapotec language areas—Nexitzo, Cajonos, and Bixanos—have their homeland in the area encompassed by the colonial Villa Alta district.[8] Although there are great linguistic differences among all four northern Zapotec groups, the languages do share some grammatical and semantic features that unite them and differentiate them from Zapotec languages elsewhere in Oaxaca. While Serrano, Nexitzo, and Bixanos Zapotec have few internal dialectical differences, Cajonos Zapotec at the time of the Conquest had strong dialectical variation that today has resulted in various nonmutually intelligible languages.

Of the five groups treated in this volume, only the Chinantecs and the Mixes were subdivided into different colonial jurisdictions. The Chinantla as a whole has been divided by Robert Weitlaner and Howard Cline into five subregions, each distinguished by certain cultural and ecological characteristics. Four of these subregions are classified as lowland, and only one of these—the Eastern Chinantec, or colonial Guatinicamanes—lies within the territorial limits of the present study.[9] The Mixes were also politically divided until the creation of the Distrito Mixe in 1938. There are several nonmutually intelligible Mixe languages, and the boundary between western and eastern language groups may have been reflected in the demarcation drawn in 1570 between the colonial jurisdictions of Villa Alta and Nejapa. Only the western Mixe groups fall within the scope of this study.

Colonial administrators in Villa Alta paid considerable attention to language differences. Communities were invariably classified according to language spoken (see table 9, in chapter 3, for a complete breakdown), and Dominican missionaries found it necessary to specialize in one language or another to proselytize. Mixe and Chinantec always posed the greatest problems for the colonizers, Chinantec for its tones and Mixe for its difficult grammar. These languages are different from the Zapotec family as well as from each other, and most Spaniards found them more difficult to master.

I have chosen to organize this book around these five linguistic groups, but in doing so I do not want to give them more significance than is their due. We must heed Laura Nader's warning that linguistic and cultural areas in the Sierra do not coincide. The Bixanos Zapotecs, for example, may have more in common culturally with the Chinantecs, with whom they share a similar ecology, than with other Zapotec groups.[10] Just how cultural and ecological factors combine in the Sierra to form distinguishable groupings, and the relationship of these to the language map, has yet to be worked out in detail and will require further ethnographic and linguistic research. For now, then, I use terms such as "Cajonos" or "Bixanos" as ethnolinguistic categories whose cultural content must remain to a degree unspecified.[11]

But what about the ethnic component of these categories? Were these five linguistic groups also important units of ethnic identification? As is so often the case in colonial documentation, direct information on this topic is lacking. It is clear, however, that two important bases of ethnic identity were language and community of origin, and there is little reason to believe that colonial ethnicity in the Sierra differed fundamentally from the midtwentieth-century pattern described by the ethnographer Julio de la Fuente.[12] His data indicate that language is the primary basis of ethnic identification above the level of the community. Each Zapotec linguistic group has a Zapotec term for itself and terms for the others. These are invariably composed of a word meaning "people" (*bene,* or some variation), and one additional term that refers to a common language (*did zaa, ditza,* etc.). For example, Bixanos Zapotec speakers in the vicinity of Choapan call themselves *beneziɟa,* "people of the Zapotec language." The corresponding term used in the Cajonos zone is *benedizun,* and in the Rincón it is *buinirshidza.*[13] The generic self-designation in use among the eastern Chinantecs is *wa-hmi,*[14] though it is not clear whether this term has a linguistic referent. In the sixteenth century the term *guatinicamanes* was adopted by the Spaniards, apparently in reference to the fact that several eastern Chinantec towns were situated in a valley.[15] The highland Mixes call themselves *ayuuk,* glossed by Etsuko Kuroda simply as "Mixe," though again we are unsure of the role of language in this self-appellation.[16]

Ethnic identity among the Zapotec groups is clearly the most problematic, for unlike the Chinantecs and Mixes they share linguistic affinities with speakers of other Zapotec languages in diverse parts of Oaxaca. Julio de la Fuente found a gradient of identification and classification, beginning with one's *pueblo* or community, progressing to the language group (Cajonos, Nexitzo, Bixanos), and at the most general level encompassing all Zapotec speakers everywhere. Dress and custom are also used to distinguish people from outside one's pueblo. While all groups view themselves as *serranos* (as opposed to people from the *valle*), the Sierra Zapotec groups identify more closely with Zapotec speakers elsewhere than with their Mixe and Chinantec neighbors.

Ethnicity was probably more salient in the Sierra in pre-Hispanic times than it was during the colonial period. Native warfare seems to have had an ethnic basis, and language was a common element around which people could unite, even in the face of cultural differences. The Conquest changed all this, however, for while the Spaniards did not disregard the ethnolinguistic groups, colonial policy treated each Indian community as a quasi-independent *república de indios.* In time this policy of divide and conquer pushed regional ethnic ties into the background and heightened identification with one's community of origin. In the chapters that follow I will refer to the five groups as "ethnic groups," but in this qualified sense.

PRE-HISPANIC SOCIETY

It is not possible to portray the pre-Hispanic societies and cultures of the Sierra Zapoteca (a term I use interchangeably with the colonial Villa Alta political district) in any detail, for little direct information is available. Though many sites are known locally, no systematic archaeology has been carried out anywhere in the region. Nor do documentary sources provide firm clues to what the region was like before Spanish penetration in 1521. No native documents—either pre-Hispanic or colonial—that have much bearing on pre-Hispanic times have come to light. A total of four *lienzos* are known: one from San Miguel Tiltepec in the Rincón, one from the Tlaxcalan barrio of Analco established at Villa Alta after the Conquest, and two from San Juan Tabaa, a Cajonos Zapotec town. None of these has been studied in detail, but it is doubtful that any date from before the 1550s. All appear to deal with post-Conquest affairs in local communities and were probably produced not for native purposes, but to meet specific colonial administrative needs. In the words of Howard Cline, "they are generally a pictorial appendix or analogue to documentary judicial petitions of one sort or another."[17]

Nor are Spanish colonial chronicles or the *relaciones geográficas* of the sixteenth century of much help for the Sierra Zapoteca. Francisco de Burgoa's works, valuable as they are, contain only scattered references to Sierra communities, as does Agustín Dávila Padilla's chronicle. Not a single *relación geográfica* is available for any town in the Villa Alta district. Given these severe limitations, I can make only general observations based largely on inferences. A number of more specific points will also be discussed topically in succeeding chapters.

Given the total lack of archaeological knowledge of the region, discussion of the origins of Sierra ethnic groups must be highly speculative. On the basis of oral tradition, ethnography, and a few colonial documents, De la Fuente suggests that the Chinantecs, Zapotecs, and Mixes may have been driven southward by population pressure in the lowlands of Veracruz and northern Oaxaca, although it has also been suggested on the basis of linguistic evidence that the Nexitzo and Bixanos Zapotecs came from the Valley of Oaxaca.[18] In a similar vein, Ralph Beals has theorized that the western Mixes were influenced more by peoples to the north and east of them than by the Zapotecs to the south and west.[19] Also relevant is Oscar Schmieder's observation that a broad belt of unsettled mountainous land separated the Sierra Zapotec communities from the nearest settlements in the Valley of Oaxaca.[20] Until recently, most of the Sierra Zapoteca traded more with the lowlands of Veracruz than with the Valley of Oaxaca.[21] Only now is this beginning to change with the construction of vehicular roads connecting many sierra communities with the city of Oaxaca.

Pre-Hispanic interaction with Veracruz becomes more intelligible when we consider that the pre-Conquest population of the Sierra Zapoteca was substantially greater than it was in the colonial period, or even today. In chapter 3, I postulate a 1520 district estimate that is three times greater than the 1970 figure. Most of the depopulation occurred in the sixteenth century, and it was sharpest in the lowlands in the northern and northeastern parts of the district. In pre-Conquest times this territory supported the populous Zapotec kingdom of Xaltepec in the tropical rain forest of the northeast, its dependency Nanacatepec directly to the south, and Guaspaltepec to the

north (see map 3).[22] The available documentation also indicates that the
strongest Indian caciques and *cacicazgos* (cacique estates) were in Bixanos
Zapotec country in the vicinity of Choapan.[23]

Characterizing the differences between the Sierra Zapoteca and the Valley
of Oaxaca at the time of Spanish contact, Burgoa noted that the peoples of
the Sierra, because of their poverty and the imperviousness of their homeland, were generally less civilized, less politically developed, and more in-
clined toward "idolatry" and "superstition" than their Valley counterparts.[24]
While the friar's ethnocentrism is evident, the early colonial documentation
I have surveyed confirms the view that the Sierra was an area of "simple
peasant settlement" lacking elaborate social stratification or large political
units.[25] It is in these respects that the Sierra differed most noticeably from
the more developed Valley of Oaxaca and Mixteca Alta. Certainly none of
the mountain communities could be classified as urban, and it may even be
appropriate to raise the question of whether the political units best approxi-
mated a state or "chiefdom" level of organization. Sierra settlements were
generally smaller, much poorer, and only incipiently stratified and possessed
less specialized economies than those of the Valley. A brief list of characteristics that set off the Sierra from the more developed regions of Oaxaca at the
time of the Conquest includes the following:

1. Despite the presence of a major Aztec trading post at Tuxtepec to the
north and battles with Aztec troops at San Miguel Tiltepec and Jaltepec de
Candayoc,[26] none of the five ethnic groups studied here was ever incorporated into the tribute empire of the Triple Alliance. The map of Aztec territory drawn by Robert Barlow excludes the Mixe and Sierra Zapotec areas,
which he describes as "uneasy frontiers."[27] Some Chinantecs had more direct contact with the Triple Alliance, which tried and failed to subject them
to its will. While some of their towns (such as Usila) did pay tribute,[28] the
Chinantecs were better known as enemies of the Aztecs; the eastern Chinantecs, dealt with in this study, seem to have remained relatively unaffected.
Two points are worth making regarding the lack of Aztec penetration of the
Sierra Zapoteca. First, one reason the Triple Alliance did not try harder to
subdue this region was probably its poverty—there was not as much potential tribute for the taking as elsewhere in Oaxaca. Second, local Sierra caciques did not have the advantage of patronage ties with Aztec rulers. Had
these existed, they might have served to strengthen the local nobles' power
bases within their own communities. This may help explain the weakness of
the caciques during the initial *entradas* of the Spanish in the sixteenth century (see chapter 2).

2. In the highland portions of the district, the steep, mountainous terrain
coupled with Neolithic technology placed limits on the size and complexity
of the population that could be supported. Here no extensive valley floors
are conducive to intensive agriculture as in the Valley of Oaxaca or the
Nochixtlán and Tamazulapan valleys in the Mixteca Alta. The Bixanos and

Chinantec lowlands contain more level land, but soils are poor and unproductive in many areas.

3. The customary Mesoamerican settlement pattern of head town (*cabecera*) with subject hamlets (*sujetos*) was not as developed in the Sierra as it was in other parts of Oaxaca. The pattern of small, relatively independent villages intensified during the colonial period and is dealt with in some detail in chapter 3.

4. Data are sparse, but Sierra villages seem to have supported few, if any, full-time craftsmen. These were primarily agricultural settlements and lacked the high degree of economic specialization found in the Valley of Oaxaca.

5. Unlike the more developed city-states in the Valley of Mexico and Valley of Oaxaca, not all Sierra communities had distinct ruling and priestly hierarchies. At least in the Bixanos zone, it was not uncommon for political rulers and high priests to be the same person. The *vigana,* young men in training for the lesser priestly offices, were customarily recruited from the ranks of the second sons of the nobility (see chapter 6).

6. The social hierarchy was far simpler in the Sierra than it was in the Valley of Oaxaca and the Mixteca. The stratum of *mayeque* (dependent serfs, referred to as *terrazgueros* by colonial Spaniards) apparently did not exist—not a single reference to them has been found. Nor were slaves of any importance; the sole bit of information about them mentions two that were owned by a cacique of the Nexitzo community of Yagavila, but these were just small boys.[29] The commoners of the region, therefore, seem to have been minimally differentiated, most of them free peasants engaged in independent subsistence farming.

7. Finally, it is clear that the caciques of the region possessed relatively little land or other forms of wealth to set them off from the commoners, with the possible exceptions of the dynasties of Choapan and Xaltepec. Even in these cases, cacique power and prestige were probably due principally to leadership in the incessant warfare preceding the Spanish conquest. With few exceptions, early colonial caciques had little influence in their communities. They owned little land and in court were rarely able to present convincing genealogies to confirm the pre-Conquest heritage they claimed. In all, they lived in much the same manner as the *macehuales* (commoners) and their cacicazgos bore little resemblance to the larger, wealthier estates of the Valley and the Mixteca.

When the Spanish arrived in 1521, they found the Sierra Zapoteca in a state of total war. These hostilities were probably the major impetus behind the existing intercommunity and ethnic alliances, ephemeral as they were. One important center of aggressive expansion was the Bixanos Zapotec community of Choapan, which counted Comaltepec and Latani, among others, as its allies. Led by the powerful cacique Tela, the Alliance was said to consist of "seven *parentelas*" (families or kin groups), each descended from an

illustrious royal forebear. The parentelas founded several towns, Comaltepec among them.

Bixanos warriors fought both Chinantecs and Mixes, and met with some
success on both fronts. The goals of the conflict are not entirely clear, but
some land seems to have been seized by the Bixanos. For example, the area
where Comaltepec was settled, south of Choapan, may once have been Mixe
territory. Bixanos forces also conquered the Chinantec towns of Yaci (known
in colonial times and later as Jocotepec) and Lobani to the north, though
they failed to subdue Petlapa and Toavela. It is possible that these events
occurred after initial Spanish penetration of the region, for Tela lived until
about 1558, and his son Theolao, christened don Alonso Pérez, ruled in
Comaltepec. By at least the 1550s, most Chinantec nobles also spoke Bixanos Zapotec, the language of their overlords.[30]

Turbulent as matters were on the Bixanos frontier, an even wider area of
conflict pitted all three Zapotec groups against the Mixes. The Mixe wars
were raging when the Spanish arrived, and the town of Villa Alta was
founded near the principal line of combat in an effort to put an end to the
hostilities. The Cajonos Zapotecs were directly involved, and the spectacular
ruins at San Francisco Yatee may have functioned as a military garrison of
sorts. The Nexitzos of the Rincón also fought the Mixes and may have
formed an alliance with the Bixanos for this purpose, as the Bixanos pueblo
of Yetzelalag and Nexitzo Lahoya (today Otatitlán) and Yatoni are said to
share some sort of common history.[31] Oral tradition in the Rincón recorded
by Rosendo Pérez García refers to the "seven pueblos" of Talea that were
fighting the Mixes of Totontepec at the time of the Conquest.[32] This may
turn out to be the same alliance as the Bixanos "seven parentelas" mentioned
above, though it was almost certainly not headed by Talea, which probably
did not exist at the time.

The nature of leadership and political integration on the Mixe side of the
conflict is even more problematic. As Ralph Beals has pointed out, the
Mixes must have had some sort of unity, even if based on nothing more than
a common language and culture, to sustain their warfare with the Zapotecs.[33]
While Peter Gerhard identifies Mixistlán as the "old Mixe capital," Padre
José Antonio Gay is closer to the mark in designating Totontepec, home of
the legendary war leader Condoy, as the most important community.[34] Totontepec was one of the largest and most influential Mixe towns during the
colonial period, while Mixistlán received little mention. At any rate, the
Spaniards found pacification of the Mixe-Zapotec conflict a difficult task indeed. The last major offensive, the so-called Mixe rebellion, occurred in
1570, more than forty years after the Spanish had settled Villa Alta.[35]

As tentative and incomplete as this brief account has been, the various
characteristics discussed suggest a special type of Contact-period society
(or societies), different in many respects from the more developed, better

known peoples of the central Mexican highlands. The familiar three-tiered stratification system of caciques, *principales* (second echelon nobles), and macehuales was present, but much less developed and not buttressed by any significant concentration of wealth at the top. Warfare, of course, was no stranger to any part of Mesoamerica in the Post-Classic era, but it seems to have persisted longer into the colonial period in the Sierra Zapoteca than anywhere else in Oaxaca. This is indicative of the slow pace at which Spanish colonization proceeded in the Sierra.

CHAPTER 2

THE CONQUERORS

THE SPANISH CONQUEST of the northern sierra of Oaxaca was one of the most brutal and protracted episodes in sixteenth-century Mexico. Other parts of Oaxaca—the central Valley, the Mixteca, and the Isthmus—fell quickly under the Spanish yoke following the first military forays in 1521. Valley and Isthmus Zapotecs were receptive to the *conquistadores,* for the powerful lord of Tehuantepec had abdicated his throne and allied himself with Fernando Cortés before the Spaniards' arrival in Oaxaca. But the Zapotecs, Chinantecs, and Mixes of the Sierra saw things quite differently. Unaccustomed to domination by outsiders, the serranos fought tooth and nail to preserve their autonomy. They largely managed to evade Spanish control until the 1550s, three decades after the more developed and geographically accessible parts of the Oaxaca region had already been incorporated into the political structure of New Spain.

The Spanish first became interested in Oaxaca's northern sierra—the Provincia de los Zapotecas, as they called it—in 1521, when Fernando Cortés learned from the Aztec emperor Moctezuma that Nahua Tuxtepec was one of the places that furnished the Aztecs with gold dust. Moctezuma's claim that mines existed in the surrounding Chinantec and Zapotec regions further stimulated Cortés's curiosity, and a small expedition was sent to look things over.[1] Subsequently, Gonzalo de Sandoval arrived to pacify Tuxtepec with an army of two hundred Spaniards, thirty-five horses, and many Indian allies. The Mexicans were quickly subdued, and Sandoval sent word to the Chinantec, Zapotec, and Mixe caciques of the Sierra that they should come to Tuxtepec and declare themselves vassals of the king of Spain. Some of them came, but many others were not prepared to surrender so easily, so Captain Briones was sent with a hundred Spaniards and as many Indians on an initial entrada into Rincón Zapotec territory. The mission was an utter failure. The Spanish soon discovered that they would have to enter the region on foot, since their horses could not negotiate the rugged mountainous terrain. The expedition came to an abrupt halt at the Zapotec town of (San Miguel) Tiltepec, where over a third of the Spanish troops were wounded in battle. After this defeat Sandoval retreated to the large Zapotec kingdom of Xaltepec in the hot country, conquered it, and went on to found the Villa de Espíritu Santo at Coatzacoalcos.[2]

The next serious attempt to conquer the Sierra Zapoteca was led by Rodrigo Rangel, an alcalde of Mexico City, who embarked in the summer of 1523 with 150 foot soldiers. But he returned just two months later, for the expedition had set out during the rainy season and the muddy mountain trails were virtually impassable. In February 1524, Rangel tried again, this time with authorization from Cortés to take Indian slaves and distribute them to the Spaniards in the party. Rangel also hoped to find gold. But this entrada also turned out to be a bust. Rangel was unable to provide strong leadership, and the Indians defended themselves well with fifteen-foot lances. The Zapotecs' favorite tactic was to hide in the mountaintops and then ambush the Spanish as they pushed through at lower elevations.[3]

Unwilling to accept defeat, Royal Treasurer Alonso de Estrada soon sent Luis de Barrios back to the Zapotecas with one hundred men. According to one account, two entradas were launched simultaneously: Barrios penetrated from the north, and Diego de Figueroa with another hundred men from the Valley of Oaxaca attacked from the south.[4] Barrios, like his predecessors, met his match at Tiltepec in the Rincón, where he perished along with seven other Spaniards. To Figueroa fell the distinction of being the first conquistador to have any success in the Sierra Zapoteca.[5] The chronicler Bernal Díaz del Castillo belittled his efforts, emphasizing that Figueroa spent much of his time digging up cacique graves in search of gold and only brought more violence and discord to the region.[6] This may have been the case, though it was Figueroa who, in 1526, founded the first Spanish settlement in the region, Villa Alta de San Ildefonso, by order of Marcos de Aguilar and Alonso de Estrada. Established as a mountain outpost some twenty leagues from Antequera (as the city of Oaxaca in the central Valley was then known), Villa Alta was initially located on lands belonging to Totontepec, a large and powerful Mixe town just east of Zapotec territory. The purpose of the garrison was to put an end to the incessant warfare in the region, for the Zapotecs and Mixes continued to war with each other as well as with the Spanish.

Permanent Spanish presence in the Sierra Zapoteca therefore dates from 1526, when Figueroa founded Villa Alta, appointed a *cabildo* (municipal council), and distributed a small number of *encomiendas* to his followers.[7] Shortly thereafter, however, Figueroa returned to Mexico City. On October 21, 1527, Alonso de Estrada replaced him by naming Gaspar Pacheco as *teniente de gobernador* (deputy governor) in Villa Alta and giving him authority to "pacify and conquest," try civil and criminal cases, assign new encomiendas, and capture slaves from "rebellious" Indian communities. Apparently some dissatisfaction with the site of Villa Alta had already developed, for Pacheco and the cabildo moved the town to its present location and distributed house lots to the Spanish *vecinos* (residents).[8] Pacheco's other accomplishments in Villa Alta, if any, remain unknown, though he redistributed encomiendas there in 1528 (see below) and held the title of *visi-*

tador in 1531 before moving on to the conquest of Yucatan with his son Melchor.[9]

The conquest of the Sierra quickened in 1529, when the First Audiencia appointed Luis de Berrio as Villa Alta's first *alcalde mayor*.[10] His three-year reign, from 1529 to 1531, was one of unremitting carnage and brutality against the Indian population of the region, particularly the Mixes and Rincón Zapotecs. Berrio obtained the post through his good connections in the capital; he was a first cousin of Oidor Diego Delgadillo and also of Juan Peláez de Berrio, who was named alcalde mayor of Antequera in the same year. Yet even before he arrived in Villa Alta, Luis de Berrio had acquired a very unsavory reputation. His greatest enemy was Fray Juan de Zumárraga, the first Bishop of Mexico, who characterized Berrio as "infamous" in his letters to the crown and finally excommunicated him following the *residencia* held at the end of his term of office in Villa Alta.[11]

The late 1520s and early 1530s in the Sierra are best described as a period of extreme terrorism, as Berrio and several others attempted to crush all Indian resistance and extract from the natives as much food, gold, and cotton goods as possible. Berrio was known for his merciless treatment of the Indians, even those in the Mixe towns of Tonaguia and Totontepec, which he appropriated from Gaspar Pacheco and made his own encomiendas. Whole Mixe and Zapotec towns were attacked without provocation (notably Chichicaxtepec, San Miguel Tiltepec, Yagavila, and Cuescomaltepec), resulting in the death of hundreds. Hundreds more, most of them free macehuales, were branded and carried off as slaves. Caciques and principales who failed to obey Berrio's orders were hanged, burned, or thrown to the dogs. At least ten individuals died in this fashion, including the caciques of Yagavila and Temaxcalapan. Even these tactics failed to produce enough slave labor for the search for mines, and on at least one occasion Berrio illegally imported slaves from the Valley of Oaxaca, outside his jurisdiction.[12]

Berrio's reputation among his fellow Spaniards in Villa Alta was not much better. During the inquiry into his performance (*residencia*), held in the summer of 1531, most of the vecinos testified against him, even some of those he was said to favor. Villa Alta during these years was a classic example of an isolated frontier town: faction ridden, lawless, and dominated by a strong individual who imposed his will by force. Among the things Luis de Berrio was charged with were failing to maintain order and punish crimes, indulging in favoritism, living openly with an unmarried *española*, failing to obey orders from the crown and audiencia, taking bribes and gifts (sometimes by force), failing to pay his debts, and neglecting to hold regular cabildo meetings. But his most controversial decision was to strip all *encomenderos* of the holdings previously awarded them by Gaspar Pacheco and reallocate them to his own supporters. In all, sixteen men lost their encomiendas, and five of them were forced out of the region altogether. Those that remained were reduced to bickering over the meager resources the region had to offer. Eventually, Berrio was roundly condemned. In 1532 he mounted a weak defense before the audiencia, claiming that all who testified against him were his "mortal enemies." But his friends in the capital were no longer in power, and on December 24, 1532, the Second Audiencia banished him from New Spain and confiscated half his property. He returned to Spain the following year.[13]

Luis de Berrio may have been an especially rapacious individual, yet other conquistadores in the Sierra used similar tactics against the Indian pueblos. Clearly, the Spanish found the conquest of this region much more difficult than they had anticipated, and the rewards fewer. The isolation of the territory further encouraged the attitude that they could employ any violent means they wished without fear of reprisal. A distinctive aspect of the conquest of the Sierra was the Spanish use of dogs, which were employed both as a means of defense and as an instrument of death for recalcitrant Indians. Indeed, according to Antonio de Herrera y Tordesillas the Indians feared the dogs more than they feared the armed men.[14] Gaspar Pacheco was said to have used greyhounds to kill and devour Mixes, and his dogs kept continuous watch over the town of Villa Alta.[15] Both fear of the conquerors and resistance to their demands were considerably greater than in other parts of Oaxaca, which had long since become accustomed to Aztec dominion. This was the first time that these serranos found their freedom placed in jeopardy, and they did all within their power to oust the foreigners. The chronicler Alonso de Zorita even claimed that the Mixes and Chontal induced abortions and for a time refused to procreate.[16]

Another early Spaniard in the area who pressed his luck too far and incurred the wrath of the audiencia was Francisco López Tenorio, a young illiterate man from León, Spain, who served as *corregidor* of Zapotec Yagavila and part of the Chinantec Guatinicamanes in 1535–37. By 1537 the audiencia had received reports of extreme cruelty toward the Indians by corregidores in the Sierra and ordered that residencias be taken on their conduct in office. At least two were conducted (the other one on Graviel de Aguilera), but only one has survived. As was customary in the region, López Tenorio exacted tribute every eighty days from several towns (Yagavila, Zoogochi, and Lobani) in the form of gold, cacao, cotton cloth, corn, turkeys, and honey. He was condemned not for this, however, but for the physical violence he inflicted on his Indian enemies. He was the first Spaniard ever to take up residence in the vicinity of Yagavila, and the caciques of several communities anticipated his arrival by ordering their people to abandon their homes and flee to the hills. Indeed, López Tenorio spent his first two months alone in Yagavila before a few principales relented and agreed to provide him with food.

The Indians first tried to scare Tenorio away by imitating the noises of ferocious animals outside his house at night. When this failed, they tried to kill him. The corregidor responded by inflicting extreme punishment on those who failed to obey his orders, hoping that a few public spectacles would encourage the rest to fall into line. A dissident Indian from Yabago (later to become San Pedro Yaneri) had his ears cut off; others had their cotton cloth burned and had to weave extra quantities to meet their tribute payments. Tenorio put his own house servants in chains so they would not escape, and anyone who did not pay tribute on time could expect to be jailed, at the minimum. Caciques and principales were especially vulnerable, for they were expected to exhibit model behavior and serve as examples for the macehuales. But they lacked the power and wealth of their counterparts in regions like the Valley of Oaxaca and the Mixteca, and if they refused to cooperate they were often killed. Thus Tenorio set his dogs on and later hanged Yagaeche, the cacique of Yagavila and a man of some influence in the area who refused to side with the Spanish. A *principal* who failed to cooperate was hanged in the village on market day. The residencia of 1537 went against Tenorio and he was jailed for a time, banished permanently from the district, and forbidden to hold public office again. Yet in the 1540s he surfaced as a *regidor* in the city of Antequera.[17]

VILLA ALTA DE SAN ILDEFONSO

The fledgling Spanish settlement of Villa Alta was built on a hillside at an altitude of 1,750 meters, and today is just a few minutes' walk from the Cajonos Zapotec community of San Cristóbal Lachirioag. There was no suitable stone in the area, so adobe became the construction material for all the houses and the few public buildings. Roofs were of thatch, after the indigenous style of the region, and Spanish vecinos frequently complained that wooden beams rotted because of the copious rains.[18] Despite the hilly nature of the site, Luis de Berrio in 1529 ordered that the standard Spanish grid plan be used to design the town, and the central plaza soon came to serve as the focal point for the residences of the alcalde mayor and other notables, the cabildo, and the church. Berrio also designated municipal common lands (*ejidos*) that fanned out to the north, west, and south, bordering on the Mixe community of Tonaguia and the Zapotec towns of Temaxcalapan and Tabaa. The legal status of these lands was in doubt, for the ejidos were not initially confirmed by the viceroy, but by 1555 they were routinely used as pasture lands for cattle by individuals who had contracted to supply the villa with meat.[19] A town government of sorts came into being at the beginning, and in 1531 the cabildo was composed of three *alcaldes ordinarios*, six *regidores*, an *alguacil mayor*, and an *alguacil*.[20] The community's population was small and remained so during the colonial period, fluctuating between twenty and thirty vecinos—or 100 and 150 inhabitants—in the sixteenth century.[21]

THE SPIRITUAL CONQUEST

Christianity came to the Sierra along with the first conquistadores, though the process of proselytization proceeded slowly during the first half of the sixteenth century. The first representative of the church in the area appears to have been Bartolomé de Olmedo, a Mercedarian friar who came with Cortés from Hispaniola in 1519. Olmedo accompanied Pedro de Alvarado in the conquest of the Mixtec kingdom of Tututepec on the Pacific coast in 1522 and may have presided over the baptism of Cosijopi, the Zapotec ruler of Tehuantepec. Shortly before his death in 1524, Olmedo participated in an early entrada into Rincón Zapotec and Mixe territory—probably that of Rodrigo Rangel—and baptized some five hundred individuals.[22] This was a brief visit with few lasting consequences, though Olmedo's name was remembered several decades later on the Lienzo de San Juan Tabaa and related documents from Talea, Yatzachi, Juquila, Solaga, and Lahoya.[23]

The next missionary to enter the region was Fray Gonzalo Lucero, appointed as vicar of the first Dominican convent in Villa Alta. Ignorant of the languages of the area, at least initially, he communicated in Nahuatl with some of the local nobility and also used pictures to get his message across.[24] His stay was brief, however, and within two years he was replaced by two secular clergy. These men spent most of their time in the Indian communities, but they also managed to build a crude church in Villa Alta.[25] Just what these two priests accomplished and in which communities is unknown, but they remained in the Sierra until 1548, when they were relieved by two unnamed Dominicans. The newcomers took over Villa Alta's church, built by their predecessors, and replaced it with a convent of adobe and thatch. While the Dominicans were apparently very popular in some of the villages, they ran into difficulties with the Spanish vecinos and left in 1552. Fray Lucero then returned with three associates for a three-year stay;[26] by this time they had acquired some facility in Zapotec and probably had more influence with the Indians than many of their predecessors.

The turning point that established Dominican hegemony in the Sierra Zapoteca came in 1556 with a royal *cédula* instructing the order to take charge of the Villa Alta district and granting them one thousand pesos per year to defray expenses. The cédula was received by the viceroy the following year, and on January 15, 1558, Fray Jordán de Santa Catalina arrived as Villa Alta's first prelate, accompanied by three other friars, Pablo de San Pedro, Fabián de Santo Domingo, and Pedro Guerrero. Work on the Dominican convent in Villa Alta was resumed, and the pace of missionization increased. Santa Catalina was fluent in Zapotec, and Guerrero immediately set about learning Mixe. When Fray Jordán left in 1561, Guerrero replaced him as prelate until 1576 and extended mission activities into the Chinantec Guatinicamanes area. Thus the "spiritual conquest" of the Sierra became largely a Dominican affair, though a few secular clergy did remain for a time in the Rincón town of Tanetze.[27]

TRANSPORTATION

Transportation proved to be a major problem for the new town of Villa Alta. Even to this day the town's lack of growth is due in good measure to its inaccessability. The principal colonial route from Villa Alta to the city of Antequera in the Valley of Oaxaca was substantially the same as it is today, passing through the pueblos of Yaa, Betaza, Yalalag, the Cajonos towns, Yaganiza, Xagacia, Santa Catarina Albarradas, San Miguel del Valle, and either Díaz Ordaz (formerly Santo Domingo del Valle) or Teotitlán del Valle and Macuilxóchitl.[28] The road covered a distance of about 22 leagues or 57.2 miles. To the north, the Spaniards made use of well-established routes used by Zapotec traders, routes still in use today.[29] The primary route departed from Villa Alta and passed through Temaxcalapan, Yatzona, Yetzelalag, and Lobani before joining up with the Río Chiquito, which it followed through Roayaga, Tonaguia, Comaltepec, Choapan, Latani, Roavela, and Jalahui; crossed the Río de la Lana; then passed through Tatahuicapa, Sochiapan, and Guaspaltepec.[30] Before its decline in the late sixteenth century, the town of Guaspaltepec, some sixty leagues from Villa Alta, was an important terminus. Supplies from Veracruz were shipped by canoe as far as Guaspaltepec (and also to the town of Chinantla), then carried the rest of the way on foot.[31]

The Europeans soon discovered that horses and often burros were virtually useless as pack animals on the steep slopes of the highlands. Vecinos of Villa Alta complained in 1533 that many of their horses had fallen off cliffs, and they asked that an exception be made to the ban on Spanish use of *tamemes* (Indian carriers). Such permission was regularly granted by viceroys in the sixteenth century, and tamemes continued to serve as a chief means of transport of Spanish goods during the entire colonial period.[32]

EARLY INDIAN UPRISINGS

Throughout much of the sixteenth century, the conquerors also had to contend with numerous Indian uprisings. While most of these were local affairs, they were nonetheless quite violent and greatly feared by the colonists. Many incidents took place in the 1530s, the worst in 1531 in Zapotec Tiltepec, which had fought so desperately when provoked by the Spaniards in preceding years. Alcalde Mayor Luis de Berrio once complimented the inhabitants of Tiltepec as "the worst Indians of the land." Seven Spaniards lost their lives in the 1531 battle, despite aid from twenty-five Spanish vecinos and some Indians from Antequera.[33] In all, about a dozen Spaniards lost their lives in conflicts with Indians between 1526 and 1533,[34] but these casualties were few indeed compared with those suffered by Indians.

The villa itself experienced two major attacks in the sixteenth century. In 1550 a group of Mixes and Chontales attacked the town. Once again, reinforcements were sent from Antequera, but not in time to prevent extensive damage.[35] A much larger undertaking was the Mixe rebellion of 1570, probably the largest of the century. This uprising was aimed not only, or even primarily, at the European intruders, but at the Mixes' old enemies, the Zapotecs. Many Zapotec villages were sacked, and it took reinforcements from Antequera and two thousand Mixtecs from Cuilapan to restore order.[36]

ENCOMIENDA AND CORREGIMIENTO

In accord with customary Spanish procedure, the twin institutions of *encomienda* and *corregimiento* were employed to subjugate the indigenous population, ensure the payment of tribute, and reward individual conquerors for their efforts. Slavery was also common before the early 1530s. Especially during the regime of Luis de Berrio, free Indians were frequently branded as slaves and put to work in mining explorations.[37] While Indian slavery diminished considerably after 1531, the alcalde mayor and others held some slaves as late as 1550.[38]

Encomiendas were first parceled out by Diego de Figueroa to his men in 1526–27. All of these were in Nexitzo territory, where most of the early Spanish-Indian conflict took place, and included Cuescomaltepec (later to become San Juan Yae), Huayatepec, Lachichina, Totolinga, and Zultepec. After Figueroa's departure, Gaspar Pacheco in 1528 redistributed these and established several others, casting his net more widely. Cacalotepec, Ixcuintepec, Teotlaxco, Tiltepec, and Yabago (Yaneri) were added to the roster of Nexitzo encomiendas. Others distributed by Pacheco included the Cajonos pueblo Zoochixtepec; Chinantec Teotalcingo and the Guatinicamanes (Petlapa, Toavela, Lobani, and Yaci [Jocotepec]); Mixe Amatepec, Jareta, Metepec, Tonaguia, and Totontepec; and perhaps Bixanos Camotlán, Comaltepec, and Choapan.

The *Suma de visitas*[39] clearly indicates that in 1548, in addition to subsistence items such as turkeys, corn, cacao, honey, chile, and beans, virtually all encomenderos required their Indians to weave cotton cloth as part of their tribute. In most cases the encomendero supplied the cotton. A few villages also gave gold dust in tribute. A good example at the upper end of the range was the Guatinicamanes encomienda. Tribute quotas for this jurisdiction were set in 1543 by Alcalde Mayor Francisco de Sevilla. Half the following goods, due every eighty days, went to the encomendero Juan Antonio, and the other half to the crown: fifty pesos' worth of gold dust, six *cargas* of cacao, thirty-nine cotton *mantillas* (shawls), twelve *arrobas* of honey, and fifty turkeys. In addition, one hundred *fanegas* of corn were due at harvest time each year and eight Indian workers on a daily basis. More typical of the tribute given by a single community was the quota for Zapotec Yagavila in the same year. This was a crown community, and the corregidor provided the cotton for twelve large pieces of cloth that were woven every eighty days. Also given at the same intervals were two large cups of cacao, twenty turkeys and chickens, and three loaves of bread. Yagavila also provided one hundred fanegas of corn each year and four laborers daily.[40]

It is clear that encomenderos in the Sierra Zapoteca did not fare nearly as well economically as their counterparts in Antequera with holdings in the Valley of Oaxaca and the Mixteca. The average Villa Alta encomendero received annually: 186 turkeys, 79 pieces of cotton cloth, 176 fanegas (117 bushels) of corn, and unspecified quantities of cacao, bread, beans, and honey.[41] He was not entitled to any gold dust, however, whereas most Antequera encomenderos with holdings in other regions were receiving an average of 254 pesos' worth each year. Furthermore, while the city encomenderos had at their disposal from ten to fifteen day laborers, Sierra encomiendas furnished no more than six, on the average.[42]

In 1548 twenty-nine encomiendas had been established in the district. Distribution by ethnic group, dates, and sujetos of the thirty-eight Villa Alta encomiendas is given in table 1. Roughly two-thirds of the total were located in Nexitzo Zapotec and Mixe territory, although the Chinantec Guatinicamanes encomienda was one of the largest and most remunerative. Other large encomiendas included Zultepec, Cuescomaltepec, and Ixcuintepec, all of them Nexitzo. By law, all twenty-nine encomenderos were required to reside in Villa Alta, but until the mid 1550s few of them did, much to the consternation of local vecinos. In 1551 the town's attorney (*procurador*), Juan Gómez, complained to the viceroy that many encomenderos were living in Antequera and other places. He claimed that Villa Alta was constantly short of provisions because the absentees had all their tribute shipped to Antequera by mule train. The viceroy's response was to order all encomenderos to move to the villa within two months. He also required them to dispose of their excess tribute by public auction in Villa Alta.[43] Several years would pass, however, before such decrees had any effect.

The corregimiento in the Villa Alta district, as Gerhard has pointed out, was from the beginning also intended to support the vecinos of the villa.[44] Like the encomiendas, corregimientos were most heavily concentrated in Nexitzo and Mixe villages. Table 2 lists corregimientos in the sixteenth century by ethnic group. The eleven shown for the 1530s were established by the Second Audiencia; most had previously been in encomienda. By 1545,

TABLE 1. Encomiendas in the Villa Alta District[a]

Ethnic Group	Encomienda	Population 1568[b]	Date[c]
Cajonos	S. Francisco Cajonos, S. Pedro Cajonos, S. Miguel Cajonos, Sto. Domingo Xagacía, S. Pablo Yaganiza, S. Mateo Cajonos	394[d]	1548–1768
	Nestepec, Zoochila, Yohueche, Yalalag, Zoogocho, Yatzachi, Yaa	1,531[e]	1548–1604
	Zoochila, Zoochina, Quetache (?), Oyasache (Yatzachi?), ½ Tiltepec (Mixe), Yaa		1677–77
	Tabaa		E 1548
	Zoochixtepec	215	1528; E after 1548
Nexitzo	Cacalotepec	281	1528–97
	Cuescomaltepec (S. Juan Yae)	564	1527; E 1550
	Huayatepec[f]	254	1527; E before 1534
	Ixcuintepec,[g] Juquila, Yachas, Mixistlán[h] (Mixe), Talea,[h] Sayultepec[h]	2,230[i]	1528; E ca. 1578
	Lalopa	423	1540s; E 1545
	Josaa		1579–79
	Lachichina	478	1526–1653
	Temaxcalapan	168	1548–60
	Teotlaxco	168	1528; E after 1548
	Tepanzacualco	141	1540s–1653
	Tiltepec[j]	622	1528–97
	Totolinga,[k] Zultepec,[l] Zoquio,[m] Tultitlan[m]	296[n]	1526–97
	Yabago (Yaneri)	282	1528; E ca. 1534
	Yatzona (with 6 Cajonos pueblos)		1748–48
Bixanos	Camotlán, Comaltepec	494	E before 1545
	Choapan	676	E before 1545
	Lazagaya,[o] El Tagui[o]	252	1548; E before 1609
	Roavela (Malinaltepec)	283	1548–97
	Tizatepec[p]	337	ca. 1529; E 1550s
	Yovego		1680–80
Chinantec	Guatinicamanes (Petlapa, Yaci [Jocotepec], Lobani, Toavela)[q]	4,231	1528–97
	Tlapanalá (Lachixila)	706	1548–1679
	Teotalcingo[r]	(2,695)	1528–70
Mixe	Ayacastla, Noban (Atitlán), Alotepec, Ixcocan (Guiazona)[s]	1,956	1548–1628

TABLE 1. *(continued)*

Ethnic Group	Encomienda	Population 1568[b]	Date[c]
	Amatepec	155	1528–79
	Ayacaxtepec, Metaltepec	(508)	1530s–97
	Chichicaxtepec	254	1531–97
	Jareta	254	1528–97
	Metepec	141	1528; E after 1534
	Ocotepec, Jayacaxtepec, Moctum	859	1548; E after 1652
	Suchitepec (Tlazoltepec, now Candayoc)	378	1560–92
	Tlahuitoltepec	564	after 1545; E before 1560
	Tonaguia, ½ Totontepec	(568)	1528; E before 1548

Total number of encomiendas: 38

[a] Some further details and names of encomenderos are given by Gerhard, *Guide*, pp. 369–73.

[b] Population figures from Cook and Borah, *Central Mexico, 1531–1610*, pp. 84–88. Figures in parentheses are my interpolations from data for 1548 and 1622.

[c] Date of assignment or first mention followed by date of last mention. Known escheatments indicated by "E."

[d] Figures only for San Francisco Cajonos and San Pablo Yaganiza.

[e] No figures for Yohueche or Yatzachi.

[f] Not mentioned after 1622.

[g] Merged with Tanetze after 1622.

[h] Added after midsixteenth century.

[i] No figures for Yachas or Sayultepec.

[j] Half escheated in 1532.

[k] Abandoned by 1674.

[l] Not mentioned after 1568.

[m] Added in 1560, but not mentioned again.

[n] No figures for Zoquio or Tultitlan.

[o] Not mentioned after 1622 (not to be confused with Nexitzo San Juan Tagui).

[p] Disappeared after 1622.

[q] Half escheated before 1534.

[r] Half escheated before 1534.

[s] Disappeared after 1600.

Sources: *Cajonos.* AJVA Civil 1708–1825, *3;* AJVA Civil 1682–1882, *55;* Gerhard, *Guide*, p. 372; AGN Indios 10, Cuaderno 3, *54;* AGI Justicia 230; AGN Reales Cédulas Duplicadas 19, *615;* APVA *Papeles de Analco;* ENE, 9:38–40.

Nexitzo. AGI Justicia 230; AGI Patronato 183, *219;* AGI Justicia 135, *1;* AGI México 96, 91, 242; AGI Escribanía de Cámara 159A; AJVA Civil 1579–1825, *3;* AJVA Civil 1672–1799, *2;* AJVA Civil 1708–1825, *39;* AGN Indios 6, primera parte, *372;* AGN Inquisición 437, *17;* AGN Mercedes 3, *785:307–8;* Zavala and Castelo, 7:35; ENE, 9:38–40; Icaza, 1:89; PNE, 1:278; CCG *Libro de la Hermita.*

Bixanos. AGI Justicia 230; AGI México 242; AGN Indios 7, *249;* AJVA Civil y Criminal 1701–50, *22;* Gerhard, *Guide*, pp. 370–72.

Chinantec. AGI Justicia 205, *5;* AGI Justicia 230; AGN Reales Cédulas Duplicadas 19, *624;* CCG *Libro de la Hermita;* Gerhard, *Guide*, pp. 370–72.

Mixe. AGI Justicia 230; AGI México 242; AGN Mercedes 26:100v–114; AJVA Civil 1682–1882, *13;* AJVA Civil 1708–1825, *3;* ENE, 9:38–40; Gerhard, *Guide*, pp. 370–71.

the number had grown to twenty, and appointment of corregidores was made by the alcalde mayor in Villa Alta. Incumbents were rotated annually and probably had little real political power.[45] The low salaries listed for the first half of the sixteenth century indicate that these corregimientos, like the encomiendas, were not especially remunerative. Indeed, in 1545 the tribute collected in these villages was not even sufficient to pay these low salaries, let alone provide any income for the crown.[46] This did not negate opportunities for illicit forms of exploitation, of course, though it will be shown later that the alcaldes mayores effectively dominated illegal trade and were not disposed to leave much for others. This was one of the reasons why the early corregidores, like the encomenderos, were reluctant to take up residence in the villa, preferring to live in Antequera and elsewhere.[47] In 1533 the vecinos of Villa Alta complained that all the corregimientos of the district

TABLE 2.   Corregimientos in the Villa Alta District

Ethnic Group	Corregimiento[a]	Population in 1568[b]	Corregidor Salaries in Pesos[c]		
			1530s	1545	1609
Cajonos	⅓ Nestepec, ½ Teotalcingo (Chinantec)	(1,825)[d]	n/d	—	—
Nexitzo	Tiltepec, Yagavila	(1,103)	200	50	110
	Huayatepec, Lahoya	479	200	150	—
	Ixcuintepec, Juquila, El Tianquez	2,032[e]	200	150	—
	Yagavila, ½ Guatinicamanes (Petlapa, Yaci [Jocotepec], Lobani, Toavela)	(4,712)	—	200	200 (Yagavila only)
	Yabago (Yaneri)	282	—	100	
	Teotlaxco	168	—	150	
	Lalopa	423	—	150	
	Yaxila (Yagila)	169	—	70	
	Vechinaguia and Yatoni	163	—	70	
	Cuescomaltepec (S. J. Yae)	564	—	—	200
	Tagui and Yalahui	142[f]	—	—	140
Bixanos	Choapan	676	—	100	200
	Camotlán (& Comaltepec?)	494	—	50	—
	Zapotequillas	338	—	—	200
	Lazagaya,[g] El Tagui[g]	252	—	—	130

TABLE 2. (*continued*)

Ethnic Group	Corregimiento[a]	Population in 1568[b]	Corregidor Salaries in Pesos[c]		
			1530s	1545	1609
Chinantec	Lalana and "other pueblos"	—	150	—	—
	½ Guatinicamanes	4,231	150	—	—
	Teotalcingo, El Tagui (Bixanos)	(2,835)	—	150	—
Mixe	Tlahuitoltepec, Huitepec	986	150	150	200
	Metepec, Alotepec	479	200	—	—
	Yatove (?), Yacochi	168[h]	—	70[h]	150[h]
	Totontepec (& Tonaguia?)	(598)	—	—	200
	Otzolotepec	—	—	150	—
Other & Unidentified	½ Quilapa (Quezalapa), Nanacatepec, Xaltepec	—	200	100	—
	Suchitepec, Aguayo (Yagallo?)	—	200	100[i]	
	Balachita	—	—	150	
	Suchitepec	—	—	20	
	Guaxilpa	—	—	n/d	—
	Tecomatlán	—	—	150	120

Total number of corregimientos: 30

Note: Gerhard, *Guide*, p. 369, states that in 1545 there were 21 corregimientos in the district, but I have confirmed only 20. He further notes that in 1560–70 the number had "levelled off" at 25 (I confirm 23) and that towards 1600 the suffragan corregimientos (those that were subject to the alcalde mayor) were abolished.

[a] In many cases, only the name of the head town is given.

[b] Population figures are from Cook and Borah, *Central Mexico, 1531–1610*, pp. 84–88. Figures in parentheses are my interpolations from data for 1548 and 1622.

[c] "n/d" means the corregimiento existed in that year, but the salary is unknown. A line indicates that the pueblo was not in corregimiento in that year or that information is lacking. Several pueblos were in encomienda before becoming corregimientos (see table 1).

[d] Applies only to Teotalcingo.

[e] No figure for El Tianguez.

[f] Tagui only.

[g] Not mentioned after 1622 (not to be confused with Nexitzo San Juan Tagui).

[h] Yacochi only.

[i] Suchitepec only.

Sources: AGI Patronato 183, *2, ramo* 9 (Second Audiencia); AGI México 91, *1* (1545); AGN Tierras 2951:196–200, 202–7 (1609).

taken together did not produce enough tribute for one. Furthermore, the Indians were in the habit of fleeing the villages whenever an attempt was made to collect.[48]

EARLY ECONOMIC AND POLITICAL PROBLEMS

The picture that emerges of life in Villa Alta before 1556 is one of a reluctant settlement of about twenty Spanish vecinos, some of them with Spanish wives,[49] totally dependent on the Indians for subsistence and constantly on the verge of depopulation. One observer noted in 1544 that the vecinos lived on "gold, cotton, and corn."[50] Gold was never plentiful. Although a decade earlier the vecinos had declared they wanted to mine gold "because there is nothing else in the region,"[51] there is no evidence that mining was an important part of the economy at that time. That left corn and cotton, which were grown, and in the latter case woven into cloth, by the Indians. But the productive capacities of the pueblos were limited and the Indians often loathe to part with foodstuffs. Encomenderos complained in the 1530s that they could not get enough to eat and that they often had to buy food because their Indians would not give it to them. A few even abandoned their encomiendas because they could not support themselves.[52]

Cotton was another matter. Much, if not most of it was grown under the supervision of the vecinos, encomenderos, and corregidores. It was then sold or otherwise distributed to the Indian pueblos, for women to weave. By 1555, most pueblos were paying tribute only in money and cloth. Spanish peddlers who sold church ornaments and other goods to the Indians were customarily paid in cotton cloth, a practice that angered corregidores and encomenderos, since often pueblos did not have enough cloth left to pay their tribute quotas on time. Since it had become a scarce commodity, the price of cotton in the villa rose precipitously, and the cabildo began looking for ways to control prices and at the same time to force the Indians to part with more of their corn. It was finally decreed in 1555 that all villages must pay part of their tribute in corn, as specified in the quotas. In the case of encomenderos who did not reside in the villa—and there were several—their corn was to be sold at public auction and they would be given the proceeds. Only in this way, the cabildo declared, could the town provision itself.[53]

Villa Alta's problems were further compounded by the *in absentia* administrations of most of its alcaldes mayores during the first half of the sixteenth century. Following the departure of Luis de Berrio in 1531, only one of his eight or nine successors before 1556 appears to have spent much time in the villa.[54] Like so many others, the alcaldes mayores preferred the comforts of Antequera to the harsh realities of the Sierra.[55] This meant that the Spaniards with privileged access to the region's most exploitable resource—the

Indian population—did not reside in the district. Repeated viceregal orders that the magistrates establish residence in Villa Alta had little effect.[56]

One exception to this rule was Francisco de Sevilla, who served as alcalde mayor from 1542 to 1544. Newly arrived from Spain and in his first administrative post, he approached his job conscientiously, only to incur the wrath of the vecinos who accused him of favoring the Indians. The vecinos complained to the viceroy that Sevilla (1) terminated the use of Indians for personal service, especially for building and repairing houses, (2) abolished the local tradition of using tamemes, (3) limited the amount of weaving required of Indian women by corregidores and encomenderos, and (4) set low tribute quotas for corregimientos and disallowed meals as tribute. While the viceroys were not unsympathetic with Sevilla's goals, this alcalde mayor had no lasting impact on the community, and previous ways of doing things soon reappeared after his departure in 1544.[57]

Another early official who took a genuine interest in Villa Alta's growth was Luis de León Romano, *juez de comisión* (special commisioner) for the entire Province of Oaxaca in 1550. Among other duties, he was charged with conducting a residencia on the administration of Alcalde Mayor of Villa Alta Cristóbal de Chávez, a resident of Antequera. While in Villa Alta, Romano began construction of a new church (with a wall around it to protect women and children from Indian attacks), redesigned the town plaza, initiated efforts to widen the *caminos reales* (roads) to Antequera, and began construction of two bridges. Romano soon departed, however, and when Chávez was reappointed as alcalde mayor the following year the pace of public works slackened once again. Municipal officials were even driven to request the viceroy to direct any future aid or provisions directly to the cabildo itself, not to the alcaldes mayores, because they could not be trusted to follow through on orders.[58]

THE LATE SIXTEENTH CENTURY

Given these many problems and limited possibilities, it is a wonder that this fledgling Spanish outpost did not disappear altogether during the early sixteenth century. At the outset there were selective exploitation of Indian pueblos by Spanish officials and merchants and some ineffective attempts at proselytization by a few clergymen, but the conquerors did not succeed in establishing political control. Indian pueblos remained substantially autonomous and, even though they were paying tribute, were not yet incorporated into the colonial structure in any meaningful way. Spanish control, of an indirect sort, was not far off, however. As mentioned above, the arrival of the Dominicans in Villa Alta in 1558 was a turning point in the church's operations in the region. On the secular side, Spanish control advanced appreciably with the appointment of Juan de Salinas as alcalde mayor in 1555. Taking office the following year, Salinas served until 1560. He was a former vecino and regidor of Antequera and then corregidor of Teutila before arriving in Villa Alta. By 1563 he had left Oaxaca and become a resident of Puebla, where he was granted some land.[59]

Little specific is known about Salinas's activities as alcalde mayor, but his name is mentioned prominently in five related documents, originally written in Zapotec, that record the baptism of caciques and the measurement of community lands in five Zapotec pueblos. One of them mentions the Dominican Fray Jordán de Santa Catalina as well. The visits of these two individuals are conceptually merged in the documents with events of the 1520s, and it appears that Salinas was the first alcalde mayor to give formal legal recognition of cacique status and Indian communal landholdings.[60]

The splitting off of the Alcaldía Mayor of Nejapa, most of it formerly a part of the Villa Alta district, also occurred during the Salinas years. This large territory, inhabited by Zapotec, Mixe, and Chontal speakers, became a separate jurisdiction in 1560, though for the next decade the same alcaldes mayores served simultaneously in Villa Alta and Nejapa.[61] Missionaries were active in this region as early as 1554, and the Dominicans had begun construction of a convent in the town of Nejapa four years later.[62]

The Spanish town of Nejapa was founded about 1533, but was subsequently abandoned.[63] In 1560, with the creation of the new district, the majority of the vecinos of Villa Alta moved to Nejapa, which was located on a river next to a Zapotec town of the same name. Many of the settlers found the climate there inhospitable, however, and soon returned to Villa Alta.[64] By 1563, the four Dominicans in Nejapa were attending twenty-four Indian pueblos, the district contained sixteen corregimientos and seven encomiendas, and the Spanish vecinos who remained were already in conflict with their Zapotec neighbors.[65] Later in 1614, with the Zapotec pueblo greatly reduced in size, the Spanish moved their settlement and occupied the indigenous site, which had better access to land and water.[66]

The structure of encomienda and corregimiento in the Villa Alta district changed little during the second half of the sixteenth century. The figures in table 3 show that by the 1560s the number of encomiendas had dropped to twenty-three (down from twenty-nine in 1548) and that the number of corregimientos had risen from twenty (in 1545) to twenty-three. It appears that during this period, virtually all the villa's twenty to thirty vecinos were either corregidores or encomenderos; the remaining holders probably lived in Antequera. As the Indian population declined (see chapter 3), the amount of tribute that could be collected sank even lower and complaints from the vecinos about their poverty became more numerous. By 1599, all tribute was still being paid in cotton cloth and corn, and the vecinos frequently found themselves at odds with the alcaldes mayores when there was not enough to go around.[67] Towards 1600 the alcaldes mayores lost their privilege of distributing corregimientos,[68] but the problem of scarce resources continued to limit the size of the Hispanic community. In the first decade of

TABLE 3.   Encomiendas and Corregimientos in the Villa Alta District in the Second Half of the Sixteenth Century

Ethnic Group	Number of Encomiendas (Towns in Encomiendas)	Number of Corregimientos (Towns in Corregimientos)	Population 1568	Population in Encomiendas (%)	Population in Corregimientos (%)
Cajonos[a]	3 (12)	1 (2)	2,729	1,925 + [a]	215 + [a]
Nexitzo	8 (14)	11 (12)	7,566	3,820 (50.5%)	3,320 (43.9%)
Bixanos	2 (3)	3 (6)	3,978	535 (13.4%)	2,014 (50.6%)
Chinantec	3 (6)	3 (5)	7,632	4,604 (60.3%)	3,028 (39.7%)
Mixe	7 (15)	5 (8)	7,243	4,346 (60.0%)	1,893 (26.1%)
District Total	23 (50)	23 (33)	29,148	15,230 (52.3%)	10,470 (35.9%)

[a]Population data for and knowledge in general about the Cajonos pueblos are very fragmentary for the sixteenth century. I estimate that about half the Cajonos towns and population were in encomienda. Apart from the two towns in corregimiento, the remaining twelve pueblos were apparently still outside Spanish control.
Sources: Same as for tables 1 and 2, but especially ENE, 9:38−40 (1560) and AGI México 242 (1564) for encomiendas and AGN Tierras 2951:196−200, 202−7 (1609) for corregimientos.

the seventeenth century, the alcalde mayor drew up an annual list of *vecinos beneméritos y necesitados* who received a sum of money, *ayudas de costa*, from Mexico City. To join this select group, one had to be both in need and a descendant of conquistadores, and most vecinos easily met both criteria.[69]

The late sixteenth and early seventeenth centuries saw many of the usual sorts of Spanish abuses of Indian labor—Indians were forced to perform unpaid labor in the villa, had to carry their tribute there, and were illegally jailed when they refused to cooperate.[70] But in this region the abuses were often worse than in others because the colonists were permitted to use Indians as tamemes.[71] As the Indians put it in 1590, "the Spaniards make use of the macehuales as if they were horses."[72]

Abuse of Indian labor in Villa Alta was especially evident during the "building campaign" launched by Luis de León Romano in the 1550s[73] and again three decades later when the town had to be rebuilt following a disastrous fire on March 11, 1580.[74] Their convent in ruins, the Dominicans began to rebuild the following year, drawing on Indian labor from all parts of the district. Fourteen Mixe and fifteen Nexitzo pueblos were called on to supply raw materials, while twenty-five Bixanos and Cajonos towns together furnished a crew of fifty laborers each week.[75] At the same time still other Indians were conscripted to rebuild different structures in the villa. Laborers came from as far away as the Chinantec towns of Lobani, Yaci (Jocotepec), and Tepinapa, where it was said that many workers became ill and died on the way back home to the lowlands.[76]

The result of these efforts, and others that came later, was not a town of imposing dimensions. All structures were small and built of adobe, for the region lacked lime, and stone construction remained unfeasible. House roofs continued to be of thatch. The lack of skilled labor also placed strict limits on what could be accomplished architecturally. Even the Dominicans, who in the Valley of Oaxaca brought in outside architects to design their churches and convents, depended entirely on their own personnel in Villa Alta.[77]

Villa Alta did have its Indian allies, however.[78] The conquest of the Sierra Zapoteca was accomplished with the aid of Nahuatl-speaking *indios naborías* (free Indians required to work for Spaniards) from central Mexico, especially Tlaxcala. While they do not appear frequently in colonial records, Tlaxcalans were very much a part of Villa Alta from the beginning. Their roles as messengers, carriers, workers, and general intermediaries were similar to those they filled in other Spanish settlements in the colony, from Guatemala in the south to Santa Fe in the north.[79]

Virtually nothing is known of the activities of Villa Alta's naborías during the first half of the sixteenth century,[80] but they were surely an important pool of labor for the Spanish and probably played a key role, as they did later on in putting down and staving off local rebellions against the colonizers. We first hear from the naborías in a viceregal decree in 1549 that records their complaint that they were treated like slaves by the Spaniards, forced to work against their will, and not permitted to live where they wanted. Viceroy Antonio de Mendoza ordered that they could not be forced to work and that they must be paid for their labors. Evidently, the proddings of the viceroy—and probably population growth as well—had some effect, for in 1552 the cabildo of Villa Alta authorized a living site to the west of town for the naborías "and others who may want to come." In exchange for this land the cabildo imposed six conditions: (1) the naborías were to remain part of Villa Alta and subject to its authorities; (2) they could not take water illegally; (3) they could not plant crops in the ejidos of the villa; (4) they must not crowd the roads entering and leaving the villa; (5) they must provide messenger service to Antequera and Mexico City and repair the roofs of the church and Dominican convent when needed; and (6) they must help extinguish fires. This arrangement was approved by Viceroy Luis de Velasco I, but only on condition that the cabildo also assign some land to the naborías for cultivation.

The cabildo was reluctant to comply, for it did not want to part with any of its own ejidos, and all other land in the area was claimed by various pueblos. By 1555, however, the naboría barrio had grown sufficiently to be known informally as the pueblo of Nuestra Señora de la Concepción, with a Nahuatl-speaking *gobernador* and two alguaciles. In that year another viceregal order arrived, insisting that the Indians be granted some land. Knowing that the cabildo was unwilling to cooperate, the Indians presented the order to Marcos Ruiz de Rojas, the corregidor of Cuicatlán who was serving as *juez de residencia* in Villa Alta at the time. The naborías asked for some lands located a league from the villa near the road to Antequera, and their request was granted by Ruiz de Rojas on June 10, 1555. The cabildo claimed that most of this land belonged to the villa but said it had no objection since the vecinos were not using it. Some of the land, however, was claimed by Mixe Totontepec and the Cajonos Zapotec towns Yaa, Yohueche, and Nestepec.[81] Although an agreement of sorts was worked out in August 1555, it did not hold and protracted litigation ensued. Officials of San Andrés Yaa even visited the audiencia in Mexico City in 1567, but the naborías were never dislodged.

By the late 1560s the naboría settlement had evolved into the "estancia and pueblo of Papalotipac" and had its own alcaldes, a regidor, and a *mayordomo*. Soon thereafter it acquired the name of Analco,[82] and eventually adopted the Virgen del Rosario as its patron saint. While the new town maintained its Nahua character, Zapotec migrants from the hinterland were arriving steadily. By 1571 the Zapotecs had established their own barrio, known as Elotepec or simply Las Milpas, within the *traza* (the central, Spanish portion) of Villa Alta but subject to the political authority of Analco. Ethnic friction between the two was considerable in the 1570s. One faction in Las Milpas, the smaller of the two settlements, urged that it separate from Analco and incorporate as a distinct pueblo. Receiving no support from the alcalde mayor, the Zapotecs petitioned the viceroy, who handed down a compromise decision in 1575. There was to be only one naboría cabildo—in Analco—but Las Milpas could have its own *alguacil mayor* (police chief) since its people were of a different "nation and language" than the *mexicanos* of Analco.[83] This policy failed, however. The alcaldes mayores continued to insist that Las Milpas be subject to the police authority of Analco, and the two appear to have merged completely by the end of the sixteenth century. Nahua and Tlaxcalan dominance in Analco remained, but Zapotec and Mixe influences increased as migrants arrived from pueblos in the region.

When it stabilized in the late sixteenth century, Analco came to be officially known as a barrio of Villa Alta. Though it had its own political officials, it did not acquire the status of pueblo until much later in the colonial period. The Indians of Analco occupied a unique and in some ways privileged niche in the colonial society of the Sierra Zapoteca. As naborías of Villa Alta, they were freed from paying tribute in 1572.[84] They may also have been granted the right to use firearms.[85] But in return for this privileged status they were expected to perform "voluntarily" a myriad of services for the Spanish vecinos on whom they were dependent. The reality was just a different form of exploitation, as Villa Alta's vecinos ignored the law and forced the people of Analco to work as tamemes, messengers, and servants without pay.[86]

THE SEVENTEENTH AND EIGHTEENTH CENTURIES

Villa Alta in the seventeenth and eighteenth centuries was not a very different place than it was in earlier years. While it was established as a permanent settlement, it remained a small, isolated outpost still economically dependent on the Indians of the province. The population estimates in table 4 suggest that the number of Hispanic inhabitants changed little between 1565 and 1742, remaining at about 150. The figures for Analco are less reliable, but it is clear that during much of Villa Alta's colonial history its Spanish residents were definitely outnumbered by their Indian naborías.

Some political and economic changes occurred. The eleven remaining corregimientos in 1609 (see table 2) seem to have been abolished soon thereafter, following the decision to remove them from the control of the alcalde mayor.[87] The number of encomiendas in the jurisdiction dwindled steadily in the middle and late colonial period (see table 1). Nine survived the sixteenth century, but only one persisted until the eighteenth century. Most of these encomiendas were too small and their inhabitants too poor to provide much remuneration for their holders, most of whom were vecinos of Villa Alta in the seventeenth century.

The Nexitzo pueblos Tepanzacualco and Lachichina (whose inhabitants complained of being overworked in mines in 1633) were still in encomienda to vecinos Nicolás de Chávez and Juan Próspero as late as 1653, and Chinantec Lachixila was in the hands of Gonzalo de Alcántara and later (1679) his widow Ana María de Chávez. Mixe Ayacastla and sujetos belonged to Francisco López Muñíz as late as 1628, though this was the last record we have for this pueblo. The Ocotepec encomienda escheated shortly after 1652 with the death of Antonia de Angulo, widow of Juan Gutiérrez Gigón. Juan Andrés Coronado was encomendero of the Bixanos pueblo Yovego in 1680, the latest mention of this encomienda. The only documented holding still in

TABLE 4.   Colonial Population of Villa Alta and Analco

Year	Villa Alta	Analco	Source and Method of Calculating
1565	145		AGI Patronato 20, *5, ramo* 1 (5 × vecinos)
1568	150		Cook and Borah, *Central Mexico, 1531–1610*, p. 58 (5 × 30 vecinos)
1703		271	AGI México 881, *12* (4.6 × casados)
1742	148	135	AGI Indiferente 108 (Villa Alta: 6 × families less 5%; Analco: 5 × families)
1781	184	355	CCG "Estado o plan de las ciudades . . ." (full count)
1826	289	156	Murguía y Galardi, "Extracto general" . . .

existence in the eighteenth century comprised the six Cajonos pueblos (see chapter 3) plus San Juan Yatzona. In 1748 it belonged to a minor in Ante-quera, don Manuel Joaquín Nieto de Silva y Moctezuma. Twenty years later, when he had become the proprietor of a store in the city, half of his encomienda rent was sequestered, but he controlled the remaining half for some years to come.[88]

With the demise of the encomiendas and corregimientos, many vecinos of the villa departed, and the seventeenth century was not much more pros-perous for the community than the sixteenth had been. There were indica-tions by 1606 that the villa lacked the necessary critical mass of permanent vecinos for an effective municipal government. In that year the alcalde mayor annulled the municipal elections, following a *real provisión* from the audiencia that forbade regidores to vote for their relatives or boarders. Elec-tions were again annulled the following year, this time by the viceroy, be-cause they were made by only a single regidor in the presence of the alcalde mayor's lieutenant.[89] Despite these problems, the cabildo continued to exist for a few more decades with two alcaldes ordinarios, six regidores, and an *escribano* (secretary).[90] But by 1640 it had become moribund and was abol-ished. This same year saw the founding of the chapel of Santo Domingo, with its own *cofradía*, or brotherhood, that formally took over the admin-istration of the villa's ejido lands. Alcalde Mayor Almirante don Gerónimo Bañuelos y Carrillo attended the first mass on August 4, 1640, and declared the chapel a *capilla real*. In 1673 vecinos of the villa donated additional land to the chapel, which remained in existence until about 1790. In 1796 a large part of the ejidos of Villa Alta were still referred to as "lands of Santo Domingo Soriano."[91] Not until after independence in the 1820s would Villa Alta revive its municipal council.

One of the reasons the cabildo was suspended for so long was that the alcaldes mayores wanted it that way. With no town officials and few enco-menderos to placate, the magistrates could wield more power in the district and aim for a virtual monopoly on the biggest prize of all: the lucrative trade in cochineal dyestuff and cotton cloth. In a letter to the crown in 1663 the bishop of Oaxaca observed that the post of alcalde mayor of Villa Alta was by far the richest in the entire Province of Oaxaca because of the com-mercial possibilities it offered. He added that the villa's population of forty-five vecinos had been halved due to the threatening behavior of the alcaldes mayores. Many Spaniards had left to seek their fortunes elsewhere, and con-sequently the town's Hispanic population remained smaller than those of Yanhuitlan and Teposcolula in the Mixteca Alta.[92]

During the sixteenth and much of the seventeenth centuries alcaldes may-ores were appointed by the viceroy. Sixteenth-century appointees tended to be local men from Antequera. Later on, as the possibilities for enrichment in Villa Alta increased, high-ranking officials in Mexico City came to domi-nate the post (Appendix A lists all confirmed alcaldes mayores and subdelegados of Villa Alta). It had become one of the most remunerative offices in the land, and to be considered for it one had to be very well connected in the patronage networks of the capital. For example, Alcalde Mayor don Pedro Fernández de Villaroel y de la Cueva (1659–61) had served as a general in the Philippines and was a nephew of Viceroy Francisco Fernández de la Cueva, the Duque de Albuquerque (1653–60).[93] His successor in Villa Alta in 1662 was don Felipe de Leyva de la Cerda, relative of Viceroy Juan de Leyva y de la Cerda (1660–64) and son of don Felipe Morán de la Cerda, who held the title of Sargento Mayor de la Gobernación y Guerra de Nueva España.[94] The following year Viceroy Leyva appointed his own son, Pedro de Leyva, as alcalde mayor of Villa Alta, the post regarded by the viceroy as the best in all of New Spain (another son, Gaspar, served as magistrate in Xicayán, Oaxaca). However, Pedro had no intention of putting up with the hardships of life in the Sierra Zapoteca. He never went to Villa Alta but sent his personal barber, Joseph Martínez, as his lieutenant.[95]

In 1677 the privilege of appointing alcaldes mayores passed to the crown.[96] Beginning with don Cristóbal de Castillo Mondragón (1668, 1677–82), the magistrates sent to Villa Alta tended to be peninsular noblemen, most of them military men and Caballeros of the Orden de Santiago. The customary term of appointment was for five years (see Appendix A). Some examples: don Miguel Ramón de Nogales (1692–96) had previously served for several years in Veracruz as Capitán de Infantería Española; Maestre de Campo don Francisco Benítez Maldonado (1701–2), also a military man, had served for twenty-two years in the Armada del Océano and as Corregidor Interino in Veracruz; Capitán don Diego de Rivera y Cotes (1703–8) had served in Naples and in the Armada Real del Océano; don Joseph Francisco de Madrigal (1719–23[?]) had been Teniente General de Guerras in Cartagena; don Antonio Blanco de Sandoval (1730–34 [?]) was a Teniente Coronel de Caballería with many years of service in Seville and Calatrava; don Alonso de Basco y Vargas (1762–65[?]) was a Teniente de Navío de la Real Armada in the peninsula.[97]

The list goes on but the pattern never changed: these were men who had served their king well, usually in military service, and were sent to Villa Alta late in their careers as a reward for services rendered. These officials may have known or cared little about Indian administration, but they took full advantage of the trading opportunities that came with the office. In 1767 the post was still ranked administratively at the top of the "first class" alcaldías mayores of New Spain, with neighboring Nejapa as number two.[98]

Throughout the entire colonial period—and today as well—Villa Alta was the only Hispanic community in a vast Indian region. No precise information is available on the ethnic and racial composition of the villa in the sixteenth and seventeenth centuries, but some fragmentary figures exist for the late colonial period. These show—as a visit to the area today confirms—that most of the non-Indians in the alcaldía mayor lived in Villa Alta. A census of adult mulattoes in the district in 1806 turned up only twenty-eight individuals. Only four communities had more than two each: Villa Alta (5), Choapan (6), Ayutla (4), and Solaga (3).[99] The best overall profile of the late colonial population of the district is furnished by an *alcabala* (sales tax) census of 1781, summarized in table 5. Only those pueblos with any recorded non-Indian inhabitants are listed; the rest were entirely Indian. The figures indicate that blacks were practically nonexistent and that recognized *mestizaje* was minimal. Most of the Spaniards living outside Villa Alta were either priests or merchants.

A partial view of the racial composition of the villa itself can be derived from parish church records. Of the registers of vital statistics, the marriage books were the only ones that recorded racial affiliation, and even these did not do so consistently. The figures in table 6, fragmentary as they are, do tell us a few things. During the eighty-one years between 1729 and 1810 marriages averaged two per year in Villa Alta's parish church. During the last twelve years (1789–1810) the number of marriages increased to an average of 4.3 per year. The small number of peninsular grooms and the complete absence of peninsular brides is noteworthy. Most persons were placed in the three main categories of creole (*español*), mestizo, and Indian, with creoles predominating. The categories of castizo and mulatto were little used, and blacks were absent altogether (or at least the few there may have been did not marry in the church). Since nearly three-quarters of all marriage partners in the sample were not identified by race, it is not possible to draw any firm conclusions other than that Villa Alta was a predominantly creole community and that race in itself was not a terribly important element in the town's social structure. Much more salient and of far greater import was the cultural division between Hispanics and Indians.[100]

A final bit of information that can be gleaned from the marriage records concerns the places of origin of brides and grooms. These are listed in table 7. Some 58 percent of the identified marriage partners were natives of Villa Alta, and 85 percent were native to the Oaxaca region. A significant number had come from Antequera, and the eight peninsular men represented widely different parts of Spain. While it might appear from these figures that the villa's population had finally stabilized after the more turbulent and transient years of the sixteenth and seventeenth centuries, there is no reliable way to gauge the size of the villa's transient population in the eighteenth century, for temporary residents would rarely consider marrying there. To judge from the frequent complaints about the trading monopolies of the alcaldes mayores (to be discussed in chapter 4) and the lack of a cabildo in the town, however, the number of transients and their rate of turnover must have been substantial. All indications are that no vecino could remain long in Villa Alta and hope to sustain himself without establishing some sort of exploitative relationship with some of the Indian pueblos of the district. The town was not large enough to demand the services of many full-time craftsmen

TABLE 5.   The Non-Indian Population of the Villa Alta District, 1781[a]

Town	Españoles or Gente de Razón	Castas	Indians	Total
Villa Alta	64	92	28	184
Analco	1		354	355
Cajonos Zapotec Towns				
San Melchor Betaza[b]	4		1,165	1,169
San Pedro Cajonos	1		462	463
San Juan Tabaa	2		697	699
San Juan Yalalag[c]	3		2,102	2,105
San Francisco Yatee[d]	4		518	522
Santiago Zoochila	28	6	448	482
Nexitzo Zapotec Towns				
San Miguel Talea[e]	4	10	570	584
San Juan Tanetze[f]	9		363	372
San Juan Yae[g]	2		852	854
Santa Cruz Yagavila	2		365	367
Bixanos Zapotec Towns				
San Juan Comaltepec	2		1,003	1,005
Santiago Choapan	7		1,440	1,447
Santo Domingo Latani	5		927	932
Santa María Yahuive	6		661	667
Chinantec Towns				
Santa María Lachixila	2		860	862
San Juan Teotalcingo	2		311	313
Mixe Towns				
Santiago Atitlán	3		489	492
San Pablo Ayutla	2		710	712
San Cristóbal Chichicaxtepec	1		69	70
Santa María Puxmetacan	2		533	535
Santo Domingo Tepuxtepec		1	623	624
Santa María Totontepec[h]	4		960	964
Total	160	109	16,510	16,779

[a]Only towns with resident non-Indians are listed. In table 9 slightly different figures are given for Betaza, Yalalag, Yatee, Talea, Tanetze, Totontepec, and Yae for 1781. They represent an averaging of the 1777 and 1781 censuses and include only Indians.

[b]1777 (AGI México 2589, 56): 2 españoles and 2 mulattoes.

[c]1777 (ibid., exp. 58): 1 priest and 1 free black.

[d]1777 (ibid., exp. 56): lists no non-Indians.

[e]1777 (ibid. 2591, exp. 2): 2 españoles, 16 mestizos, 2 mulattoes.

[f]1777 (ibid.): 5 españoles and 4 mestizos.

[g]1777 (ibid. 2589, exp. 50): 4 españoles, 5 mestizos, 2 mulattoes.

[h]1777 (ibid. 2590, exp. 4): 2 españoles and 35 mestizos.

Source: CCG "Estado o plan de las ciudades . . ."

TABLE 6.   Racial Composition of Marriage Partners in Villa Alta,
1729–1810

Classification	Men	Women	Total
Peninsulars	8		8
Creoles	24	11	35
Castizos	1	2	3
Mestizos	9	12	21
Free Mulattoes	2		2
Mulatto Slaves	1		1
Indians	6	15	21
Unidentified	115	126	241
Total	166	166	332

Source: APVA "Libros de Casamientos," 1729–1810.

TABLE 7.   Places of Origin of Marriage Partners in Villa Alta, 1729–1810

Place of Birth	Men	Women	Total
Villa Alta	70	78	148
Analco	17	30	47
Antequera	18	6	24
Indian pueblos in district	9	13	22
Spain (Asturias, Pamplona, Navarra, Vizcaya, Jerez de la Frontera, Sevilla)	8		8
Puebla	2		2
Mexico City	3		3
Guanajuato	1		1
Unknown	38	39	77
Total	166	166	332

Source: APVA "Libros de Casamientos," 1729–1810.

and artisans. The first item of priority for household provisionment was, of course, food. But the obstacles to obtaining basic staples were often challenging, since none of the Spaniards or creoles of the villa was willing to grow crops, and the town had no market during most of its colonial history. As late as 1690, the alcalde mayor claimed that since there was no *tianguis* (Indian market) in the villa, all his provisions had to be brought in from Indian pueblos.[101] Mention is made of a weekly Sunday market in 1724 and again in 1769 (at which meat from Tehuantepec was sold), but it was small and probably did not satisfy all the vecinos' needs.[102]

During much of the colonial period, but almost certainly not before the Mixe rebellion of 1570, Villa Alta had a special relationship with several Mixe towns, including Totontepec, which at the beginning had ceded some of its land for the founding of the intrusive Spanish community. In the

1690s considerable wrangling arose over whether or not Mixes should continue to be obligated to sell corn to the vecinos of Villa Alta as part of their
tribute obligations. The communities in question included Jayacaxtepec, Totontepec, Tamazulapan, Alotepec, Cotzocón, Chisme, Candayoc, Zacatepec,
Ayacaxtepec, and Metepec. Fray Bartolomé de Alcántara noted that since
the 1630s it had been customary for all the tributaries from these pueblos to
sell half a fanega of corn to the villa at the rate of nine *reales* per fanega. The
corn was in turn redistributed among the vecinos. The friar claimed that
lands in the Mixe pueblos were especially fertile and produced two harvests
each year. He then sounded what by then had become a familiar refrain:
since the vecinos grew no crops of their own, the villa might depopulate
altogether unless the Mixes were forced to continue selling their corn. The
friar added that some vecinos had already left for Antequera.

The Mixes, on their side, saw these demands as excessive, for they were
not always able to produce enough corn to feed both themselves and the
Spaniards comfortably. At times they had to purchase corn at a higher price
than that for which they sold it in the villa. At some time before 1693, the
Mixe pueblos had convinced the audiencia that they should not continue to
pay tribute in corn. But after the vecinos protested vigorously of their *ex-
trema calamidad*, the audiencia reversed itself a year later and reinstituted
the old system. In a few months, however, it became clear that there was just
not enough corn for everyone and the Mixes were once again paying tribute
in money to the alcalde mayor.[103] Since the vecinos produced little food of
their own except for small quantities of meat, they continued to pressure the
Mixes for corn whenever it was available.

Two other services traditionally performed by the same Mixe pueblos—
and upheld by the audiencia in 1694—were repairing the thatched roofs of
the vecinos' houses ("because no one else knows how to do it except the Indians") and *repartimiento* labor service.[104] During the seventeenth century,
the ten communities furnished, on a rotating basis, two workers each week
to each Spanish vecino. The alcaldes mayores received an even greater variety of services from the Zapotec pueblos of Roayaga, Tagui, Temaxcalapan,
Yalahui, Yatzona, Yaa, Yatee, and Lachitaa. Besides furnishing servants for
the magistrate's household, these villages also supplied tamemes, horses, and
mules for frequent trips to Antequera.[105]

Much to their annoyance, Indians of the region were also forced to take
part in numerous political and religious festivities in the villa all through
the colonial period. The two most important occasions were the fiestas of San
Ildefonso in January and Corpus Christi in the spring. By 1685, Villa Alta
had at least two cofradías—de la Veracruz and de las Benditas Animas del
Purgatorio—to aid in sponsoring religious fiestas. But the alcaldes mayores
adroitly used these occasions to symbolically commemorate the Spanish conquest and the subordination of the Indians. Villagers were required to come
from as far away as twenty to thirty leagues and to spend five or six days in

the villa carrying flags, drums, and other musical instruments. They had to bring their own provisions with them, and many village governments developed a custom of imposing *derramas* (levies) in their communities to pay for these travel expenses of town officials.[106]

Villa Alta also had a small Indian population of its own that served the Spaniards in a menial capacity. Toward the end of the colonial period in 1806 it numbered 161 persons, or 25.5 tributaries.[107] Some of these were known as *indios terrazgueros:* displaced families from different pueblos who rented small parcels of land from the villa. In the 1790s one subdelegado decided to rescind their rent payments as long as they continued to work on communal projects. In the words of the terrazgueros in 1796: "We have always recognized this Villa in our work. It is well known that we have always worked in the church, in the plaza, on the roads, and in other specific duties. We contribute with good will for the benefits we receive, for the right to live in places that the vecinos give us without pay, and also for the lands we have where we plant corn and other crops."[108]

These terrazgueros were far outnumbered by the naborías of the Barrio of Analco, however, which during most of the eighteenth century was larger than Villa Alta. In 1664 Analco received permission to build a chapel to Nuestra Señora de los Remedios, who became patron saint of the community when it emerged as a separate pueblo sometime before 1787.[109]

Over the years Analco maintained its special relationship with the Hispanic community in Villa Alta. Even after it became a pueblo, Analco's inhabitants were still forced to perform a variety of services for the Spaniards. In addition to traditional messenger service, Analco also provided watchmen to patrol the streets of the villa at night with the authority to arrest unruly vecinos.[110] Analco also played a key role in maintaining order in the district. In 1684 the community boasted of its effectiveness in quelling local rebellions against Spanish mistreatment in Choapan, Lachixila, San Francisco Cajonos, Yalalag, Huitepec, Yagavila, and Yojovi.[111] Alcalde Mayor Francisco Marty observed a century later in 1782:

> The Indians of this province are so afraid of the [Analco officials] that the pueblos have remained in peace and tranquility, and with good government. In whatever they are called upon or commissioned to do [the people of Analco] are given respect, for they are descendants of the first Indians who aided the *conquistadores* in this province. For that reason they are exempt from the payment of royal tribute and enjoy other privileges.[112]

While they enjoyed some privileges, the naborías of Analco were still Indians and therefore still subservient. Four years later, Marty's successor, Pablo de Ortega, decided that a shortage of provisions in the villa could be overcome by distributing seed to all the residents of Analco and ordering each household to plant three *almudes* of corn.[113]

The Tlaxcalan heritage of Analco was never forgotten, though by late colonial times it remained little more than a memory. According to neighboring Mixe Totontepec, in 1772 Analco had only four men who were directly
descended from original Tlaxcalan inhabitants in the sixteenth century.[114]
Most residents by that time were descendants of migrants from Jalatlaco (a
barrio of Indian naborías adjacent to Antequera), Totontepec, the Cajonos
pueblos, Yaxila, and others.[115]

Surviving marriage registers from Analco's parish church for 1747–96
show that with an average of 4.1 marriages per year, the community was
more populous than Villa Alta. It was certainly a less transient settlement.
Table 8 shows the places of birth of all people married in Analco between
1747 and 1796 (all were Indians). Of the 312 individuals whose places of
birth are known, fully 73 percent were natives of the barrio. The community was also significantly endogamous: 76.3 percent of the grooms born in
Analco married women who were also natives. As was seen in table 7, some
Analco natives married in Villa Alta and had probably moved there, but
they were few. While the Nahuatl language and a relatively cosmopolitan
culture persisted in eighteenth-century Analco, the community had clearly
been considerably transformed by extensive in-migration, especially from
Zapotec towns in the district. These migrants, however, do not appear to
have maintained close ties with their native villages. By moving to Analco
they became naborías. The *padrinos* selected for the 253 baptisms performed
in Analco between 1777 and 1800 were local residents in over 75 percent of
the cases. The sponsors from outside the community (57, or 22.5 percent)
were predominantly creoles and peninsulars from Villa Alta.[116] Similar to
these relations of compadrazgo between Indians and Spaniards, Analco remained very much a client community dependent on its patron, Villa Alta.
Much later, in the 1940s, Analco ceased to be a separate community and
merged with Villa Alta.

CONCLUSION

The picture that emerges of the Spanish presence in Villa Alta throughout
the colonial period is one of a small, often transient group of colonists constantly struggling against great odds to fulfill their dreams of conquest and,
if not to get rich, to at least make some money. Very few of them succeeded.
The chief arena of Spanish economic, political, and religious activities was
not in Villa Alta itself, but in the Indian communities, and these topics will
be discussed in detail in subsequent chapters. After a prolonged and bloody
conquest and a period of tenuous Spanish control that lasted thirty-five
years, Villa Alta in the midsixteenth century found itself in very precarious
circumstances. Though it established itself better in the seventeenth and
eighteenth centuries, this fragility always remained.

TABLE 8. Places of Origin of Marriage Partners in Analco, 1747–96

Place of Birth	Men	Women	Total
Analco	114	114	228
Villa Alta	2	6	8
Antequera	6		6
Jalatlaco	2		2
Ciudad de Tlaxcala		1	1
Cajonos Zapotec Towns			
San Cristóbal Lachirioag		4	4
San Andrés Solaga	1		1
San Andrés Yaa	1		1
Santa Catarina Yahuio	1		1
San Francisco Yatee	2	1	3
San Baltazar Yatzachi Alto	1	1	2
Santiago Zoochila	1		1
San Bartolomé Zoogocho	1		1
Nexitzo Zapotec Towns			
Santiago Lalopa		1	1
Santo Domingo Roayaga	3	2	5
San Juan Tagui		1	1
San Juan Tanetze		1	1
Santa María Temaxcalapan	2	4	6
Santiago Yagallo	1	1	2
Santa Cruz Yagavila		2	2
San Juan Yalahui		1	1
San Juan Yatzona	3	4	7
Santa María Yaviche	1		1
San Juan Yetzecovi	3	2	5
Bixanos Zapotec Towns			
Santiago Choapan	1		1
San Juan Roavela	1		1
Chinantec Towns			
Santiago Jocotepec		1	1
Mixe Towns			
Santa María Totontepec	3	6	9
Santa María Tonaguia	2		2
Santiago Zacatepec	1		1
San Pablo Ayutla	1		1
Santo Domingo Tepuxtepec	1		1
District of Teutila			
Tlacoatzintepec (Chinantec)	1		1

TABLE 8.   (*continued*)

Place of Birth	Men	Women	Total
District of Nejapa			
Lapaguia (Chontal)	1		1
Zoquitlan (Zapotec)		1	1
District of Teococuilco			
Teococuilco (Zapotec)	1		1
Unknown	41	45	86
Total	199	199	398

Source: APVA "Libros de Casamientos de Analco," 1747–96.

Almost wholly dependent on the Indians for sustenance, the villa possessed a makeshift character more reminiscent of a trading outpost than a permanent community. This was reflected not only in its tiny population and lack of a cabildo after 1640, but also in the steadfast refusal of the colonists to grow their own food even in times of scarcity. Indeed, 170 years after Spanish penetration of the region, the people of Villa Alta still had not learned how to repair the leaky roofs on their houses. This indicates a curious refusal to adapt to the local environment. Whenever practical problems emerged—which was quite often—the solution inevitably proposed was: "Let's have the Indians do it." Hence the colonists were fated to remain as parasites on Indian society, through what could be siphoned off by encomienda, corregimiento, repartimiento, and other means of appropriating Indian tribute. When this failed, small-scale mining with Indian labor and trade with the Indians (mostly forced) were the only economic alternatives.

The political economy of the region placed most of the power and wealth in the hands of a few individuals who would come and go—the alcaldes mayores—while condemning those who stayed to perpetual poverty. Given the virtual nonexistence of a Spanish market economy in the district, it was perhaps inevitable that the flow of power and resources would be determined principally by the structure of political administration controlled from Mexico City and Madrid. This situation, coupled with a very large Indian population that could be compelled to cultivate cochineal and weave cotton at home, made the Alcaldía Mayor of Villa Alta distinctive in colonial Mexico.

CHAPTER 3

POPULATION AND SETTLEMENT

To STUDY FULLY the impact of Spanish colonialism on the people of the Sierra Zapoteca, it is necessary to know something about population trends in the region. It will also be helpful to construct an estimate of the indigenous population of 1520, on the eve of the conquest. Other related topics to be examined in this chapter are settlement patterns, epidemics, and *congregaciones*, the attempts at forced settlement by the Spaniards.

POPULATION

Any attempt to reconstruct contact-period and colonial population levels in Mexico is bound to be controversial. For the Alcaldía Mayor of Villa Alta, like other regions, reliable counts were few and were usually expressed as numbers of tributaries, families, or *casados* (household heads). Conversion of such figures to estimates of total population requires certain assumptions about household size and the ratio of tributaries to total population in different periods. Further assumptions are necessary to make use of colonial data to derive estimates for the pre-contact period. In the discussion and tables that follow, I have attempted to apply the methodology, and some of the substantive results, of the landmark studies of Sherburne F. Cook and Woodrow Borah.[1]

Table 9 gives population figures for towns in the Alcaldía Mayor of Villa Alta in eighteen different years, beginning in 1548 and ending in 1970. For the colonial period, counts are available for 1548, 1568, 1622, 1703, 1742, 1781, 1789, and 1820. The sources for 1548, 1568, 1622, and 1742 are now well known and have been studied extensively by Cook and Borah, Peter Gerhard, and others.[2] Those for 1703, 1781, 1789, and 1820 are specific to the Villa Alta district.

With the exception of 1781, all the counts through 1820 were of tributaries or families, and methods must be devised to convert these into estimates of total population. Furthermore, the sources for the earlier years do not give counts for all the communities, and a way to fill in these gaps is needed. From 1826 on, however, the sources give total population counts and few adjustments are necessary. While this book is concerned with the colonial period, I have included population figures for the nineteenth and twentieth centuries for the sake of completeness and also for comparison. The following analysis of population trends begins with a description of sources and methods for each year, then moves on to consider the significance of the data for the various ethnic groups and the district as a whole.

1548

The source for 1548 is Borah and Cook's analysis of the tribute counts in the *Suma de visitas de pueblos*, the only general survey of the Mexican Indian population before 1560.[3] The *visita* (tour of inspection) in the Villa Alta district covered approximately fifty towns and was carried out between 1548 and 1550. While the counts in the *Suma* are much lower than later ones, Borah and Cook hold that this was because the *Suma* was intended to determine only the tributary population, and they estimate that in regions like the Zapotecas where there were no mayeques, 35 percent of the population was exempt from tribute at that time.[4] They calculated the tributary population by multiplying the number of casados for each town by the factor of 3.3. The figures not in parentheses in table 9 represent Borah and Cook's calculated tributary population for each town, plus 35 percent.

Many communities are still unaccounted for, however. The *Suma* was far from complete, especially for marginal regions like the Sierra Zapoteca that were not yet firmly under Spanish control. In order to correct for this deficiency, I have selected forty-two towns (excluding the atypical Guatinicamanes, which was really a group of four towns, and Choapan, Xaltepec, and Nanacatepec) for which counts are available both in the *Suma* and also for 1568 (see below). Dividing the total population estimate for each town by the corresponding 1568 estimate and then taking the average yields a ratio that can be used to fill in the blanks for 1548, provided that figures exist for the communities in question in 1568. Cook and Borah expressed the rationale for this procedure:

> The underlying principle may be conceived as the tendency of population ratios to remain stable in space and time and may be expressed thus: With respect to whole populations, or subordinate categories thereof, the ratio between two components, or between two spatial entities, remains relatively constant through an appreciable interval of time. This principle is very versatile and is applicable to a wide range of situations.[5]

In the case at hand, the mean ratio of 2.719 is used to produce estimates for twenty-two towns in 1548.[6] These appear in parentheses in table 9.[7] For these twenty-two, the Cook and Borah estimate for 1568 is multiplied by the ratio of 2.719 to get an estimated population count for 1548.

1568

Figures for this year are the total population estimates constructed by Cook and Borah, using a variety of data from the years 1565–70.[8] By this time,

TABLE 9.   Population of the Alcaldía Mayor of Villa Alta, 1548–1970[a]

Name	Sta-tus	Dis-trict	1548	1568	1622	1703	1742	1781	1789
Cajonos Zapotec Towns									
Betaza, San Melchor	M	V	—	—	—	935	1,234	1,287[b]	1,049
Cajonos, San Francisco (Tehuilotepec)	M	V	706	254	1,002	506	735	456	440
Cajonos, San Mateo	M	V	—	—	—	184	452	342	311
Cajonos, San Miguel (1970: S.F. Cajonos)	A	V	—	—	—	129	121	138	74
Cajonos, San Pedro (Yaechi)	M	V	—	—	—	258	382	463	440
Guiloxi, San Sebastián (1970: Laxopa)	A	I	—	—	—	133	37	392	363
Lachirioag, San Cristóbal	M	V	—	—	—	1,242	1,434	1,285	1,321
Lachitaa, Santo Tomás (1970: Betaza)	A	V	—	—	—	178	419	508	211
Laxopa, Santiago	M	I	—	—	—	166	512	647	601
Miahuatlán (sujeto of Tabaa)	—	—	683	(251)	—	—	—	—	—
Solaga, San Andrés	M	V	—	—	—	299	801	913	749
Tabaa, San Juan	M	V	1,012	338[c]	570	699	1,019	697	568
Tavehua, Santa María (1970: Solaga)	A	V	—	—	—	129	354	387	368
Xagacia, Santo Domingo (S.D. Cajonos)	M	V	—	—	—	129	124	174	165
Yaa San Andrés (Yao)	M	V	(767)	282	495	240	419	604	699
Yaganiza, San Pablo (S.P. Cajonos)	M	V	(381)	140	(124)	363	237	271	244
Yahuio, Santa Catarina (1970: Laxopa)	A	I	—	—	—	216	466	199	229
Yalalag, San Juan (Villa Hidalgo)	M	V	(460)	169	306	1,577	1,752	2,280[b]	2,220
Yuguiba (Trapiche)	—	—	—	—	—	193	(287)	55	—

1820	1826	1882	1900	1910	1921	1930	1940	1950	1960	1970
1,066	1,425	1,505	1,275	1,246	1,252	1,286	1,328	1,300	(1,294[c])	1,236
333	361	630	572	581	476	518	537	559	560	751
296	362	549	575	618	536	558	588	665	862	978
168	161	345	363	598	424	403	466	466	431	144
533	455	775	802	822	911	867	1,083	1,255	1,287	1,276
215	276	294	317	402	263	269	297	315	316	346
1,147	1,431	1,895	1,967	1,978	1,566	1,844	1,761	1,675	1,748	1,679
(245)	251	255	247	247	235	253	251	260	(329[d])	398
411	492	671	837	890	764	860	767	1,125	1,138	1,063
—	—	—	—	—	—	—	—	—	—	—
392	902	1,460	1,251	1,202	1,111	1,171	1,110	1,134	1,157	1,148
392	428	681	691	686	673	758	858	892	964	1,064
355	361	451	378	406	430	410	409	423	431	464
237	305	515	719	830	771	866	879	1,139	1,484	1,453
592	947	1,085	992	874	825	519	774	797	838	769
329	300	728	712	719	667	733	844	979	1,070	1,095
228	270	334	314	370	355	368	410	491	434	476
1,972	3,232	3,458	3,238	3,261	3,407	3,320	3,020	3,000	3,117	2,848
—	—	—	—	—	—	—	—	—	—	—

TABLE 9.   (*continued*)

Name	Sta-tus	Dis-trict	1548	1568	1622	1703	1742	1781	1789
Yalina, Santa María	M	V	—	—	—	175	(260)	416	442
Yatee, San Francisco (1970: Villa Alta)	A	V	—	—	—	327	(487)	559[b]	496
Yatzachi El Alto, San Baltazar (1970: Yatzachi El Bajo)	A	V	—	—	—	458	410	366	296
Yatzachi El Bajo, San Baltazar	M	V	—	—	—	—	605	557	535
Yohueche, Santa María (1970: Yatzachi El Bajo)	A	V	—	—	—	163	284	257	246
Yojovi, Santo Domingo (1970: Solaga)	A	V	—	—	—	375	442	407	305
Zoochila, Santiago	M	V	(919)	338	789	253	563	482	383
Zoochina, San Gerónimo (1970: Yatzachi El Bajo)	A	V	—	—	—	184	279	239	165
Zoochixtepec, Santa María (1970: Yatzachi El Bajo)	A	V	120	215	313	(81)	121	177	155
Zoogocho, San Bartolomé	M	V	2,334	742	502	368	982	971	905
Total			**7,382**	**2,729**	**4,103**	**9,960**	**15,218**	**15,529**	**13,980**
Nexitzo Zapotec Towns									
Cacalotepec, Santo Domingo (1970: Ixtlán)	A	I	923	281	87	(391)	582	705	862
Cuescomaltepec (see S. J. Yae) Huayatepec	—	—	(728[f])	254	119	—	—	—	—
Ixcuintepec (see Tanetze)									
Josaa, Santa María (1970: Ixtlán)	A	I	—	—	44	(197)	293	229	250
Juquila, San Juan	M	V	(919)	338	(299)	(313)	466	471	422
Lachichina, Santa María (1970: Yae)	A	V	854	478	(423)	(194)	289	266	298

1820	1826	1882	1900	1910	1921	1930	1940	1950	1960	1970
259	378	665	823	851	948	868	654	789	713	585
562	829	749	661	688	392	588	664	645	629	764
296	(296)	378	336	340	(342)	343	405	376	372	247
511	509	599	499	531	517	524	488	570	579	426
283	228	262	263	240	299	292	304	269	424	367
278	330	601	486	455	430	513	574	616	645	651
283	289	450	433	479	550	550	575	588	716	421
207	(207)	250	230	236	228	238	225	287	180	103
209	(209)	200	194	186	211	213	234	236	284	303
940	1,070	1,098	814	845	893	946	1,004	1,052	1,083	965
12,739	**16,304**	**20,883**	**19,989**	**20,581**	**19,476**	**20,078**	**20,509**	**21,903**	**23,085**	**22,020**
616	766	940	956	997	831	866	829	705	637	497
—	—	—	—	—	—	—	—	—	—	—
196	186	109	93	78	77	67	76	103	103	112
424	623	1,012	1,133	1,098	1,099	1,143	1,319	1,292	1,244	1,383
167	223	379	449	443	407	418	401	371	416	397

TABLE 9. (*continued*)

Name	Sta-tus	Dis-trict	1548	1568	1622	1703	1742	1781	1789
Lahoya, San Francisco (Reveag, Xaca, Otatitlán; 1970: Talea)	A	V	(1,158[g])	225	43	(110)	163	203	196
Lalopa, Santiago	M	V	1,075	423	167	(401)	596	801	705
Roayaga, Sto. Dom.	M	V	—	—	—	409	615	601	553
Tagui, San Juan (El Tagui) (1970: Villa Alta)	A	V	610	142	310	584	140	86	68
Talea (de Castro), San Miguel	M	V	(307)	113	(100)	(350)	521	687[b]	590
Tanetze (de Zaragoza), San Juan (Ixcuintepec)	M	V	3,297	1,694	1,312	(235)	349	414[b]	401
Temaxcalapan, Santa María	M	V	197	168	(149)	398	633	501	233
Teotlaxco, Santiago (1970: Ixtlán)	A	I	455	168	122	(210)	312	233	228
Tepanzacualco, San Juan (1970: Yaneri)	A	I	415	141	(125)	(163)	242	246	270
Tiltepec (del Rincón), San Miguel (1970: Ixtlán)	A	I	906	622	352	(736)	810	410	296
Totolinga	—	—	683	155	88	—	—	—	—
Yae, San Juan (Cuescomaltepec)	M	V	1,625	564	400	(296)	666	911[b]	860
Yagallo, Santiago (1970: Yae)	A	V	1,155	169	206	(338)	503	546	514
Yagavila, Santa Cruz (Yahualica) (1970: Ixtlán)	A	I	1,309	(481)	(304)	(238)	354	367	429
Yagila, San Juan (Yaxila) (1970: Ixtlán)	A	I	525	169	166	(460)	684	489	555
Yaneri, San Pedro (Yabago)	M	I	394	282	136	(306)	456	432	470
Yalahui, San Juan (1970: Villa Alta)	A	V	—	—	—	205	205	172	118
Yatoni, San Bartolomé (1970: Talea)	A	V	242[h]	163[h]	163	(178)	265	167	168

1820	1826	1882	1900	1910	1921	1930	1940	1950	1960	1970
144	212	344	356	346	369	381	323	321	344	280
414	576	959	1,111	1,086	1,071	1,101	1,011	934	863	676
(489)	489	532	618	572	598	618	806	528	586	644
37	134	191	190	152	160	198	227	276	275	290
518	823	1,833	1,963	1,697	1,729	1,692	1,735	1,865	2,228	2,044
448	641	1,114	1,011	1,029	1,061	1,063	1,162	1,009	1,070	1,167
407	482	575	586	585	601	616	679	741	779	702
200	242	189	240	268	(265)	261	316	295	253	320
239	243	417	365	471	504	529	466	454	390	418
379	284	503	398	185	256	147	150	132	150	147
—	—	—	—	—	—	—	—	—	—	—
659	999	881	896	892	888	956	858	883	839	753
411	434	472	484	460	457	508	460	442	395	399
213	260	328	370	368	424	514	502	492	479	560
518	674	446	361	340	310	321	397	396	385	375
315	444	386	378	471	420	434	380	378	382	247
130	166	350	377	297	325	273	300	297	263	291
152	225	177	196	252	327	361	325	368	374	330

TABLE 9.   (*continued*)

Name	Sta-tus	Dis-trict	1548	1568	1622	1703	1742	1781	1789
Yatzona, San Juan	M	V	—	—	—	772	884	646	572
Yaviche, Santa María (1970: Tanetze)	A	V	(231)	85	(75)	(138)	242	164	205
Yetzecovi, San Juan (1970: Villa Alta)	A	V	—	—	—	(278)	414	246	235
Yotao, San Miguel	M	I	(460)	169	85	(329)	489	559	622
Zoogochi, Santa María (1970: Ixtlán)	A	I	(383)	141	(125)	(210)	312	389	352
Zultepec	—	—	735	141	—	—	—	—	—
Total			**19,586**	**7,566**	**5,400**	**8,389**	**11,485**	**10,941**	**10,472**
Bixanos Zapotec Towns									
Camotlan, Santiago	M	V	317	71	77	161	149	88	94
Choapan, Santiago	M	C	11,282	676	1,554	1,343	1,918	1,447	1,393
Comaltepec, San Juan	M	C	2,017	423	456	1,118	1,443	1,005	542
Jalahui, San Juan (or Santiago) (1970: Lalana)	A	C	(307)	113	(100)	207	526	328	463
Jaltepec, San Juan (1970: Yaveo)	A	C	—	1,007	(891)	14	84	71	81
Lachixova, San Bartolomé (1970: Comal-tepec)	A	C	—	—	—	120	177	180	176
Latani, Santo Domingo[P] (1970: Choapan)	A	C	—	—	—	1,136	1,541	932	464
Lazagaya	—	—	(243[i])	112	(44[i])	—	—	—	—
Lealao, San Juan[P] (1970: Comaltepec)	A	C	—	—	—	396	773	462	572
Maninaltepec, San Juan (Roavela) (1970: Choapan)	A	C	1,549	283	226	133	293	201	242
Reagui, San Miguel (1970: Camotlán)	A	V	—	—	—	212	233	77	93
Tagui (El Tagui)	—	—	(448[j])	140	(128[j])	—	—	—	—

1820	1826	1882	1900	1910	1921	1930	1940	1950	1960	1970
474	491	661	625	523	454	501	543	553	563	526
122	155	259	166	383	355	383	245	390	375	415
126	152	342	209	171	132	136	132	134	204	241
333	414	632	444	388	455	521	510	485	478	450
305	352	465	438	525	400	422	432	398	461	462
—	—	—	—	—	—	—	—	—	—	—
8,436	**10,690**	**14,496**	**14,413**	**14,077**	**13,975**	**14,430**	**14,584**	**14,242**	**14,536**	**14,126**
126	188	477	434	373	524	417	355	360	458	859
1,038	1,425	665	634	738	1,537	751	634	1,254	1,476	1,812
829	920	764	634	608	451	375	380	368	444	673
302	422	234	364	261	105	122	183	261	322	680
46	82	119	185	210	349	475	601	819	968	1,258
52	97	95	130	150	109	160	232	292	367	131
470	538	36	71	111	158	182	215	251	311	327
—	—	—	—	—	—	—	—	—	—	—
414	494	449	312	308	313	316	384	443	586	599
152	189	(117)	45	47	49	43	56	66	84	117
105	134	225	246	186	243	271	230	(287)	344	360
—	—	—	—	—	—	—	—	—	—	—

TABLE 9. (*continued*)

Name	Sta-tus	Dis-trict	1548	1568	1622	1703	1742	1781	1789
Tizatepec	—	—	802	337	253	—	—	—	—
Xagalazi, San Gaspar (1970: Ixtlán)	A	I	—	—	48	138	331	417	414
Yahuivé, Santa María (1970: Choapan)	A	C	—	—	—	621	1,024	667	696
Yaveloxi, San Jacinto (1970: Choapan)	A	C	—	—	—	281	335	179	142
Yaveo, Santiago	M	C	k	169	(150)	373	684	568	648
Yaxoni, San Bartolomé	—	—	(383)	141	(125)	193	196	121	(107)
Yetzelalag, Santa Catarina (1970: Villa Alta)	A	V	—	—	—	281	233	143	152
Yovego, San Francisco (1970: Camotlán)	A	V	(457)	168	(149)	322	475	607	588
Zapotequillas	—	—	332[l]	338	129	—	—	—	—
Total			**18,137**	**3,978**	**4,330**	**7,049**	**10,415**	**7,493**	**6,867**
Chinantec Towns Guatinicamanes[m]	—	—	18,462	4,231	—	—	—	—	—
Jocotepec, Santiago (Yaci)	M	C	—	—	—	(69)	102	153	200
Lachixila, Santa María Asunción (Tlapanalá; 1970: Camotlán)	A	V	538	706	473	377	624	862	993
Lachixola, San Miguel (1970: Jocotepec)	A	C	—	—	—	—	—	100	93
Lacova, Asunción (1970: Lalana)	A	C	—	—	—	—	—	78	91
Lalana, San Juan	M	C	—	—	—	(219)	326	335	416
Lobani, Santa María Magdalena (1970: Petlapa)	A	C	—	—	117	(54)	81	91	118
Petlapa, San Juan	M	C	—	—	864	(263)	391	277	339
Teotalcingo, San Juan (1970: Choapan)	A	C	7,329	(2,695)	745	(350)	521	313	370

1820	1826	1882	1900	1910	1921	1930	1940	1950	1960	1970
—	—	—	—	—	—	—	—	—	—	—
518	613	772	451	30	(83)	136	179	231	176	270
703	687	202	290	370	240	278	354	443	572	600
109	79	159	196	174	130	138	367	192	227	326
426	377	187	839	778	447	975	1,463	1,375	2,760	4,793
65	97	41	—	—	—	—	—	—	—	—
94	135	188	195	207	165	215	250	275	271	299
481	740	627	445	330	294	304	274	295	323	392
—	—	—	—	—	—	—	—	—	—	—
5,930	**7,217**	**5,357**	**5,471**	**4,881**	**5,197**	**5,158**	**6,157**	**7,212**	**9,689**	**13,496**
—	—	—	—	—	—	—	—	—	—	—
270	297	568	572	906	957	1,017	1,205	1,736	3,293	5,014
725	775	878	383	291	272	271	249	220	323	235
128	167	140	160	93	94	90	129	186	280	440
81	88	72	103	153	118	132	142	169	181	240
374	422	843	1,199	1,652	3,124	3,016	4,274	5,054	6,446	8,501
146	162	378	507	126	132	221	257	288	317	410
342	235	561	579	570	498	449	751	928	972	988
115	28	89	166	161	191	215	198	234	269	290

TABLE 9.   *(continued)*

Name	Sta-tus	Dis-trict	1548	1568	1622	1703	1742	1781	1789
Tepinapa, San Pedro (1970: Jocotepec)	A	C	—	—	—	(110)	163	281	250
Toavela, San Juan (1970: Petlapa)	A	C	—	—	—	(59)	88	71	122
Total			**26,329**	**7,632**	**2,199**	**1,501**	**2,296**	**2,561**	**2,992**
Mixe Towns									
Alotepec, Santa María	M	M	(919)	338	60	299	312	209	209
Amatepec, Santiago (1970: Totontepec)	A	M	322	155	100	327	70	346	237
Atitlán, Santiago (Noban)	M	M	(1,074)	395	250	(535)	796	492	520
Ayacastla	—	—	692	593	330	—	—	—	—
Ayacaxtepec, San Pedro (1970: Alotepec)	A	M	2,158	339	204	165	209	124	105
Ayutla, San Pedro y San Pablo	M	M	(457)	168	149	(585)	870	712	503
Candayoc, San Juan (Tlazoltepec, Jaltepec de Candayoc; 1970: Cotzocón)	A	M	1,063	378	39	354	414	295	239
Chichicaxtepec, San Cristóbal (1970: Mixistlán)	A	M	365	254	65	147	121	70	35
Chinantequilla, Guadalupe (1970: Totontepec)	A	M	—	—	—	78	—	—	—
Chisme, Santa María (1940: Cotzocón)	A[n]	C[n]	(383)	141	(125)	143	331	330	316
Cotzocón, San Juan	M	M	—	—	—	235	396	645	623
Huitepec, Santa María (1970: Totontepec)	A	M	297	422	82	212	163	185	165
Ixcocan	—	—	1,713	(630)	—	—	—	—	—
Jareta, Santiago (1970: Totontepec)	A	M	314	254	54	285	182	253	231

1820	1826	1882	1900	1910	1921	1930	1940	1950	1960	1970
296	313	311	389	163	164	184	147	148	235	333
102	86	121	184	126	89	148	120	140	208	203
2,579	**2,573**	**3,961**	**4,242**	**4,241**	**5,639**	**5,743**	**7,472**	**9,103**	**12,524**	**16,654**
222	299	650	822	889	579	592	704	763	1,870	1,429
244	301	251	273	386	210	166	216	299	284	284
320	373	719	808	925	745	1,191	1,182	1,667	1,595	1,795
—	—	—	—	—	—	—	—	—	—	—
(95)	90	224	284	340	290	266	263	336	350	383
494	583	1,472	1,625	1,733	1,421	2,168	2,516	3,293	3,865	4,636
255	345	279	343	252	284	214	171	247	536	698
76	110	321	305	243	229	312	308	345	348	376
—	—	—	—	—	174	215	318	384	388	402
278	372	314	392	476	435	450	456	—	—	—
749	933	1,308	1,513	1,514	1,336	1,382	1,213	1,924	8,356	11,554
179	230	171	177	123	117	230	241	294	290	291
—	—	—	—	—	—	—	—	—	—	—
181	278	258	148	184	137	156	190	297	293	241

TABLE 9.   (*continued*)

Name	Sta-tus	Dis-trict	1548	1568	1622	1703	1742	1781	1789
Jayacaxtepec, San Francisco (1970: Totontepec)	A	M	(609)	224	(198)	294	363	256	239
Metaltepec, San Juan (1970: Zacatepec)	A	M	(460)	169	(150)	129	182	192	187
Metepec, San Miguel (1970: Totontepec)	A	M	374	141	97	147	154	(140)	137
Mixistlán, Santa María (de la Reforma)	M	M	140	85	99	239	289	499	401
Moctum, San Marcos (1970: Totontepec)	A	M	(307)	113	(100)	143	791	54	26
Ocotepec, Santa María Asunción (1970: Toton-tepec)	A	M	1,746	522	241	396	191	111	83
Otzolotepec, San Juan (1970: Cotzocón)	A	M	—	—	—	51	47	—	—
Puxmetacan, Santa María (1970: Cotzo-cón)	A	M	(305)	112	(99)	396	344	535	579
Tamazulapan, Espiritu Santo	M	M	—	—	—	(469)	698	678	383
Tepantlali, Santa María	M	M	—	—	(120)	(272)	405	288	385
Tepitongo, Santiago (1970: Totontepec)	A	M	229	141	43	230	251	90	57
Tepuxtepec, Santo Domingo	M	M	(462)	170	(285)	(78)	116	624	516
Tiltepec, Santa María (1970: Totontepec)	A	M	—	—	—	216	154	155	185
Tlahuitoltepec, Santa María	M	M	1,155	564	590	(595)	600	821	455
Tlazoltepec (see Candayoc)									
Tonaguia, Santa María (1970: Roayaga)	A	V	918	282	235	460	144	216	105
Totontepec, Santa María (Villa de Morelos)	M	M	858	(316)	294	920	135	1,036[b]	599

1820	1826	1882	1900	1910	1921	1930	1940	1950	1960	1970
244	324	487	209	293	712	834	434	500	530	561
198	294	348	423	485	526	539	571	692	893	941
150	138	97	108	105	98	131	178	219	220	174
546	721	749	737	668	926	957	1,235	1,289	1,467	1,390
20	31	57	80	68	87	61	48	58	76	70
43	86	63	51	59	76	127	183	228	250	239
—	—	84	92	116	148	216	274	319	444	598
551	888	179	267	423	233	367	496	602	784	976
411	646	1,482	1,666	1,693	1,439	1,889	2,172	2,041	3,390	3,904
207	350	674	758	385	778	804	690	1,141	1,419	1,342
48	79	144	203	235	232	254	250	261	249	255
555	804	1,334	1,675	776	743	1,146	554	1,456	1,670	1,620
(181)	179	321	318	315	386	465	385	442	403	433
585	784	2,259	1,734	2,490	2,887	2,200	2,498	3,462	3,168	4,628
46	94	236	263	291	228	204	(210)	216	250	270
677	847	1,641	1,750	1,609	1,767	1,720	1,403	1,405	1,544	1,427

TABLE 9.   (*continued*)

Name	Sta-tus	Dis-trict	1548	1568	1622	1703	1742	1781	1789
Yacochi, Santa María (1970: Tlahuitoltepec)	A	M	228	168	92	363	163	257	165
Zacatepec, Santiago	M	M	(460)	169	(150)	313	535	459	466
Total			**18,008**	**7,243**	**4,251**	**9,076**	**9,426**	**10,072**	**8,151**
Other and Unidentified									
Villa Alta, San Ildefonso	M	V	(150)	150°	(150)	(150)	148	184	(177)
Analco, Nuestra Señora de los Remedios (1940: Villa Alta)	Aᵖ	Vᵖ	(200)	(200)	(177)	271	135	355	(176)
Xaltepec	—	—	1,545	460	—	—	—	—	—
Nanacatepec	—	—	1,642	495	141	—	—	—	—
Tlaxuca	—	—	2,872	(1,056)	—	—	—	—	—
Total			**6,409**	**2,361**	**468**	**421**	**283**	**539**	**353**
Summary: Totals by Ethnic Group									
Cajonos Zapotec Towns			7,382	2,729	4,103	9,960	15,218	15,529	13,980
Nexitzo Zapotec Towns			19,586	7,566	5,400	8,389	11,485	10,941	10,472
Bixanos Zapotec Towns			18,137	3,978	4,330	7,049	10,415	7,493	6,867
Chinantec Towns			26,329	7,632	2,199	1,501	2,296	2,561	2,992
Mixe Towns			18,008	7,243	4,251	9,076	9,426	10,072	8,151
Other and Unidentified Towns			6,409	2,361	468	421	283	539	353
Grand Total			**95,851**	**31,509**	**20,751**	**36,396**	**49,123**	**47,135**	**42,815**

[a] This table attempts to trace through time the population of the geographical region encompassed by the Alcaldía Mayor of Villa Alta as it existed after 1570, when the separate Alcaldía Mayor of Nejapa was created. The area today is divided among the districts of Villa Alta, Ixtlán, Choapan, and Mixe. Until the twentieth century there were few changes in the names and number of towns. However, new agencias that have appeared since 1910 are not listed in this table. Their populations have been merged with those of the cabeceras of their municipios. Where formerly independent towns survive in modern times as dependent agencias, they continue to be listed separately. In the column labeled Status, M indicates that the town was a municipio in 1970; A, that it was an Agencia Municipal or Agencia de Policía. In the column labeled District, V indicates that the town was located in the District of Villa Alta in 1970; I, in the District of Ixtlán; C, in the District of Choapan; and M, in the District Mixe. Appearing in parentheses after the names of towns are other names by which they have been known at various times, or in the case of agencias in 1970, the municipios to which they belonged in that year. Numbers in parentheses were arrived at by interpolation (see chapter 3).

[b] An average of the 1777 and 1781 censuses; includes only Indians.

[c] Counted with Lachitaa.

1820	1826	1882	1900	1910	1921	1930	1940	1950	1960	1970
168	131	348	368	322	345	352	434	531	547	635
666	(666)	1,302	1,347	1,261	1,312	1,519	1,767	3,065	2,922	2,766
8,389	**10,976**	**17,772**	**18,739**	**18,659**	**18,880**	**21,127**	**21,560**	**27,776**	**38,401**	**44,318**
(379)	289	538	653	298	548	610	676	756	883	914
83	156	171	77	139	123	90	102	—	—	—
—	—	—	—	—	—	—	—	—	—	—
—	—	—	—	—	—	—	—	—	—	—
—	—	—	—	—	—	—	—	—	—	—
462	**445**	**709**	**730**	**437**	**671**	**700**	**778**	**756**	**883**	**914**
12,739	16,304	20,883	19,989	20,581	19,476	20,078	20,509	21,903	23,085	22,020
8,436	10,690	14,496	14,413	14,077	13,975	14,430	14,584	14,242	14,536	14,126
5,930	7,217	5,357	5,471	4,881	5,197	5,158	6,157	7,212	9,689	13,496
2,579	2,573	3,961	4,242	4,241	5,639	5,743	7,472	9,103	12,524	16,654
8,389	10,976	17,772	18,739	18,659	18,880	21,127	21,560	27,776	38,401	44,318
462	445	709	730	437	671	700	778	756	883	914
38,535	**48,205**	**63,178**	**63,584**	**62,876**	**63,838**	**67,236**	**71,060**	**80,992**	**99,118**	**111,528**

[d] Counted with Betaza.
[e] Includes Lalana.
[f] Counted with Lahoya.
[g] Counted with Huayatepec.
[h] With Vichinaguia.
[i] Counted with Tagui.
[j] Counted with Lazagaya.
[k] May be included with Zapotequillas.
[l] May include Yaveo.
[m] Included Jocotepec (Yaci), Lobani, Petlapa, and Toavela.
[n] In 1940.
[o] Cook and Borah *Central Mexico, 1531–1610*, p. 58, multiply 30 vecinos by their Indian multiplier of 2.8 for and estimate of 85. I have multiplied by 5, for Spanish households were larger.
[p] In 1940.
[q] Speaks Chinantec today, although was grouped with Bixanos Zapotec towns in colonial period.

the tribute system had been modified significantly. Few Indians were now exempt, and the multiplying factor used by Cook and Borah to convert tributaries to total population is 2.8. Excluding Spanish Villa Alta, Cook and Borah provide estimates for seventy-two communities.[9] Estimates for six more (in parentheses in table 9) that had 1548 tributary counts in the *Suma* are derived by dividing the 1548 estimates by the ratio of 2.719. Analco is arbitrarily assigned a population of 200.

1622

These data come from Cook and Borah's study of a tribute document dated 1646, though the counts most likely were made between 1620 and 1625.[10] To convert tributaries to total population, they used a factor of 3.4, derived from their previous Mixteca Alta study.[11] Excluding once again Villa Alta and Analco, which are assigned largely arbitrary populations, we have estimates for fifty-three towns. Estimates for twenty-four more (in parentheses in table 9) are calculated using the mean ratio (0.885) of the total population estimates of forty-nine town pairs in 1568 and 1622. Thus, by multiplying the 1568 population estimates for these towns by 0.885, we get reasonable estimates for 1622.[12]

1703

The document used for 1703 is in the Archivo General de Indias, Audiencia de México 881, *expediente* 12, and bears the title "Testimonio del cuarto cuaderno de los autos hechos sobre la división de los beneficios de la jurisdicción de Oaxaca que administran religiosos de Santo Domingo." It is dated 1705 but contains a report by the *contador mayor* of the Antequera Cathedral that gives numbers of casados in communities in 1703. To convert casados to total population, I consulted Cook and Borah's Mixteca Alta study and selected the factor 4.6.[13] Data are available for seventy-four towns, including Analco.[14] Estimates are derived for thirty-four additional communities by applying a mean ratio (1.488) based on a comparison of the total population estimates of seventy-two town pairs in 1703 and 1742. Thus, estimates for blanks in 1703 are obtained by dividing the 1742 estimates for those towns by 1.4888.[15]

1742

For 1742 my source is the Fuenclara census published by Joseph Antonio Villaseñor y Sánchez.[16] It gives a count of families in each community, which can be treated the same as casados. Following Cook and Borah, I reduce the number of families by five percent to allow for those that were headed by widows and widowers.[17] Then the result is multiplied by 4.9 (5 for Spanish Villa Alta), the factor established by Cook and Borah as the population-to-casado ratio in the Mixteca Alta for this period. This census (and, happily, all succeeding ones) is quite complete, providing data for 107 towns.[18] The mean ratio (1.4888) for 1742 to 1703 village populations is used to produce estimates for only three missing communities.

1781

The main source for this year is a report on town populations by José María Beltrán, *administrador de alcabalas* in the Villa Alta district. This is one of several surviving district reports prepared in 1781 by *alcabala* (sales tax) administrators in Oaxaca, and the document was kindly made available to me by Lic. Luis Castañeda Guzmán of Oaxaca. The report was prepared in Villa Alta on April 5, 1781, and the printed title on the standardized form reads: "Estado o plan de las ciudades, villas, o lugares correspondientes en lo eclesiástico a la Mitra de Oaxaca que existen situados en el distrito de la administración reunida a Villa Alta. . . ." It is a count of total population, with separate columns for "Españoles o Gente de Razón," "Indios," and "Otras y Castas."[19] Only two settlements are missing.[20]

Another important group of sources which may serve as a check on the 1781 census is the collection of church censuses of 1777, housed in the Archivo General de Indias, Audiencia de México 2589, 2590, 2591. These are thorough, house-by-house listings of all inhabitants, conducted by parish priests, and censuses are available for twenty-five towns (in addition to the Trapiche de Yuguiba) in the Villa Alta district.[21] The 1781 figures for these towns in table 9 represent the average of the 1777 and 1781 counts. It is noteworthy that in all but two of these twenty-five cases, the 1777 church censuses record significantly higher populations than the 1781 alcabala census. The differences range from a low of 1.4 percent higher for Tonaguia to 210 percent higher for Yaa. The mean is 20 percent. This discrepancy is difficult to explain. The 1777 censuses would appear the most trustworthy. Perhaps the 1781 census was too hastily done and underrepresented the true population. Yet increasing the grand total for the district in 1781 by 10 percent yields a population of 56,562, a figure significantly higher than our totals for 1789, 1820, and 1826. On the other hand, it is possible that the 1777 censuses counted former parishioners who were absent from the region, thus inflating the totals. A final resolution of this problem will require further study; for the time being, we must rely principally on the 1781 census.

1789

The source for 1789 is a tributary count located in the Archivo General de la Nación, Tributos 25, expediente 19. It is complete except for the pueblo of Yaxoni, for which an interpolation is given. The estimates for Villa Alta and Analco include only the Indians; the single tributary figure for both has been divided equally between them, though most of the tributaries were probably residents of Analco. Once again I follow Cook and Borah in selecting the factor 3.7 for converting tributaries to total population for this period.[22] The 1789 counts are generally lower than those for 1781, the main reason being an epidemic that struck the district in 1788–89. This epidemic was very likely associated with the great famine that occurred in Mexico in 1785–86.

1820

In December 1819 and January 1820 the subdelegado of Villa Alta surveyed the *bienes de comunidad* (community revenue) and the number of tributaries in the pueblos of the district; the surviving paperwork exists in the Archivo del Juzgado de Villa Alta, Civil 1819–21, expediente 30. Interpolations are necessary only for Lachitaa, Ayacaxtepec, and Santa María Tiltepec. The figure given by the subdelegado for Roayaga was obviously in error, so the 1826 count is substituted. The estimates for San Miguel Cajonos and Yatee are averages of the 1820 count and another one conducted independently by a parish priest in the same year (this can be found in the Archivo General de la Nación, Tierras 847, expediente 1). The multiplier 3.7 is again used to convert tributaries to population.

1826

The source for 1826 is the total population count assembled by the Oaxaca hacendado and intendente, José María Murguía y Galardi, "Extracto general que abraza la estadística toda en su primera y segunda parte del estado de Guaxaca y ha reunido de orden del Supremo Gobierno y yntendente de provincia en clase de los cesantes José María Murguía y Galardi" (unpublished manuscript, 1827. Benson Latin American Collection, University of Texas at Austin). This is an abbreviated version of Murguía y Galardi's five-volume "Estadística de Oajaca," now located in the library of the Sociedad Mexicana de Geografía y Estadística in Mexico City. The only adjustments needed are for Yatzachi El Alto, Zoochina, Zoochixtepec, and Zacatepec; the census is incomplete for these communities, so the 1820 estimates are substituted.

1882

Manuel Martínez Gracida's well-known *Colección de "cuadros sinópticos" de los pueblos, haciendas y ranchos del estado libre y soberano de Oaxaca* (Oaxaca, 1883) is the source for 1882. Total population counts are given, and only one interpolation (for Roayaga) was necessary.

1900–70

The sources for the twentieth century are the national censuses, all of them virtually complete.[23]

Despite the rather exhaustive appearance of table 9, one cannot take these town-by-town population counts as definitive. The enormous obstacles involved in obtaining accurate census figures in remote areas like the Villa Alta district, even today, are well known. For the colonial period, my efforts have been hampered by incomplete data. As there was no complete census of the district on a community basis until 1742, I used ratios to construct estimates for twenty-two pueblos in 1548, twenty-four in 1622, and thirty-four in 1703. Nonetheless, I think the figures in table 9 are the most accurate that are currently obtainable for the Villa Alta district. The grand totals for the colonial period conform in a general way to the population profile constructed by Cook and Borah for central Mexico as a whole. Between 1548 and 1568, the population declined by over two-thirds, reaching its nadir in the early or mid-seventeenth century. It had rebounded somewhat by 1703 and continued to increase into the late eighteenth century until disease reduced it in the 1780s (see below). The 1820 count seems low when compared with the more accurate census of 1826. If we disallow the 1820 figures, a trend of further growth can be discerned from the late eighteenth century until the late nineteenth. From 1882 until 1921, no significant change in either direction occurred, but soon thereafter growth began again. It continues unabated today.

Several general matters deserve comment. The first is that the eighteenth-century district totals in table 9 differ from those published by José Miranda for the same period.[24] Miranda used different sources and worked only with district totals; his figures appear in table 10. The discrepancy between Miranda's figures and those in table 9 are due mainly to differences in method (except for the apparent error inherent in his data for 1793). Miranda used the multiplier of five in all cases to convert families and tributaries to total population, while I have relied on Cook and Borah's Mixteca Alta study, which employs lower factors. I believe these are more analytically sound because they are based on rigorous empirical testing. It can safely be concluded, therefore, that Miranda's estimates are probably too high.[25]

The second general issue, and one much more difficult to resolve, is the question of the population of the district before 1548. No additional data can be brought to bear on this matter. Documentary sources for the early period provide few clues, and there have been no archaeological settlement surveys in the region. Given this unfortunate state of affairs, the one method that remains open is to use the techniques of extrapolation developed by Cook and Borah for central Mexico.[26] Cook and Borah use data on seven town pairs to construct a ratio of the 1532 population to the 1568 population in their Zapotecas region.[27] Their mean ratio is 10.009. If this ratio is applied to the 1568 total in table 9, the result is an estimate of 315,374 persons for 1532. In their reconstruction of the aboriginal population of central Mexico at the time of the Conquest, Borah and Cook would increase the

TABLE 10.   Estimates by José Miranda of the Indian Population of the Villa Alta District, 1742–94

Year	Population Estimate	Miranda's Source
1742	51,735	Villaseñor y Sánchez, *Theatro americano.*
1767	55,910	Cuentas del medio real de ministros, AGN Tributos 2, 36.
1788	55,920	Ibid.
1793	50,900	AGN Historia 523 : 94.
1794	58,280	Ibid., totals by race.

Source: José Miranda, "Evolución cuantitativa," pp. 133–35.

1532 figure by only 10 percent for isolated regions like the Sierra Zapoteca where the early effects of Spanish penetration may have been less than in well-traveled areas.[28] Increasing the 1532 figure by 10 percent yields a 1520 estimate for the Villa Alta District of 346,911.

Finally, it is possible to construct a district estimate for the year 1595. Cook and Borah provide estimates of total population for sixteen pueblos in the Alcaldía Mayor of Villa Alta in 1595.[29] Dividing the 1568 estimate by the 1595 estimate for each one of these, then taking the average, yields a mean ratio of 0.679.[30] Multiplying the 1568 district estimate by 0.679 produces a 1595 estimate of 21,395.

Table 11 sums up all the Villa Alta district estimates for the colonial period, rounded to the nearest hundred. The numbers indicate that the population declined by 94 percent between 1520 and 1595 (with a depopulation ratio of 16.2 : 1) and that it did not begin to increase again until some time after 1622, perhaps in the mid-1600s. It is conceivable that the low point was reached in the late sixteenth century, for the 1595 and 1622 estimates are nearly identical. It is just as likely, however, that the nadir came some time after 1622. Between 1532 and 1548, the total fell by a little over two-thirds; it continued to decline at roughly the same rate between 1548 and 1568, then slowed to a depletion rate of about one-third between 1568 and 1595.

Keeping in mind that the Spanish had only ephemeral control over the region until at least the 1550s and that few Spaniards or blacks inhabited the area at any time in the sixteenth century, it is remarkable that the decline was so steep and that it occurred so early (just how much of it happened between 1520 and 1532 we cannot be sure). Most of the depopulation can undoubtedly be attributed to epidemic disease. On the other hand, the district is in many ways more like the lowland and coastal regions of central Mexico than the high plateau. Cook and Borah have demonstrated that, compared with those on the plateau, the lowland and coastal populations generally deterio-

TABLE 11.   Population of the Alcaldía Mayor of
Villa Alta, 1520–1820[a]

Year	Estimate
1520	346,900
1532	315,400
1548	95,900
1568	31,500
1595	21,400
1622	20,800
1703	36,400
1742	49,100
1781	47,100
1789	42,800
1820	38,500

[a]Figures rounded to nearest hundred.
Sources: Table 9 and extrapolations in the text, chapter 3.

rated faster and earlier, though they began to recover sooner.[31] After 1580
the decline was faster in the highlands and slower in the lowlands. The Villa
Alta district would seem to conform fairly well to these trends, though recovery in the lowland portions has been very slow and is still going on today.
Differential population trends within the various subregions of the district
will be discussed in the section on settlement below.

SETTLEMENT

During its entire recorded history, the Villa Alta region has been occupied
by numerous small, shifting settlements. This generalization applies to all
five ethnic groups included in this study, as well as to others in northern
Oaxaca. The population figures in table 9 show very few colonial communities that exceeded one thousand inhabitants. In 1781, for example, the
average size of the district's 121 towns was only 390, and only six villages
had populations of 1,000 or more. Nader observed that the entire Rincón
region, extending into the Chinantla, has a history of changing pueblo locations because of soil or water exhaustion or epidemics.[32] This statement can
be applied to virtually the entire Villa Alta district. Few pueblos for which
information is available occupied their original sites in the eighteenth century. Many were forcibly relocated during the Spanish congregación campaigns, but many others moved voluntarily at various times. Throughout
the Sierra are found numerous tracts of abandoned villages, most of them on
tops of mountains and other inaccessible places.[33] Few towns, it seems, lack
oral traditions about their former *pueblos viejos*,[34] and many can show the
visitor the remains of earlier sites. This pattern of shifting settlement is not

a reaction to the European conquest and its aftermath, but a centuries-old adaptation to the ecology of the region.

While villages moved frequently, remarkably few disappeared altogether once the trauma of the sixteenth century had passed. Apart from recent *ranchos* founded in lowland areas, the roster of communities in the region today is little different from what it was in the seventeenth century. Even the epidemic of 1788–89 (see below) failed to erase any towns from the map. Encomiendas, corregimientos, and Dominican *doctrinas* (parishes) grouped and regrouped many communities in ways that often ignored indigenous linguistic, cultural, and political boundaries. But for administrative purposes, the alcaldes mayores always treated each community listed in table 9 as a separate unit, and the lists they used differed little, if at all, from one year to the next.

Thirty known communities that became extinct at one time or another in the colonial period are listed in table 12. It is immediately apparent that most of them disappeared during the sixteenth century, under the combined assaults of military conquest, epidemic disease, and the congregaciones. Only seven are known to have expired in the seventeenth century, and four in the eighteenth. It may also be the case that some of these communities survived longer under different names. The names in table 12 are predominantly Nahuatl, but they were rarely used by the inhabitants themselves, who continued to employ the indigenous names in their own languages. There has been a tendency over time for indigenous names to disappear and be replaced with Nahuatl or other names,[35] but this process is far from complete, even today.

The highland regions of the Sierra impress the modern visitor as being well populated, and land there is generally scarce.[36] Most villages are no more than a two- or three-hour walk from their nearest neighbors.[37] The trip may be a difficult one, though, for arduous ascents and descents are the rule. Most communities are situated on mountain slopes in *tierra templada* (the temperate zone), though municipios frequently encompass some *tierra fría* (cold country) and *tierra caliente* (hot country) as well. Pueblos themselves often seem vertically constructed, as in the Rincón, where a drop of two to three thousand feet between the highest and lowest houses is not unusual.[38] For this reason the Spanish grid pattern of streets was never successfully imposed in the region (except in Villa Alta) and most towns are still irregular in plan.[39]

Settlement patterns today range from the compact communities of the highland Cajonos and Nexitzo zones to a more dispersed pattern at lower elevations in Chinantec and Bixanos territory. Yet the degree of nucleation is not a simple function of highland-lowland differences, for the Mixes, who inhabit a mountainous environment similar in some respects to that of the highland Zapotecs, are more dispersed in their style of living.[40] The reasons for this contrast are not entirely clear. Schmieder suggested that, in arrang-

TABLE 12.   Extinct Communities in the Colonial District of Villa Alta

Town	Ethnicity	Last Mention	Source
Andaama	Mixe	1597	Gerhard, *Guide*, p. 371.
Ayacastla	Mixe	1622	Cook and Borah, "Royal Revenues."
Ayutustepec	Mixe	1548	Gerhard, p. 371.
Balachita	?	1545	AGI México 91.
Daga, S. Miguel	?	1618	Zavala and Castelo, 6:307.
Guaxilpa	?	1545	Gerhard, p. 370.
Guiazona (Ixcocan)	Mixe	1568	García Pimentel, p. 73.
Hueyacatepec	Nexitzo?	1534	Gerhard, p. 371.
Javee	Bixanos	1726	AGN Tierras 442, 7.
Lazagaya	Bixanos	1622	Cook and Borah, "Royal Revenues."
Mayana	?	1564	AGI México 242.
Mazuich	Mixe	1570	Gerhard, p. 370.
Miaguatlan	Cajonos	1568	Gerhard, p. 371.
Nestepec	Cajonos	1579	AJVA Civil 1708–1825, 3.
Sayultepec	?	1578	Gerhard, p. 371.
Suchitepec	Mixe	1733	AJVA Civil 1635–1803, 49.
Tagui	Bixanos	1622	Cook and Borah, "Royal Revenues."
Tatahuicapa	Bixanos	1712	AGN Tierras 442, 7.
Tecomatlan	?	1545	AGI México 91.
Tecpanac	Mixe	1592	AGN Indios 6, primera parte, 199.
Tetze	Nexitzo	1604	De la Fuente, "Algunos problemas," p. 244.
Tizatepec	Bixanos	1622	Cook and Borah, "Royal Revenues."
Totolinga	Nexitzo	1597	Gerhard, p. 372.
Yachas	Nexitzo	1578	Gerhard, p. 371.
Yachave	Cajonos	1567	Gerhard, p. 372.
Yadube (2)	Nexitzo	?	De la Fuente, p. 244.
Yetza	?	1748	APVA Bautizos, Yetzecovi
Zoquio	?	1564	AGI México 242.
Zultepec	Nexitzo	1567	Gerhard, p. 373.
Zapotequillas	Bixanos	1622	Cook and Borah, "Royal Revenues."

ing themselves in compact villages, the Sierra Zapotecs were simply imitating their Valley counterparts and were actually going against environmental influences.[41] Beals, writing on the Mixes, saw them as not particularly well adapted to their environment either.[42] In his opinion, their culture is but a "weak reflection" of that of the Zapotecs and more suited to lowland humid tropics (their possible ancestral home, according to Beals) than to their present mountain environment. More recently, Nader has suggested that the differences between Sierra Zapotec and Mixe settlement can be best explained by cultural rather than environmental variables, though she fails to specify what they might be.[43]

Because of their vagueness, none of these hypotheses is particularly compelling. A firmer grasp of settlement differences in the region must be based on more extensive ethnographic and archaeological research than we now possess. I would suggest that environmental differences may not turn out to be irrelevant to the problem. A case in point is soil productivity. As compared with Sierra Zapotec territory, the Mixe homeland is a little higher, more rugged, more heavily forested, and wetter.[44] But the lush forestation and high volume of rainfall do not imply high agricultural productivity, for the Mixes today have little good soil, and this only in patches.[45] Under such conditions, Schmieder is probably correct in asserting that the relatively scattered Mixe settlement pattern is ecologically adaptive.[46] The Rincón Zapotec region, on the other hand, is often described as one of the most fertile areas in the state.[47] Such conditions could help promote the more compact style of settlement that exists there.

We are still left with the problem of discerning what settlement patterns were present at the time of Spanish contact. What exists today has been influenced to a considerable degree by the colonial congregaciones, to be discussed shortly. It is fairly clear that the aboriginal Mixes must have lived in small, scattered rancherías.[48] There are differences of opinion, however, regarding the Zapotecs. Gerhard has recently disputed Schmieder's claim that the Sierra and Valley Zapotecs both had nucleated settlement patterns in pre-Hispanic times.[49] Unfortunately, however, he presents no data for aboriginal communities in the Villa Alta district. The chronicle of Bernal Díaz contains a passage referring to one of the early entradas led by Rodrigo Rangel that states that pueblos were deserted by the time the Spaniards reached them.[50] Díaz, who participated in the ill-fated expedition, goes on to say that houses in the Sierra Zapoteca were not bunched together, but rather some were in valleys and others on tops of mountains. This implies some degree of dispersal, although it is not clear what sort of territorial units Díaz was describing. Until some archaeological settlement surveys are attempted in the Sierra, I can do little more than repeat De la Fuente's observation that Zapotec pueblos must have been more dispersed before the colonial congregaciones, though probably less dispersed than Mixe settlements.[51] I will now take a closer look at colonial population and settlement trends at the subregional and local levels. For convenience, each ethnic group will be discussed separately.

CAJONOS ZAPOTECS

In his brief survey of oral traditions about pueblo origins in the Cajonos zone, De la Fuente found that different towns tell different stories.[52] The Cajonos territory lies just to the west of Mixe country, and frequent contact between the two groups has led some Cajonos pueblos to claim Mixe origins, as in the case of San Miguel Cajonos and Zoochixtepec. No documentary evidence supports these beliefs, however. San Miguel, for example, was founded in the seventeenth century on lands of San Pedro Cajonos, and in the late eighteenth century it was still commonly referred to as a *barrio* of San Pedro.[53] It is very probable, however, that in pre-Hispanic times Cajonos towns absorbed some Mixe population. In Tavehua it is said that a number of Mixe prisoners held there during the pre-Hispanic wars decided to stay and eventually blended with the local Zapotec population.

The precise nature of Cajonos settlements before the Conquest is not well known, but it is clear that most pueblos were not in their present locations. Modern inhabitants of San Francisco and San Mateo Cajonos, Lachirioag, and Yaganiza say that their towns were once located on the tops of nearby mountains.[54] Other evidence for mountaintop pre-Hispanic town sites is available for San Francisco Cajonos, Yahuio, Yatee, and Yaa.[55] High, inaccessible locations afforded a degree of protection and strategic advantage in the incessant wars with the Mixes that were at their peak when the Spaniards arrived. Both Cajonos and Nexitzo Zapotecs were heavily involved in the hostilities, and Pérez García draws the principal line of conflict though territory now occupied by Yatee, Lachirioag, Villa Alta, Temaxcalapan, and Yatoni.[56] He goes on to state, without citing his source, that the Cajonos pueblos of Zoogocho, Tavehua, Solaga, and Tabaa were founded in the midst of the Zapotec-Mixe wars shortly before the Conquest. The spectacular ruins at San Francisco Yatee testify to the considerable building effort stimulated at least in part by defense needs. Remains of other mountain "fortresses" may exist near Temaxcalapan and Yetzecovi, though they have yet to be investigated.

The *Suma de visitas* of ca. 1548 is the earliest written source available for Cajonos territory, but it is incomplete and provides little information. The principal foci of Spanish attention in the first half of the sixteenth century were the Rincón and Mixe territories, the Cajonos area being somewhat neglected. Only two Cajonos towns are mentioned in the *Suma* as having sujetos: Tabaa with its dependency of Miaguatlan (never to be heard from again) in the hot country, and Zoogocho with six *estancias*.[57] These were the important power and population centers in the Cajonos zone at the time of the Conquest, Zoogocho perhaps serving as a new advance town against the Mixes.

The Dominican clergy took more of an interest in the Cajonos region in the sixteenth century than any other group of Spaniards, and the two major congregaciones carried out during this period appear to have been created at the behest of the friars. Congregaciones were actually quite extensive throughout the Sierra Zapoteca, despite the remoteness of the region. There is no doubt that the Indian population was severely affected and suffered greatly. Burgoa remarked that the congregación campaign in the area about 1600 was a major tragedy involving many deaths and "other horrors."[58] The fragments of information we have for the Villa Alta district add up to a picture that is similar in some respects to that described for Yucatán by Nancy Farriss.[59] In both cases, the missionaries played a key role in carrying out the congregaciones. Ecclesiastical criteria for congregación were strongly emphasized, and the clergy remained a very potent source of social and political control over the Indians. These matters will be discussed at greater length in chapter 6.

The first colonywide congregación program, led by the civil government in 1550–64,[60] had little impact in the Villa Alta district, for the area was just beginning to be brought under Spanish control. The first of the two Cajonos congregaciones dates from about 1572. Tehuilotepec, an important *cabecera* that had already moved from a former location on the Cerro de Tiltepec, was relocated again along the principal road from Antequera to Villa Alta and renamed San Francisco Cajonos. Congregated nearby as sujetos were San Pedro Cajonos (which retained its Zapotec name, Yaechi, through the seventeenth century), Santo Domingo Xagacia, San Pablo Yaganiza, and San Mateo Cajonos. Later in the seventeenth century, San Miguel Cajonos was established on lands belonging to San Pedro. These six settlements became known collectively as the "six Cajonos pueblos."

The principal instigators behind this enterprise were the Dominican friars, who wanted the Indians in a more accessible place for proselytization purposes. A complaint was lodged by Francisco Sánchez Jara, encomendero of the Cajonos towns and a vecino of Villa Alta, that it would be a mistake to move Tehuilotepec, for the land at the new site was not as good as at the old. But the friars had the backing of the alcalde mayor and the congregación went ahead as planned. The move did not create any new towns but simply transferred five existing ones to new locations. Their cohesiveness as a unit with San Francisco as cabecera does not seem to have been affected by the congregación, despite later land litigation between San Pedro and San Francisco in 1692. In fact, San Francisco's status as a cabecera was probably strengthened, for it gained in population and in 1623 became the seat of a Dominican doctrina. It remained the largest of the six Cajonos pueblos until 1789, when it was eclipsed in size by San Pedro (see table 9). The Cajonos towns continued to be assigned as a group to a single encomendero—Fernando de Silva in 1692 and in 1768 to a descendant, don Manuel Joaquín Nieto de Silva y Moctezuma, both vecinos of Antequera.[61]

Much less is known about the other Cajonos congregación that took place seven years later, in 1579–80.[62] The town that benefited most was Yalalag, probably a post-Conquest community[63] but in existence as early as 1563 and probably before.[64] As shown in table 9, Yalalag's population increased dramatically between 1568 and 1622. Its attractiveness to the congregators, no doubt, was due to its proximity to the road to Antequera. In 1567 Yalalag was in encomienda to Juan Martín de Viloria, a vecino of Villa Alta, along with Zoochila, Zoogocho, Yohueche, Nestepec, and Yachave. In 1579 he was succeeded by his son, Juan de Viloria, who was still encomendero in 1604. All these towns, plus Yatzachi El Alto, were probably affected by congregación efforts. Zoochila and Zoogocho lost population, while Nestepec and Yachave disappeared altogether. Yohueche was congregated as three barrios, two of them forming the pueblo itself with the third, Zoochixtepec, located apart as a sujeto. Thus, the strategy in this case involved the elimination of some towns and the enlargement of another that was more conveniently located. It is not unlikely that the Dominicans were behind this congregación as well, coming as it did so soon after the one at the Cajonos pueblos.[65] Finally, a passing reference has also been located to a congregación at Lachirioag about 1600.[66]

Other Cajonos communities are known to have moved in the early colonial period, though the circumstances in each case are unclear. Yahuio was relocated from a mountaintop at Cerro de Yahuio Viejo,[67] and Yaa also changed location some time before 1567. Access to land was the chief motivation in the latter case, the pueblo claiming that it lost some of its lands to Totontepec during the Zapotec-Mixe wars.[68] Pérez García noted that the three linked pueblos of Laxopa, Guiloxi, and Yalina formerly occupied a place call Betaelaga.[69] A "barrio" was still there in 1673 when it obtained a license to build a chapel.[70] A document in 1661 contains a request from some residents of Santa María Yachibi (Yohueche?) that they be permitted to move from their cold, windy mountain location to a lower spot called Yaglina, a league away on their own land.[71] Finally, the pueblo of Yatzachi expanded and divided into two pueblos, El Alto and El Bajo, during the first half of the eighteenth century (see table 9).

Another important aspect of settlement pattern is the extent and nature of cabecera-sujeto relationships. Little can be added to what has already been noted for the Cajonos zone. Tabaa and Zoogocho both had sujetos in 1548, though Tabaa's dependency of Miaguatlan soon disappeared. San Francisco Cajonos and Yohueche continued as cabeceras of sorts, though the former owed much of its prominence to the Dominican activities there.

In general, the cabecera-sujeto pattern was not well developed anywhere in the Villa Alta district, a reflection of the Sierra's lower degree of sociopolitical development as compared with the Valley of Oaxaca, the Mixteca, and especially central Mexico. Spanish colonial officials in the district preferred to deal with each town as an independent pueblo, and this is how records were kept in the office of the alcalde mayor. The policy reflected an element of the time-honored strategy of divide and conquer, but this administrative style was also influenced by indigenous forms. Small outlying sujetos or barrios undoubtedly existed in many places, especially in the areas of less nucleated settlement in the Mixe, Bixanos Zapotec, and Chinantec zones. But they were so small that their names and affairs rarely surface in the documentation, much less in the tribute and census counts listed in table 9. If these tiny and often transitory settlements are set aside, it can be said that most pueblos were their own cabeceras. In the second half of the colonial period the term *cabecera* was used more frequently, and claims to that status were presented by a larger number of pueblos. The bases of their claims, however, were usually of colonial origin: they were cabeceras because the Dominicans decided they would be or because the alcalde mayor approved a market there and so on. These topics will be discussed in subsequent chapters.

The early colonial population figures for the Cajonos zone in table 9 are less complete than those for the other four ethnic groups. The total of 7,382 for 1548 is undoubtedly on the low side; a marginal note in the Tehuilotepec entry in the *Suma* reads: "It is believed that there are more people in these towns and this province."[72] After bottoming out in the late sixteenth century, the population gradually increased to a high of 15,529 in 1781.

Unfortunately, information on the epidemic diseases that swept the Villa Alta district in the early colonial period is lacking, especially for the Cajonos zone. The population totals indicate that of the five groups, only the Cajonos and Bixanos Zapotecs reached the nadir of their populations before the end of the sixteenth century. However, one cannot be sure in these cases what proportion of the totals was due to actual decline and what proportion to underreporting, for the Spanish were more involved with the Nexitzo Zapotec and Mixe pueblos in the early years.

Scattered references to epidemics in the seventeenth century have been located for three Cajonos towns. Betaza suffered a six-month siege of an unknown malady in 1666. It brought many deaths and caused the villages to build a chapel devoted to the Dulce Nombre de Jesús.[73] A severe epidemic and many deaths affected Tabaa in 1698.[74] Yalalag lost 250 people to an attack of measles in 1692, and 60 more to a wave of *gorrotillo* (probably croup) in 1700.[75] The entire zone was decimated by an especially brutal attack of *matlazáhuatl* (probably typhus or yellow fever) between June 1788 and February 1789. The losses in the Cajonos towns were second only to those among the Mixes. Table 9 shows the population of the Cajonos zone in 1789 to be down ten percent from the 1781 figure. Declines were registered in most communities; only Lachirioag, Yaa, Yahuio, and Yalina seem to have remained unaffected. Interestingly, the chief source on this epidemic noted that no non-Indian deaths occurred in the entire alcaldía mayor.[76]

One Cajonos pueblo that was considerably transformed in the late colonial period was Santiago Zoochila. Never a large town, it had nonetheless become a Dominican cabecera de doctrina by 1742. It hosted a thriving market throughout the eighteenth century, including several shops in the 1770s that sold goods from Choapan, Tehuantepec, and Antequera.[77] By 1781, its population of 448 Indians was augmented by 28 Spaniards and 6 *castas* (mixed-bloods), more non-Indians than were found in any other pueblo in the district outside of Villa Alta itself. With the advent of independence in the 1820s, the Alcaldía Mayor of Villa Alta was divided for a time into two *partidos*, with Yalalag and Zoochila as twin cabeceras of the first partido and Choapan as the cabecera of the second. *Jueces de primera instancia* resided in Zoochila and Choapan until at least 1834. By 1883, however, Zoochila had reverted to the status of *agencia*.[78]

NEXITZO ZAPOTECS

Rincón Zapotec settlements at the time of the Conquest, like those in the Cajonos zone, were very much affected by the constant wars with the Mixes.[79] It is possible that a number of Nexitzo communities were established at that time, though no hard data are available. Once again evidence indicates that settlements formerly in defensible mountaintop locations were moved to tierra templada on the slopes. Ruins near Temaxcalapan and Yetzecovi, east of the Río Cajonos, are two tangible examples, while Talea de Castro, west of the river, is said to have been founded in the 1520s by people who came from a settlement on the side of a mountain that Talea now faces.[80]

The most populous and powerful communities in the Rincón at the time of the Conquest were Ixcuintepec (later renamed Tanetze), Cuescomaltepec (later to become Yae), Tiltepec, and Yagavila. While Tiltepec's importance as a cabecera dimmed after the bloody battles fought there during the Conquest, the other three continued as important central places long into the colonial period. Ixcuintepec had several dependencies in the early sixteenth century, including Juquila and Yachas. Cuescomaltepec claimed Lachichina and Yagallo as sujetos, and Yagavila had Zoogochi and Yazelo.[81] In 1548, Yagallo arose as a cabecera of sorts with three barrios. Zultepec also had two barrios and El Tagui was described as "five *pueblezuelos* in total."[82]

Ixcuintepec was the largest Nexitzo community in 1521 and was taken as a private encomienda seven years later by the conquistador Diego de Figueroa.[83] By about 1578 the pueblo had become a crown possession and in 1592 was referred to as Tanetze Ixcuintepec.[84] By that time, the second colonywide effort of congregación was already in the planning stage and Ixcuintepec was a likely prospect. In 1592 the town's corregidor, Pedro Pérez de Zamora, informed the viceroy that some residents had already moved to a new location. The viceroy approved but then reversed himself when he received a protest from Bishop of Antequera Bartlomé de Ledesma. The gobernador of the pueblo, don Diego de Mendoza, tried to work out a compromise, but his efforts were in vain and on July 3, 1593, the viceroy ordered that the pueblo not be moved.[85] Just five years later, however, Ixcuintepec was one of twenty-one towns in the district, along with the other Rincón communities Yagavila and Tiltepec, scheduled for civil congregation under the direction of Francisco Pachecho.[86] The fact that Tanetze was by far the largest town in the Rincón in 1622 (see table 9) suggests that a significant number of people were in fact congregated at Ixcuintepec and that the community became known only as Tanetze. By then the Dominicans had made it one of their cabeceras de doctrina.[87]

By all accounts, the congregación at Tanetze was devastating for the Indian population. The communities most severely affected were Yae (formerly Cuescomaltepec), Lalopa, Lahoya, and Xaca (perhaps a sujeto of Lahoya). Indian officials from these villages claimed that most of the Indians in the partido died in the process. After the congregación, new tribute quotas were set in the first three towns in 1612, 1611, and 1616 respectively. Their combined population was only about 435, substantially below the later 1622 figure of 610.[88] Town officials argued in 1617 that a large number of the tributaries counted in the *tasación* (valuation) were no longer there, having fled because of the demands imposed on them by the clergy.[89]

These demands must have been considerable, for at about the time of the congregación, the Dominicans decided to split the Doctrina of Tanetze in two. Tanetze remained as cabecera of its own doctrina, while the new one was headed by Yae.[90] This would prove to be a fateful decision in later years, for the Dominicans gave Yae the status of cabecera, which was not universally recognized by its neighbors. This led to protracted conflict in the eighteenth century, to be dealt with further in chapter 4.

Another town whose regional status was bolstered by the Dominicans was Yagavila, also designated early on as a cabecera de doctrina. Its "sujetos" in the seventeenth century included Zoogochi, Tepanzacualco, Yaneri, Teotlaxco, Quezaltepec, Josaa, and Tiltepec.[91] Both Yagavila and Tiltepec were on Francisco Pacheco's list of towns to the be congregated in 1598, though the outcome is not known.[92] Perhaps Pacheco's efforts also extended to Yaneri (formerly Yabago), for in 1709 the townsite and its lands were said to be the result of a congregación. Cacalotepec was apparently also affected.[93] Another town in this region that was designated as a cabecera for church purposes in the eighteenth century was Yagila (written Yaxila in colonial times). Although it lay within the Doctrina of Yagavila, it was a secondary center of church administration and in 1753 claimed Tiltepec and a settlement called Yaze (perhaps the same as sixteenth-century Yazelo) as sujetos.[94]

An additional congregación in the Rincón took place some time before 1744, when Santa Lucía Xaque ceased to exist and became part of Yatoni. Xaque was located close to the east bank of the Río Cajonos, and in 1746 its former lands were given to Yatoni.[95] Yatoni itself considered changing its location in 1700 to be closer to its ranchos, located one league from the pueblo. It had received viceregal permission, but when some of the inhabitants protested, the move was suspended. Five years later the alcalde mayor and the bishop of Antequera (Yatoni at that time was in the Jurisdiction of Antequera) were asked to give their opinions, but it is not clear whether the move ever took place.[96]

To the east of the Río Cajonos, the Nexitzo-speaking communities of Yatzona, Temaxcalapan, Yalahui, San Juan Tagui, Yetzecovi, and Roayaga were linked in varied and complex ways. Tagui's status as a sujeto of Yalahui apparently dated to pre-Hispanic times, and inhabitants of the two pueblos frequently intermarry today.[97] Both were affected by a failed attempt to congregate them together with Temaxcalapan at a place called Chiqui in 1604.[98] Another congregación occurred at Yatzona, probably at about the same time.[99] A settlement that disappeared in the congregaciones was San Juan Tetze, located a half hour's walk north of Roayaga. Only one document mentioning Tetze has been found, but oral tradition collected by De la Fuente states that Tetze gave birth to Roayaga, Tagui, "Tagui el Viejo," Yalahui, Yetzecovi, and the two deserted pueblos of San Miguel and San Pedro Yadube. In modern Roayaga it is said that the inhabitants of Roayaga, Tagui, and Yetzecovi are all the same people.[100]

Yetzecovi, in fact, was founded in 1697 by a contingent of residents of Tagui who sought a place to live at a lower elevation with better access to water. Permission was obtained from the audiencia; land was purchased, or otherwise obtained, from Roayaga; and a significant proportion of Tagui's 140 casados moved to a site near Roayaga called Lachiyesobao.[101] In 1707 Yatzona, Temaxcalapan, and Yalahui banded together to request a priest of their own who was to reside at Yatzona (until that time they had been part of the parish of Villa Alta). Their request was granted, and presumably the same priest visited Tagui and Yetzecovi as well.[102]

One other community in the Rincón that appears to be of post-Conquest origin is San Miguel Talea. Nader observes that Talea is considered an intrusive element in the region today, and its neighbors in Juquila refer to it as a "new town."[103] Referring to a document in the town's municipal archive, Nader claims that Talea was founded in 1525 on the border between Yatoni and Juquila when Fray Bartolomé de Olmedo came to baptize people in the area.[104] The document in question, however, turns out to be one of a group of five that were apparently prepared from painted lienzos in the latter half of the sixteenth century. Their dates of 1521, 1522, and 1525 are belied by the fact that they mention Spaniards who did not arrive in the Sierra until the 1550s (see chapter 2, note 60). Perhaps the Talea document, like the others, was prepared after a congregación, for all devote much space to descriptions of *vistas de ojos* (visual inspections) of their communities' lands. That Talea is of early colonial (pre-1548) foundation is very probable, but the date and circumstances continue to elude us. While the town grew to be a relatively large and important trading center in the nineteenth century (see table 9), during most of its colonial history it was overshadowed by nearby Tanetze and Yae.

Little information is available on the effects of disease on the colonial Nexitzo population. Yet we do know that the process of reduction began early. An Indian from Yagavila in 1537 stated that the community had few people compared with former times because of the ravages of disease.[105] Although Yagavila was the third largest town in the Rincón, similar losses must have been occurring in other communities. Tepanzacualco complained in 1579 that it could no longer meet its tribute quota because so many of its inhabitants had either died or fled. Only thirty-four tributaries remained.[106] Much later, in 1762–63, Juquila suffered from an epidemic of an unknown disease. This was not an isolated incident, for the parish priest noted that deaths had been frequent since 1757. The toll between 1757 and 1764 reached 151 persons.[107] The Nexitzo population was not unaffected by the districtwide matlazáhuatl epidemic of 1788–89, but the losses here—469 persons or 4.3 percent of the population—were considerably lower than among the Cajonos, Bixanos, or Mixes (see table 9).

BIXANOS ZAPOTECS AND CHINANTECS

The Bixanos and eastern Chinantec territory, most of which today lies within the District of Choapan, differed in important ways from the Cajonos and Nexitzo regions. One now enters a more lowland ecology where settlements, on the average, tend to be less nucleated and less stable. A glance at a modern map shows that this zone has many fewer municipios and is more sparsely settled than the relatively crowded Cajonos and Rincón regions. Yet the lowlands are today the fastest-growing parts of what was once the Alcaldía Mayor of Villa Alta. The Bixanos and Chinantec towns more than doubled their populations between 1940 and 1970, though not all of these new people were Bixanos and Chinantec speakers. During this same period, the population of the Cajonos zone increased only modestly, and the Rincón actually lost population (see table 9).

Table 9 shows that neither the Bixanos nor the eastern Chinantec areas had large populations during most of the colonial period. But if the 1548 estimates approximate reality at all, they indicate that the pre-Hispanic population of these regions was quite large indeed. The inordinately large size in 1548 of Zapotec Choapan[108] and the Chinantec Guatinicamanes—11,282 and 18,462 respectively—is noteworthy. The Guatinicamanes were composed of four communities, but even with some 4,500 inhabitants apiece, they were very large by colonial Villa Alta standards. Each pueblo probably had a number of sujetos similar to the many ranchos and rancherías found in the region today. In 1970, for example, the actual settlements of Petlapa, Toavela, Lobani, and Jocotepec had a combined population of only 1,411. But if we include the twenty-two ranchos and congregaciones in the municipios of Petlapa and Jocotepec, we get a total of 7,388. The modern municipios of San Juan Lalana and Santiago Yaveo provide even more striking examples. The cabecera of Lalana in 1970 had 543 inhabitants, though the entire municipio with its twenty-seven settlements totaled 9,421. The municipio of Yaveo listed twenty-three populated places with a combined population of 6,051, though only 727 of these lived in the cabecera. The pattern in Santiago Choapan in 1970 is similar; the municipio contained seven settlements with a population of 3,472, with only 835 in the cabecera.

To second-guess the exact pre-Hispanic settlement pattern in this region requires more information than is currently available. Yet there is no reason to believe that it was much different in general outline from what exists today. The *Suma* of 1548 is sketchy because the region was not well known to the Spanish at that time. Choapan was said to have only two barrios and the estancia of Zapotequillas, which itself contained two barrios, though surely other dependencies were not mentioned. Malinaltepec (later renamed Roavela) was said to have five barrios. In the Chinantec zone, the relatively large Teotalcingo had five estancias in 1548 and Tlapanalá (later renamed Lachixila) had four.[109]

The foregoing may seem to conflict with the point made earlier that the cabecera-sujeto style of settlement was relatively undeveloped in the Villa Alta district, but such is not the case. Ranchos may have been plentiful in the lowlands, but they were small, unstable, and of little political significance. Colonial census takers routinely lumped rancho populations together with those of their cabeceras, and tributary counts seem to have done the same. Even if all the names and places could be identified, such a list would have far less significance than, for example, the one that appears in Charles Gibson's study of the Valley of Mexico.[110] Furthermore, some of the colonial Bixanos cabeceras appear to have been of the "vacant center" type. Santo Domingo Latani, for example, was a Dominican cabecera de doctrina in 1783, but it was also a center of cotton production and its inhabitants spent most of the year at ranchos thirty leagues from the cabecera.[111]

Some colonial congregaciones existed in this region, though few details have come down to us.[112] Scheduled congregaciones in 1598 included Lachixila, Tatahuicapa, Malinaltepec (Roavela), Jaltepec, Zapotequillas, and Choapan.[113] Various Chinantec settlements had also been moved down from hilltop sites to valley locations in 1574.[114] Some towns may be of post-Conquest origin, but the only one that can be confirmed is Lachixova, founded shortly before 1625 by Choapan cacique don Bartolomé de Mendoza (his father, Francisco de Mendoza, was the family's first Christian) on his cacicazgo lands.[115] San Juan Lealao was perhaps established in a similar fashion sometime in the seventeenth century.[116]

At least seven Bixanos communities disappeared altogether: Lazagaya, Tagui (different from Nexitzo San Juan Tagui), Tizatepec, Yaxoni, Tatahuicapa, Javee, and Zapotequillas. The first four were last mentioned in 1622. Most of the population of San Pedro Javee perished in an eighteenth-century epidemic, and in 1725 the surviving household heads moved "with their wives, children, and church ornaments to the pueblo of Santiago Jalahui, which belongs to the *curato* of Latani. . . , leaving their said pueblo deserted and unpopulated." The viceroy, annoyed that the town had been abandoned without his permission, ordered the people to return to Javee, but they never did.[117] Tatahuicapa also fell victim to an epidemic in 1712, its survivors also going to Jalahui. Its lands were divided among Jalahui, Latani, Roavela, and Santiago Sochiapa.[118] San Bartolomé Yaxoni hung on until the late nineteenth century, its survivors and lands going to San Miguel Reagui sometime between 1882 and 1893.[119]

Two other recorded epidemics that took many lives in Bixanos pueblos occurred in Yovego between 1648 and 1660 and in Choapan and its "entire jurisdiction" in 1668.[120] The matlazáhuatl epidemic of 1788–89 reduced the population of Bixanos communities by roughly 626 persons (8.4 percent), though the Chinantec zone actually gained in population by 16.8 percent between 1781 and 1789 (see table 9).

MIXES

It has already been noted that at the time of the Conquest, Mixe settlement patterns were considerably dispersed. Citing Burgoa, Beals contended that aboriginal ranchería settlement groupings were coterminous with kin groups.[121] The Mixe "town," he believed, was introduced by the Spanish, and in the 1930s Beals distinguished among nucleated towns (Totontepec, Metaltepec, Zacatepec, Atitlán, Juquila); vacant center towns (Tlahuitoltepec, Cacalotepec, Ayutla); and dispersed settlements (Mixistlán).[122]

Such towns are in good measure the result of a series of congregaciones carried out shortly after 1600.[123] Before that, the number of small estancias, as the Spaniards called them, was quite high. According to the *Suma*, in 1548 Ayacaxtepec had seventeen estancias, one of them being Metaltepec.[124] (Yet by 1694 Ayacaxtepec and Mecatepec were listed as sujetos of Zacatepec.)[125] Ixcocan (alias Guiazona) had five estancias in 1548, though the cabecera disappeared after 1568. Metepec had two estancias and Totontepec three barrios—Yacochi, Amatepec, and Huitepec—which continued to form a unit well into the colonial period.[126] Noban (later renamed Atitlán) and Alotepec were estancias of Ayacastla in 1548. Alotepec was founded on lands donated by Atitlán and may be post-Conquest in origin. As late as 1638 the two were acting legally as one pueblo.[127] Their cabecera, Ayacastla, survived the congregaciones of 1600 but is not mentioned after 1622.[128] Another large settlement at the time of the Conquest was Santa María Ocotepec (different from San Pedro Ocotepec in the District of Nejapa), which had eleven estancias in 1548 including Ayutustepec (not mentioned subsequently), Moctum, Jayacaxtepec, and perhaps Jarcta and Metepec.[129] Ocotepec, Jayacaxtepec, and Moctum formed a unit until 1684, when they were acknowledged as independent pueblos and requested separate lands.[130] Finally, Tlahuitoltepec had eight sujetos in 1548, though their identities are not clear.[131] It should be emphasized that the proliferation of estancias and barrios among the Mixes, similar in many respects to the pattern in the Bixanos Zapotec and eastern Chinantec zones, is simply an indicator of a dispersed settlement pattern. It does not imply a high degree of political development or the massing of social power in cabeceras.

As in other parts of the Villa Alta district the Dominicans, with the backing of the alcaldes mayores, succeeded in the sixteenth century in moving some pueblos from inaccessible mountaintop locations to more convenient lower sites. Confirmed instances of this are Mixistlán, Ocotepec, and Tlahuitoltepec.[132] Tlahuitoltepec was moved in 1572 by order of Fray Jordán de Santa Catalina, prior of the Dominican monastery in Villa Alta, and Alcalde Mayor Bartolomé Tofiño. The decision to move was not popular with the town's inhabitants because it meant giving up their tierra fria environment for a new, uncomfortable one in tierra caliente. After four years, only half the population had in fact moved, and twenty of these people had died. Then in 1576 Fray Lorenzo Sánchez and Fray Juan Pavio, both stationed at Totontepec, forced the issue and insisted that all the holdouts transfer to the new lowland location. They removed the church bell and ornaments and whipped people who resisted, causing some residents to flee altogether. The Indians appealed, however, and won viceregal permission to remain at their traditional location. As late as 1580 the town was divided into "Alto" and "Bajo" sections, though the ill-fated venture in tierra caliente was apparently abandoned soon thereafter.[133]

Movement of people and pueblos in the Mixe zone occurred on a much more ambitious scale with the launching of the government-backed congregación program in 1600. Appearing on the preliminary list of targets in 1598 were Tlahuitoltepec, Chichicaxtepec, Totontepec, Tonaguia, Suchitepec, "and all the other pueblos that are included in this province of the Mixes and in the Rincón of the Zapotecs."[134] Since the early days of the Conquest, the Rincón and Mixe zones had borne the brunt of Spanish exploitation in the district, a fact that was reflected in the goals of the congregación program.

The most ambitious—and least successful—congregación in Mixe territory began in August 1600 and straddled the border between the Districts of Villa Alta and Nejapa. San Juan Juquila, a sujeto of San Pedro Ocotepec, was selected as a desirable population center because of its proximity to trade routes and the transportation advantages this offered. The Dominicans would later make Juquila a cabecera de doctrina and it is very probable that they were involved in planning the congregación. The cabecera of San Pedro Ocotepec was to be congregated at Juquila, as were Ocotepec's other sujetos, Acatlán and San Vicente. Also to be moved to Juquila were the cabeceras of Tepuxtepec, Cacalotepec, and Tepantlali. Altogether, some 631 tributaries would be affected. The project failed, however, probably because of Indian resistence. Juquila did in fact increase substantially in population; before 1600 it had only 300 inhabitants, but by 1661 its population had grown to 1,741.[135] San Pedro Ocotepec and Acatlán were merged with Juquila for a time, though Ocotepec had reasserted itself by the early eighteenth century and Acatlán would do the same in the nineteenth. But the other three cabeceras refused to be moved. An alternative plan was soon worked out that would accommodate two of them.[136]

The alternative was to make Tlahuitoltepec a congregation center and reestablish nearby the pueblos of Tamazulapan, Ayutla, Tepuxtepec, and Tepantlali. Each town retained its own cabildo, but Tlahuitoltepec was designated as cabecera and its gobernador had authority in the other four sujetos.[137] Perhaps this particular configuration of towns was chosen for congregación because they already exhibited a sort of unity. Beals noted in the 1930s that all five communities today have a linguistic cohesiveness as compared with other Mixe towns in the region.[138] More recently, Iñigo Laviada has reported on the basis of oral tradition that the four sujetos were founded in pre-Hispanic times by four sons of a cacique of Tlahuitoltepec.[139] He further asserts that the five pueblos still share the use of some communal lands. The latter point is most interesting because the 1600 congregación later fragmented, at least administratively. By 1721, Ayutla was no longer a sujeto, but a cabecera with Tlahuitoltepec, Tepantlali, Tepuxtepec, and Tamazulapan as its sujetos. Since Ayutla was also designated as a cabecera de doctrina, it is safe to conclude that the impetus behind this reconfiguration was the Dominican Order once again.[140] This is yet another example of clerical interference in the administrative and territorial affairs, not to mention other aspects of life, of pueblos in the district. The work of the friars had a lasting impact, but as the ethnography of Beals and Laviada suggests, church policy did not entirely suppress indigenous ethnic and linguistic ties.

Other congregaciones were carried out around 1600 in Totontepec, Atitlán (Noban), and Alotepec.[141] Though the details of these are not known, it is no coincidence that in the seventeenth and eighteenth centuries the Dominicans built a church at Alotepec that Laviada has described as "the largest and most beautiful of the sierra."[142] One last documented Mixe congregación in the Villa Alta district centered on the pueblo of Suchitepec, located about seven leagues from Villa Alta at a place whose location in the late sixteenth century corresponds roughly to the 1548 description of Tlazoltepec.[143] Whatever its original name, this was a large community with over one thousand inhabitants at the time of the Conquest. In 1592 the order was given to congregate the estancias of Chiltepec, Tulapa, and Candayoc at Suchitepec, their cabecera.[144] In the early eighteenth century, however, Suchitepec was abandoned. Its last three or four families left their church, their homes, and their lands in 1733 and went to live in Quetzaltepec in the District of Nejapa. Subsequently, Cotzocón and other pueblos sought to control the abandoned lands.[145] The eventual descendant of Suchitepec was San Juan Candayoc, today an agencia in the municipio of Cotzocón (see table 9).

One other Mixe pueblo in this region with a very checkered history is San Juan Otzolotepec. Its existence as a Mixe community was first reported in 1545.[146] It was subsequently abandoned, only to be reestablished in 1680 by twenty Nahuat-speaking families, refugees from the Gulf coast who sought escape from the continual assaults and robberies by pirates. The alcalde mayor gave the Nahuas permission to reoccupy Otzolotepec, just half a league from the Mixe pueblo of Puxmetacan, and granted them exemption from tribute for four years while they built their new community.[147] Otzolotepec prospered for a time, reaching a peak of 107 tributaries in 1730.[148] Soon thereafter, however, it went into decline and was abandoned once again in the mideighteenth century. By 1779 the village lay in ruins and its former residents were living in nearby Puxmetacan.[149] Otzolotepec was not heard from again until 1882, when it was once more supporting a small population. Today it survives as an agencia of San Juan Cotzocón (see table 9).

Sources on epidemic disease in the Mixe zone begin in the latter half of the eighteenth century, when the inhabitants proved especially vulnerable to attacks of smallpox and matlazáhuatl. Smallpox struck Tlahuitoltepec, Tepuxtepec, Tepantlali, and Tamazulapan in 1763, causing many deaths and a shortage of food.[150] These same towns were also hard hit by the matlazáhuatl epidemic that swept most of the Villa Alta district in 1788–89. The Mixes suffered more than any other group, and their population was reduced by about 19 percent. The partidos most affected were those of Ayutla, Totontepec, and Chichicaxtepec. Table 13, composed of figures assembled by curates from their parish registers, shows a total of more than 1,900 deaths in nineteen towns. Collectively, these communities lost 28 percent of their population to the disease. The records in table 9 suggest that this was the last calamity of such proportions to befall the Mixe territory. After 1789 the population resumed its growth, and except for the years 1900–21 it has continued to increase up to the present.

THE NORTHEASTERN FRONTIER

The northeastern boundary of the Alcaldía Mayor of Villa Alta extended beyond the Río de la Lana down into the Gulf coastal plain into what is now Veracruz. At the time of the Conquest this was a well-populated region with three good-sized, though little known, settlements: Guaspaltepec, Xaltepec, and Nanacatepec. None of these survived the sixteenth century.

Of only peripheral importance to the Villa Alta district, Guaspaltepec was in encomienda to Gonzalo de Sandoval and later to Rodrigo de Albornoz and Jorge de Alvarado, all vecinos of Mexico City in the 1520s and 1530s.[151] Originally Zapotec, by 1570 it was inhabited by 350 Chinantecs, and in 1600 by a handful of Popolucans.[152] In 1594 it was congregated at Tesechoacan in the District of Cosamaloapan.[153] Henceforth, its former territory became known as *los despoblados de Guaspaltepec*, much of which remained

TABLE 13. Deaths in the Mixe Partidos of Ayutla, Totontepec, and
Chichicaxtepec during the Matlazáhuatl Epidemic, June 1788–February 1789

	Men	Women	Boys under 14	Girls under 12	Total
Partido de Ayutla					
Ayutla	108	90	34	15	247
Tamazulapan	153	128	77	55	413
Tepuxtepec	85	113	27	27	252
Tepantlali	41	42	11	13	107
Tlahuitoltepec	108	101	46	64	319
Total	495	474	195	174	1,338
Partido de Totontepec					
Totontepec	63	83	15	6	167
Amatepec	26	25	14	15	80
Tepitongo	4	3	1	2	10
Moctum	4	6	2	1	13
Tonaguia	21	25	8	12	66
Jareta	7	10	4	4	25
Ocotepec	7	6	1	1	15
Jayacaxtepec	5	3	1	0	9
Total	137	161	46	41	385
Partido de Chichicaxtepec[a]	80	52	38	28	198
Grand Total	712	687	279	243	1,921

[a]Figures for the Partido of Chichicaxtepec are totals for the towns of Chichicaxtepec, Mixistlán, Yacochi, Huitepec, Metepec, and Tiltepec.
Source: AJVA Civil 1779–1802, 72.

uninhabited, though there is a reference to an encomienda there in 1736, part of the Marquesado of doña Blanca de Andia Álvarez de Toledo.[154] In the eighteenth century, the pueblos of Latani and Sochiapan established ranchos there for cotton cultivation.[155] Xaltepec was another large, lowland town of Zapotec ethnicity and in the early sixteenth century lay within the jurisdiction of the Villa del Espíritu Santo. It depopulated rapidly: Dávila Padilla stated that it once had four thousand vecinos but by 1560 contained only about twenty houses.[156] Originally assigned as an encomienda to Luis Marín in 1522, by 1534 Xaltepec was a crown possession, with a much reduced population scattered in ten barrios.[157] It was in corregimiento with Lalana in the 1560s and disappeared after 1568 (see table 9).

Nanacatepec, also in the hot country, rivaled Xaltepec in size and after 1580 was part of the jurisdiction of Nejapa. It is not clear whether its inhabitants in 1520 were Mixe or Zapotec.[158] In 1548 it had a population of 1,642, dwindling to 141 in 1622, after which it disappeared. Gerhard notes that by the late sixteenth century the entire tierra caliente north of the Sierra Zapoteca was virtually uninhabited.[159]

CONCLUSION

If the Cook and Borah methods for estimating aboriginal population are valid for the colonial Villa Alta district, the population of the same geographical area in 1970 was only one-third of what it was in 1520 (see tables 9 and 11). The first part of this chapter examined the magnitude of decline in the sixteenth and seventeenth centuries. What can be said about population growth in later years?

A close inspection of table 9 shows that of the five ethnic zones, population growth in the Cajonos territory far outstripped that in the others between 1622 and 1826. During that time, the Cajonos pueblos increased their size fourfold. The Mixes come next with an increase of two and one-half times (258 percent), then the Nexitzo Zapotecs, who roughly doubled their population. Growth was considerably slower for the Bixanos Zapotecs, and the eastern Chinantec population gained only a few hundred people during the entire seventeenth and eighteenth centuries.

Population growth in the latter half of the colonial period was most pronounced in the highlands—where Cajonos, Nexitzo, and many Mixe villages are located. No real growth spurt in the lowland Bixanos and Chinantec zones (today's District of Choapan) is evidenced until the period 1950–70. The impressive gains made in the Mixe zone in this same period are also most evident in the lowlands, especially in the municipio of San Juan Cotzocón, which borders on the southern edge of the modern Choapan district.[160]

In contrast, there was no growth at all in the Cajonos and Nexitzo zones between 1950 and 1970, primarily because these areas include little space for expansion. Both areas, along with the Ixtlán and Teococuilco regions in the District of Ixtlán, have been sending migrants to the city of Oaxaca and elsewhere since the late seventeenth century. Of the Indian migrants residing within the city limits of Antequera (excluding Jalatlaco, where there were many more) in 1661, 28 percent were Sierra Zapotecs, primarily from the Villa Alta district, while Mixes, Bixanos Zapotecs, and eastern Chinantecs were barely represented at all. Essentially the same pattern obtained in the 1790s, and it emerged again 180 years later in a survey I conducted in a Oaxaca suburb in 1969.[161] Thus, the Sierra Zapotec groups today are migrating out of northern Oaxaca, while the other ethnic groups with better access to the northern lowlands are now expanding into regions that were severely depopulated in the early sixteenth century.

One final matter that deserves comment is the degree of effectiveness of the colonial congregaciones. The data discussed in this chapter are not as explicit as one would wish and make it difficult to arrive at any precise judgment. Moreover, we still know very little at all about the impact of congregaciones among the Bixanos Zapotecs and eastern Chinantecs. For the other three groups, however, it would seem that the congregaciones had the greatest impact on the Mixes. Nucleated towns existed in the region by the early seventeenth century where they were lacking in 1520. Failures occurred to be sure, such as the one at Juquila in 1600, yet the congregaciones and the missionizing by the friars did introduce a mode of town living that had not existed before. There were, and are, limits to this process, however, for Schmieder has noted a slow dispersion of the Mixe population outward from the colonial congregación centers.[162] A major reason for this has to do with agricultural practices. Alfonso Villa Rojas observed that erosion is a common problem in many Mixe villages today.[163] Agricultural yields are low, land is soon exhausted, and new fields must frequently be cleared. Under such conditions, permanent residence in a nucleated town center is bond to become impractical for many.

In the Cajonos and Nexitzo zones, the congregaciones had the effect of regrouping peoples who had already developed on their own some degree of nucleated settlement. The congregaciones and the friars may have increased the degree of nucleation, but the pueblo as such would appear to predate the Conquest in these regions.

In all areas of the Villa Alta district, the sixteenth century was clearly the period that brought the most far-reaching changes. Many of the smaller settlements, and a few of the medium-sized ones, disappeared altogether to a degree unknown in more developed regions like the Valley of Oaxaca. Stability did not come until the 1630s, after the conclusion of the last major civil congregación campaign and the bottoming out of the Indian population. The next three hundred years saw occasional extinctions and movements of pueblos, but on the whole the number of towns, and what is more important, pueblo identities, persisted with remarkably little change. One might sum up the changes this way: the sixteenth century critically altered the settlements and relations between them, while the most significant changes during the remainder of the colonial period were more internal to the pueblos themselves.

Finally, the settlement history of the colonial Villa Alta district testifies to the thoroughgoing influence of the clergy, especially the Dominicans, on the Indians and their communities. Many, if not most, of the congregaciones were planned and executed with the desires of the friars clearly in view. The Dominicans also undertook on their own to move a number of towns at various times in the sixteenth century. Even in later times, the clergy frequently altered cabecera-sujeto relationships to fit their own requirements and make transportation easier. The Indians were forced to adapt to a Dominican-inspired administrative superstructure that was always subject to change. This superstructure rarely coincided with indigenous concepts of ethnicity and political relations, but it was nonetheless an important determinant of the relative economic, political and ceremonial status of Indian pueblos throughout the colonial period.

CHAPTER 4

THE ECONOMY

RESEARCH CONDUCTED during the past twenty years has shown that the colonial economy of the Oaxaca region possessed several distinctive characteristics that set it off from other parts of New Spain. The most basic difference was that nowhere in the Bishopric of Oaxaca did Spanish haciendas or mining activity determine the rhythm of economic life—for Spaniards or Indians—to the extent found in most other parts of central and northern Mexico. Mines were never sufficiently numerous or productive to provide steady incomes for more than a handful of individuals at any time. Spanish haciendas were more common, but compared with their counterparts further north they were smaller in size, changed hands frequently, and were in more direct competition with Indian communities for land and labor. Even in the Valley of Oaxaca, where most Spaniards were concentrated, Indian communities and individuals controlled two-thirds of the agricultural land in the eighteenth century and for the most part produced crops of their own choice.[1] Indian villages retained a significant degree of economic autonomy; relatively few were involved in full-time labor or became satellites of haciendas or other Spanish enterprises.

For most of Oaxaca's Indians, therefore, a modified form of subsistence agriculture in one's native community continued as a way of life. Participation in the wider colonial economy was not unimportant, but it was always conditioned by village needs at home. To be sure, the Spanish Conquest brought with it a new agricultural technology, draft animals, and new crops. But while oxen and plow soon replaced the digging stick in many areas and the cultivation of certain indigenous crops (such as maguey and cochineal) increased, the peasant subsistence economy in independent, landholding communities continued.[2]

Oaxaca did offer certain economic possibilities that many Spaniards considered commercially attractive, and the Indian population was a key ingredient in all of them. Silk cultivation and weaving flourished in many parts of the bishopric in the sixteenth century but were later replaced by trade in cochineal dyestuff, cotton, and Indian-woven cotton cloth as the most profitable trade items. Involved in this commerce were not only the peninsular and creole merchants, most of whom lived in Antequera, but also virtually all of the regional political officials in the province—the alcaldes mayores and corregidores. As Brian Hamnett has recognized, the economy of colonial Oaxaca was dominated less by creole landowners than by the alcaldes mayores and Spanish peninsular merchants.[3]

The Alcaldía Mayor of Villa Alta exemplified all these traits to a greater degree than any other Oaxaca district. Villa Alta's remoteness, its difficult terrain, and the initial hostility of the Indians ensured that haciendas would be few and mining little developed. Few Spaniards ever went there, and those who did had little interest in land ownership, so Indian communities generally retained control of their holdings. Many aspects of peasant subsistence continued as they had been before the Conquest. Well before 1600, however, political officials discovered the substantial profits that could be made in cotton textiles and cochineal, and the Indians of the district soon ranked among the top producers of these items in all of colonial Mexico. This led to a very special form of integration into regional, colonial, and world market systems, one that had internal repercussions in virtually every native community. These trends became most evident in the late seventeenth and eighteenth centuries, and this chapter will therefore deal mainly with the second half of the colonial era.

SPANISH RANCHING AND AGRICULTURE

In contrast to the Valley of Oaxaca, very little Spanish ranching or agricultural enterprise took hold in the Villa Alta district, even in times of difficulty when the exploitation of the Indians was yielding only marginal returns.[4] The Spanish response to Indian population decline was not to acquire land, as it frequently was elsewhere, but to intensify trading activities with the survivors, hunt for mining claims, or simply leave the jurisdiction to seek one's fortune elsewhere.

Table 14 lists nineteen viceregal land grants to Spaniards in the early colonial period. Notice that only six of the recipients were vecinos of Villa Alta. Virtually all the rest were residents of Mexico City who were given cattle *estancias* in the *despoblados* of Nanacatepec in the hot country after that once populous area began to decline. The other favored place for cattle ranching was at Xaltepec, which had also lost much population. None of the vecinos of Villa Alta requested or was given land in the vicinity of the town itself, with the single exception of Hernando de Arazena's 1567 *estancia de ganado mayor* (cattle ranch) at San Francisco Cajonos. While most of the grants listed were for cattle ranching, little is known about the ultimate fate of these enterprises. The ones at Nanacatepec and Xaltepec were located at such a great distance from the villa that any successes would tend to draw their owners away from the affairs of the town and its district. Clearly, ranching was not an important activity at Villa Alta at any time in its history. Sometimes cattle had to be imported into the area simply to meet the consumption needs of the town's residents!

TABLE 14. Viceregal Land Grants to Spaniards in the Villa Alta District

Date	Type of Grant[a]	Person	Location	Source
1550	E. de ganado mayor	Contador Antonio de la Cadena	Nanacatepec	AGN Mercedes 3 : 183r–v
1550	E. de ganado mayor	Factor Hernando de Salazar	Nanacatepec	AGN Mercedes 3 : 183v
1550	E. de ganado mayor	Lope de Arellano	Nanacatepec	AGN Mercedes 3 : 183v
1550	E. de ganado mayor	Juan Velázquez	Nanacatepec	AGN Mercedes 3 : 183v
1550	E. de ganado mayor	Don Pedro de Luna	Nanacatepec	AGN Mercedes 3 : 183v
1550	E. de ganado mayor	Gaspar de San Martín	Nanacatepec	AGN Mercedes 3 : 183v
1550	E. de ganado mayor	Don Ramiro de Arellano	Nanacatepec	AGN Mercedes 3 : 183v
1550	Sitio de azúcar y tierras	Don Tristán de Arellano	Nanacatepec & Xaltepec	AGN Mercedes 3 : 182v–183
1567	E. de ganado mayor	Hernando de Arazena[b]	S. F. Cajonos	AGN Mercedes 9 : 13v
1587	E. de ganado mayor	Diego de Avila[b]	Mixes?	AGN Mercedes 14 : 91v
1591	E. de ganado mayor	Don P. Real de Oñate	Nanacatepec	AGN Mercedes 17 : 41r
1591	E. de ganado mayor	Josepe de Soto	Nanacatepec	AGN Mercedes 17 : 41r
1592	Two caballerías	Pedro de Ojeda[b]	Xaltepec	AGN Mercedes 18 : 87v–88r
1592	E. de ganado mayor	Hernando de Arazena[b]	Xaltepec	AGN Mercedes 18 : 86r–v
1592	E. de ganado mayor	Juan Antonio de Azevedo[b]	Xaltepec	AGN Mercedes 18 : 87r–v
1596	E. de ganado mayor	Juan de Espinosa	Nanacatepec	AGN Mercedes 22 : 30r
1598	Two E. de ganado menor	Daniel de Alcántara[b]	San Francisco (?)	AGN Mercedes 21 : 182r
1610	Two caballerías	Luis de Espinosa	Alotepec	AGN Tierras 165 : 2
1619	Trapiche de azúcar	Andrés de Aznar[b]	unknown	AGN Mercedes 34 : 146r–v

[a] E. = Estancia.
[b] Vecino of Villa Alta.

Only a few additional scattered references provide information on Spanish ranches and haciendas in the region for the entire colonial period. In 1579, García de Robles, a resident of Antequera, received a license to add five hundred horses to his *estancia de ganado menor* (sheep and goat ranch) in the lowland Mixe community of Puxmetacan. Just five years later, he sold half the enterprise to Melchor Paz de Ulloa, a canon of the Cathedral of Antequera.[5] In 1643 Villa Alta vecino Juan Gutiérrez Xixón owned a sugar mill on lands of the Cajonos town San Pablo Yaganiza, and in 1717 Yalalag decided to sell a cattle ranch it operated within the limits of San Francisco Yatee to the convent of La Merced in Antequera.[6] The only late colonial estate that merited the name *hacienda* was that of San Bartolomé, which bordered on the Mixe community of Ayutla. But it was not owned by a Villa Alta resident and in fact was probably located in the jurisdiction of Mitla and Tlacolula.

The sole agricultural operation in the central part of the district that displayed any longevity was a sugar mill near Yalalag, the Trapiche de Yuguiba. It is first mentioned in 1643, when it was owned by Juan Sánchez Coronel, a resident of Villa Alta. Since Sánchez had secured clear title to it during the time of the *composiciones de tierras* (legalization of land titles), he could well have been its founder. By 1675 ownership had passed to Blas de Olivera Avila, also a vecino. But by the end of the century it was in the hands of absentee owners in Antequera, doña Ana Ortiz and her husband, Capitán don Juan de Gamboa. The manager they employed, Gerónimo de los Santos y Chávez, also from Antequera, concentrated on sugar production but also raised some cattle. The trapiche is last mentioned in 1791, when its owner Fernando Márquez died, leaving the mill valued at the relatively modest sum of 5,686 pesos.[7].

MINING

Mining for precious metals in the district began simultaneously with the Conquest, though with one exception in the late eighteenth century there were no large-scale undertakings and no large fortunes reaped. Throughout the colonial period, mining was always more important in the neighboring Ixtlán region than in Villa Alta.[8] Once the initial flurry of activity in the sixteenth century subsided, mining receded into the background of the economy of the district, asserting itself only infrequently. Small strikes were worked for short periods than abandoned, and their impact on Indian communities and the overall socioeconomic structure of the district was transitory at best.

Attempts at mining gold and silver began in the Mixe and Nexitzo regions with the conquests of Gaspar Pacheco, Diego de Figueroa, and Luis de Berrio in the 1520s and early 1530s, though they never amounted to much. In 1548 reserves of gold and silver were reported in the Mixe towns of Ixcocan, Tlazoltepec, and Santa María Ocotepec, though the silver mines at the last town were not being worked. Other reports were all from lowland areas: Miaguatlan (a sujeto of Tabaa), Roavela, and Nanacatepec.[9] Shortly thereafter, however, some larger enterprises got underway. Mines were being worked in the vicinity of Nejapa in the 1550s,[10] but a larger operation was located in Mixe territory in the 1580s and 1590s on the slopes of Mount Zempoaltépetl near Totontepec. Variously known as the Mines of Zempoaltépetl or the Mines of Espíritu Santo, this claim supported a handful of Spaniards who built a small camp there in 1580. Within a few years the mine was receiving repartimiento labor drafts of 104 Indians per week from surrounding Mixe villages.[11]

Eager to promote mining in the area and anticipating a further influx of Spaniards, the viceroy in 1585 created the new office of "Alcalde Mayor of the Mines of Espíritu Santo and Province of the Mixes," headquartered at Totontepec. Its first, and probably only, incumbent was Ruy Díaz de Mendoza, who had served as alcalde mayor of Villa Alta the year before.[12] In 1589–91, however, mistreatment of Indian workers caused many Mixe pueblos to protest and the viceroy found himself opposing the Spanish miners' labor policies. For a time, Totontepec alone was forced to provide a steady labor force of sixty workers, paid at the rate of two reales for a six-day week instead of the required six reales. Espíritu Santo's luck was soon to run out, however, and it shut down before 1600. Except perhaps for a small mine at Jayacaxtepec, in operation by 1589, and another near Alotepec in 1630, no further mining activity took place in Mixe country for the remainder of the colonial period.[13]

In the Zapotec Rincón, after three decades of inactivity, mining was revived in the 1630s and 1640s. In 1633 the inhabitants of Lachichina were being forced to work in nearby mines by their encomendera Jacinta de Tarifa.[14] Two years later, the pueblos of Tanetze, Talea, and Juquila noted that they had been paid and treated well by the miners Luis Pérez and Lic. Juan Narelo Cereceda. But a new enterpreneur, Capitán Gaspar Calderón, was compelling them to work by force, sending his *mayordomos* to workers' houses to round them up.[15] Calderón may have been the proprietor of the Cerralvo Silver Mine, which flourished in the 1640s and in which Alcaldes Mayores Juan López de Oláez, Antonio de Guraya y Lezama, and Martín Robles Villafaña may have owned shares. Considerable quantities of mercury, in shipments of 20 to 70 *quintales* (2,000–7,000 pounds), arrived in Villa Alta for processing ore during this period.[16] But like the Espíritu Santo before it, the Cerralvo had a short life and closed soon after 1649. The remainder of the seventeenth century saw only sporadic activity. A strike was reported in 1670 by Fernando de Porres y Aparicio, but the extent of his operation is not known.[17] Alonso Martín Mateo Saldaña, a vecino of Antequera and resident of Villa Alta, was working a small silver mine in 1680, and Capitán don Alonso Muñoz de Castilblanque, alcalde mayor of

Villa Alta in 1684–86, registered a claim in 1700 but by that time was living in San Luis Potosí and apparently never worked it.[18]

Activity in the eighteenth century was divided between the Rincón and Cajonos zones. New mines were discovered in 1729 in Solaga and Tabaa by Diego Benítez and don Pedro Carrillo de Peralta, respectively. The Tabaa operation was the larger of the two and drew workers from several pueblos. Working conditions there were especially harsh. Yojovi, for example, was forced to provide 15–25 laborers at a salary of two reales per day without meals. The town officials protested the low pay and the sickness and death that were causing many people to leave the community. The labor drafts were so onerous that fields of corn and cochineal went unattended, corn had to be purchased, construction on the town church was halted, and ten cofradías disbanded for lack of funds.[19]

Other mines were later discovered in the Cajonos region. One of these was also in Tabaa, claimed by don Vicente Flores in 1750.[20] Francisco de Gordon y Urquijo, a Villa Alta vecino and representative of the Antequera merchant Vicente Yturribarría y Urquijo, claimed seven new silver mines in 1773, six of them in Yalalag and one in Solaga, though only two were worked.[21] The last colonial discovery in the Cajonos was once again in Solaga in 1793, made by don Diego de Villasante, an Antequera merchant. This operation also provoked complaints from Indian workers who were forced into the mine by the alcalde mayor. San Pedro Cajonos claimed that its cochineal harvest of 1793 had suffered considerably as a result.[22]

The main focus of mining activity in the late eighteenth century was not in the Cajonos, however, but in the Rincón near San Miguel Talea. New mines were established there in 1753 by Capitán don Andrés de Berdeja of Veracruz. Despite opposition from local priests, the alcalde mayor ordered up labor drafts from Nexitzo communities. Berdeja did not reside in the area himself, but employed don Pedro Melgarejo, also a peninsular Spaniard, to run the enterprise. Whether the mines were a success or a failure is unknown, but by 1777 they were abandoned.[23]

Not long after Berdeja's withdrawal, however, the largest silver mining operation the district had ever seen got underway just two thousand feet below Talea at the Río de la Cantera. This mine, known as Santa Gertrudis, and other smaller ones named Cerro, Barranca, and Dolores, were owned by wealthy Antequera merchant Colonel Juan Francisco de Echarri. He began working Santa Gertrudis about 1777 and later expanded his operations to copper mining in the Serrano towns San Mateo Calpulalpa and Ixtepeji.[24] Echarri brought a higher level of capitalization to his enterprise than any previous miner in Villa Alta and seems to have earned greater profits. By the 1780s Santa Gertrudis alone employed about seventy-six workers, plus ten more on a neighboring food-producing hacienda that served it. Table 15 shows the provenience of the labor force. All the miners were from Nexitzo communities, which had to provide weekly crews equal to four percent or

TABLE 15. Labor in the Mine and Hacienda of Santa Gertrudis, 1784

Town	Leagues from Sta. Gertrudis	No. Tributaries	Workers 2% of Pop.	Workers 4% of Pop.
In the Mine				
Nexitzo Zapotec Towns				
Tanetze	2	86.5	2	4
Juquila	3	121.5	3	5
Cacalotepec	5	174.5	3	7
Yotao	6	139.5	3	5
Talea	0.5	151	3	6
Yatoni	0.5	42.5	1	2
Yae	2	216	4	8
Lalopa	2	154.5	3	6
Lachichina	2.5	62.5	1	2
Yagallo	2	125	3	5
Yaviche	2	45	1	2
Lahoya	1	48	1	2
Yagavila	5	112.5	2	4
Yaneri	6	117	2	4
Tepanzacualco	7	55	1	2
Zoogochi	5.5	94.5	2	4
Teotlaxco	5	55.5	1	2
Yagila	6	120	2	4
Josaa	7	58.5	1	2
Total		1,979.5	39	76
On the Hacienda				
Cajonos Zapotec Towns				
Tabaa	2	131.5	3	5
Yojovi	2	81.5	2	3
Solaga	3	199	4	8
Yohueche	4	74	1	3
Zoochila	4.5	104	2	4
Yalina	5	92.5	2	4
Tavehua	5	94	2	4
Zoogocho	4	215	4	8
Zoochixtepec	4	44.5	1	2
Zoochina	4.5	50.5	1	2
Yatzachi El Alto	5	82	2	3
Yatzachi El Bajo	5	135.5	2	5
Yahuio	4.5	60	1	2
Guiloxi	4.5	74	1	3
Laxopa	5.5	136	2	5
Total		1,574	30	61

Note: Pueblos serving the mine had to provide the assigned number of workers continually on a weekly basis, 4% of their tributary populations in busy periods and 2% in slack periods. The hacienda required only ten workers each week, and the sending towns rotated in turn.
Source: AGN Civil 1607, *1*.

two percent of their populations, depending on production levels set by the mayordomo. Workers were paid but had no choice whether to participate or not, since the orders came from the alcalde mayor. It can be seen from the table that only a few Rincón communities were not forced to serve. The hacienda, on the other hand, was staffed entirely by Cajonos towns, which rotated the burden of supplying peons each week. Yalalag, the six Cajonos pueblos, and several others did not serve, probably because they were still sending workers to mines in their own vicinity.

Predictably, work at Santa Gertrudis was not popular with the Zapotecs, who composed 100 percent of the labor force. In 1782 the pueblos of Juquila, Tabaa, Yojovi, Solaga, and Yae, angered by the low wages and dangerous working conditions, threatened to kill Antonio Solano, a Nahua foreman from Analco. Alcalde Mayor Francisco Marty noted that this was one of the few expressions of defiance shown by Zapotecs to the Analco Nahuas that he had ever witnessed.[25] The following year, Tabaa, Yojovi, and Solaga filed suit against Echarri in an effort to end the labor repartimientos that were sapping their communities. When they realized they would lose the contest, the three towns began to riot in protest, but this too failed to achieve their objectives.[26] In 1788 Lalopa made a last-ditch effort on its own, arguing that the 4 percent draft should apply only to commoners and that principales should not have to work in the mines. Since a third or more of the adult males in the village belonged to the *principal* group (see chapter 5), this was an issue of some consequence, but the alcalde mayor promptly replied that all tributaries—principales included—must work.[27]

Colonel Echarri was not the only mine owner in the Rincón in the late eighteenth century. Other claims were filed in Talea and Yatoni by don Diego Antonio Fernández de Añón, a peninsular Spaniard and resident of Tanetze.[28] Don Angel Reyes also laid claim to a discovery near Santa Gertrudis in 1780, and Echarri himself formed a partnership in the same year with don José Ignacio Loperena to work a claim at Yatoni.[29] But none of these ventures came close to rivaling Santa Gertrudis, which continued as an active gold and silver mine through the nineteenth and early twentieth centuries, attracting workers from the surrounding communities as well as from the Sierra Juárez.[30] By 1910 the only other mines in the Villa Alta district were at Tabaa, the Cajonos pueblos, and Mixe Jayacaxtepec.[31]

In summary, it can be said that mining had a definite negative impact on the physical and social health of some of the towns in the district some of the time. The Mixes suffered most in the sixteenth century and the Nexitzo and Cajonos Zapotecs in late colonial times, but the Chinantecs and Bixanos Zapotecs were barely affected at all. Mining in Villa Alta was in the main a small-scale economic activity that occurred in spurts. Rarely would a mine be ascendant for more than a decade, and there were stretches of twenty to thirty years with almost no activity at all. Furthermore, the pattern of ownership of the mines was similar to the distribution of encomiendas in the midsixteenth century: most holders, particularly the successful ones, were vecinos not of Villa Alta but of Antequera, Veracruz, and elsewhere. In this economic activity, as in others to be described below, the region was plundered by entrepreneurs who sought to extract as much as they could while providing few, if any, benefits in return. The Indians could do little to influence the outcome, nor could the Spanish vecinos of Villa Alta, few of whom saw any of the profits produced by the mines.

SPANISH TRADE

While mining in Villa Alta was spotty and proceeded in fits and starts, trade with the Indians began early, increased steadily in volume as the years wore on and affected to some degree every indigenous pueblo in the district. There was no one else to trade with in the region except the Indians, and Spanish merchants were eager to supply them with a variety of goods, including food staples, household items, *aguardiente*, pulque, church ornaments, and other religious paraphernalia. At the same time, the merchants bought from the Indians for resale such products as cotton, cotton cloth and clothing, cacao, and cochineal. This trade was already well established by the 1550s, and as was seen in chapter 2, traveling merchants had begun to make their rounds and were usually paid in clothing for the merchandise they sold.

The abuses involved in this activity were considerable, and the dealings of some merchants more nearly resembled robbery than commerce. Gaspar Asensio, a resident of Villa Alta in 1592, was trading in textiles and other goods in Nexitzo Ixcuintepec, but his methods were so exploitative and disruptive that the viceroy personally ordered him to stay out of the town.[32] In remote Guaspaltepec in the lowlands, conditions were sometimes worse. The isolation of the area and its sparse population in the late sixteenth century encouraged some merchants to take extreme liberties with their customers. A common practice was to sell on credit at excessive prices to unsuspecting Indians. When payment became due, the merchant would enter his clients' homes and take whatever of their personal property that struck his fancy. The items carried off in this fashion were frequently worth much more than what the Indians owed.[33]

Spanish merchants could be found living and trading with Indians in even the most remote areas of the district. The law of the realm stated that merchants could remain no longer than three days in Indian communities; could not enter Indian homes while they were there; and, once their business was concluded, could not return to the same community for four months.[34] But such requirements were hardly possible to enforce in places like the Sierra Zapoteca. Records for the early years are scanty, but at various times in the eighteenth century Spanish merchants were living in Nexitzo Lalopa, Bixanos Latani, and Choapan, and Mixe Puxmetacan and Tepuztepec.[35] In

1739, Alcalde Mayor Juan Francisco de Puertas noted that many traveling merchants, both Spaniards and *castas,* were making forced sales of mules and horses to the Indians. Some of the traders were living with Indian women and a few had even built houses and established permanent residence in the pueblos.[36] Three decades later Alcalde Mayor Joseph de Molina y Sandoval had similar complaints. He complained that most Spaniards and castas residing illegally in Indian villages were "sailors and deserters" from Veracruz who came up the Río de Alvarado and made a living by selling liquor, playing cards, gunpowder, and other contraband to the Indians.[37]

It was not uncommon for established merchants in Antequera to employ agents to handle their trading for them in the Sierra. One such merchant, Juan Contreras, rarely went to Villa Alta himself but hired an Indian from Lachirioag to sell sugar and cacao throughout the district in 1695. Like most other traders, Contreras sold to the Indians on credit, for they rarely had cash or other goods on hand to make purchases.[38] Other merchants made a point of taking up residence in villages at harvest time, so they could be sure to collect what was due them while the Indians had some surplus at their disposal. While this practice was a flagrant violation of the law, it was fairly common in Villa Alta and the rest of the Bishopric of Oaxaca in the late eighteenth century.[39] Still other traders took advantage of special occasions, such as the installation of new Indian cabildo officials on New Year's Day, to extract illegal fees totaling as much as a thousand pesos from the pueblos.[40]

Not all merchants in the region were of the itinerant variety. Two or three stores were kept in Villa Alta, one of which was operated by the alcalde mayor.[41] These establishments catered to both Spaniards and Indians, usually on a credit basis. The magistrates' businesses were always the largest, effectively combining wholesale and retail transactions. In 1793 a Villa Alta priest remarked that Subdelegado Pablo de Ortega (1784−90) at one time had seven hundred cargas (over 78 tons) of cotton in his store. He bought it for 7 pesos per carga and resold it for 20−25 pesos, earning 10−12,000 pesos per year from this activity alone.[42] Villa Alta had two other stores in the 1750s besides the one operated by the alcalde mayor. A small shop was run by Joseph Calderón, and a larger one with an inventory valued at more than fifteen thousand pesos was owned by Joseph del Bal, juez administrator de alcabalas, and managed by Antonio Francisco de Herrera, a local vecino.[43]

The Bixanos town of Choapan was an important marketing center and crossroads for traffic between the highlands and northern lowlands, and usually hosted at least one commercial establishment in addition to the periodic Indian market. In the 1780s, one Choapan store was owned by an enterprising young bachelor from Vizcaya, don Josef (José) Carlos de Gordon Urquijo. A vecino of Villa Alta, he was also a government tax collector in the Partido of Choapan. He later served as subdelegado of Villa Alta in

1801–2.[44] In the late eighteenth century, a few stores also sprouted in the Cajonos town of Zoochila, which hosted a thriving market and, for a time, a resident Spanish community.[45] An inventory of one small Zoochila dry goods establishment that served a predominantly Spanish clientele in 1780 appears in table 16. It stocked few luxuries, but a small supply of imported items—such as plates from Talavera—was usually on hand.

TABLE 16.   Inventory of the Store of Miguel Bustamante in Santiago Zoochila, 1780

66 yards (varas) of plush woolen cloth @ 15.5 reales	127 pesos 7 reales
132 yards of Mexican-made blue woolen cloth @ 11r	181p 4r
42 yards of rough brown linen cloth @ 4.5r	23p 5r
126 yards of *chiapaneco* (Chiapas-style cotton cloth) @ 2r	31p 4r
103 yards of *cotín* @ 2½r	32p 1½r
140 yards of *jerga* (coarse frieze) @ 2r	35p
66 yards of *pontivi* @ 4r	33p
3 bedspreads from Puebla @ 12r	4p 4r
40 yards of *saya* (for dress skirts or tunics) @ 4r	20p
16 pieces of fine *chiapaneco* cloth @ 16r	32p
12 *rebozos* (shawls) from Puebla @ 12r	18p
32 blue handkerchiefs @ 1½r	6p
10 dozen blue ribbons @ 3r	3p 6r
3 pounds, 10 ounces of blue thread @ 7r	3p 1⅜r
6 pounds, 4 ounces of silk, various colors @ 15p 4r	96p 7r
2 pounds, 8 ounces of loose silk @ 8p	20p
12 belts @ 3r	4p 4r
12 colored ribbons @ 2p	24p
8¾ ounces of British thread @ 4r	4p 3r
15 ounces of sewing thread	3p
8 ounces of glitter	1p
28 dozen twisted cords for embroidery @ 1r	3p 4r
3 dozen violin strings	2p 2r
6 pairs of Spanish scissors @ 2r	1p 4r
2 reams of paper @ 9p	18p
33 sheets of gilt-edged paper @ 1½r	6p 1½r
2 pieces of fabric for straining @ 1r	2r
5 pounds of maguey thread @ 2r	1p 2r
8 dozen large and small machetes @ 11p 4r	92p
100 pounds of raw iron	30p
several iron digging sticks and *marquesotas* (branding irons ?)	42p 4r

TABLE 16.   (*continued*)

6 *cargas* (225 lbs. each) of lead discs @ 18r		13p 4r
18 plates from Talavera @ ½r		1p 1r
6 pairs of shoes @ 4r		3p
3½ dozen knives @ 18r		7p 7r
13 pieces of glass from Puebla @ ½r		6½r
7 boxes of gourd cups @ 14r		12p 2r
4 *cargas* (225 lbs. each) of wax @ 24p		96p
6 pounds of pepper @ 1p		6p
2½ pounds of cloves @ 5p		12p 4r
1 pound, 4 ounces of saffron @ 3r per oz.		7p 4r
3 pounds of cumin seed @ 2r		6r
12 pounds of starch @ 1½r		2p 2r
36 pounds of rice @ 1½r		6p 6r
26 pounds of steel @ 3r		9p 6r
4½ pounds of fine cinnamon @ 9p		40p 4r
3 pounds of course cinnamon @ 3p 4r		10p 4r
1 bundle of dried chiles		9p
4 pounds of dried chiles		9p
4 pounds of cacao @ 5r		2p 4r
84 pints of refined *aguardiente* (stocked for Spanish travelers & priests)		63p
35 pints of *mistela* (a beverage) @ 4.5r		19p 5r
4½ pints of almond oil (for curing)		4p 4r
3 pints of rose-water		1p 4r
2 vessels of *navas* oil		6p
1 vessel of cooking oil		9p 4r
3 pounds of annato @ 6r		2p 2r
338 pounds of cacao @ 4r		169p
39 *cargas* (225 lbs. each) of sugar @ 25r		121p 7r
12 pieces of copper @ 4r		6p
80 pounds of shrimp @ 1r		10p
20 bundles of fireworks @ 4p 4r		90p
31 fireworks wheels @ 3r		11p 5r
16 *fanegas* (112 lbs. each) of yellow flour @ 12p		192p
4 *fanegas* (112 lbs. each) of white flour @ 14p		56p
19 *cargas* (225 lbs. each) of tallow @ 5p 5r		106p 7r
	Total Value	2,025p 3/8r

Source: AJVA Civil 1693–1860, 5.

These shops were the only "business establishments" in the district apart from the mines and the handful of sugar mills and ranches. Other traders who resided in Villa Alta worked out of their homes and spent most of their time making the rounds of the Indian pueblos. There is no evidence that the villa had any full-time Spanish artisans. The alcalde mayor reported in 1781 that the district had seven silversmiths—one Spaniard and two mestizos in Villa Alta, a mestizo in San Juan Yae, and two Spaniards and a mestizo in Choapan. He went on to note, however, that only one of the Spaniards in Choapan did good work, none of the silversmiths worked at the trade full time, and none had a store.[46]

Somewhat surprisingly, independent Spanish merchants and peddlers appear to have traded very little cochineal dyestuff, the premier cash crop of Oaxaca.[47] This is all the more interesting when we consider that the Sierra Zapoteca was one of the leading regions of cochineal production during most of the colonial period. While the actual cultivation of the bugs was done by the Indians, Barbro Dahlgren de Jordán has estimated that about half the amount produced in all of New Spain passed through the hands of private merchants, the alcaldes mayores handling the other half.[48] If this was true in other parts of the colony, it was not the case in Villa Alta, where the alcaldes mayores monopolized the cochineal trade to an extraordinary degree. While numerous small transactions no doubt took place, beginning in the midsixteenth century and continuing at a growing pace until the late 1770s, no records mention any independent Spanish cochineal merchant who dealt directly with Indian cultivators in a business of any size. Since only Indians produced cochineal, at least until the 1780s, and since the alcaldes mayores and colonial law gave merchants only limited access to Indian communities (the magistrates did not welcome competition for their trading interests), it followed that merchants could hope to acquire large amounts of the dyestuff only through intermediaries. Indians sometimes served in this capacity, but where the potential profits were substantial and large sums were available for investment, there was no better broker than the alcalde mayor himself. This was essentially how the cochineal business operated in Villa Alta (it will be discussed at greater length below) and many other districts in Oaxaca and, as we saw in chapter 2, was one of the reasons why the villa remained small in population and without a cabildo for so long.

The only detailed accounts of a Villa Alta merchant that have been located belonged to don Joseph Martín de la Sierra y Acevedo, a very influential man and *alguacil perpetuo* of the villa in the late seventeenth century. His books for 1684–96 reveal that he specialized in the cotton textile trade and make no mention of cochineal.[49] Even so, De la Sierra must have been favored by—or in cahoots with—the alcaldes mayores to pursue his textile interests, for trade in this commodity was another specialty of the magistrates. De la Sierra's contemporaries in the villa were not as fortunate as he.

By the 1660s, the office of alcalde mayor of Villa Alta was recognized as the most lucrative political post in Oaxaca, and the dealings of the magistrates had already begun to exert a negative impact on the town itself.[50] In 1693 the vecinos of Villa Alta, led by Gabriel de Achica, complained to the viceroy that Alcalde Mayor Miguel Ramón de Nogales and his predecessors required the vecinos to have licenses to trade in the district—a brazen attempt at obstruction. Nogales also used force to prevent the vecinos from going to the pueblos to conduct their business.[51]

Things did not change, however, and Villa Alta's tiny merchant population failed to expand with the increased volume of trade in the eighteenth century, though the alcaldes mayores were making record profits. Similar protests from merchants cropped up several times in the late eighteenth century, now from Antequera. Gabriel Roldán, for example, had just managed to get a foothold in the Partido of Ayutla in 1772 when he incurred the wrath of Alcalde Mayor Sancho Pisón y Moyua. Roldán complained that the alcalde mayor prevented him from doing business and added that the magistrate's monopoly on trade in the district kept prices at an artificially high level.[52] The following year, a group of Antequera merchants protested even more vociferously about Moyua, but they made it clear that his policies were no different from those of his predecessors. All the alcaldes mayores, the merchants claimed, did everything they could to keep them out of the district. They terrorized the merchants, confiscated their goods, jailed them, and prohibited the Indians from dealing with them. Each magistrate, they protested, wanted to be the "absolute owner of the commerce his district offers," especially where cochineal (which reached its apogée at this time) was concerned.[53] As late as 1790 the story was the same, and Subdelegado Bernardo de Bonavía was attempting to carry on traditional practices even though they were specifically prohibited by the law of 1786 that established the new intendancy system. Hamnett paraphrases a remark made by the intendente of Oaxaca, Antonio de Mora y Peysal: "Fifteen private traders, all of them investors of considerable sums in cottons, textiles, and cochineal, who had ventured to Villa Alta had quickly returned to Oaxaca, and would not dare to return as long as the present Subdelegate [Bernardo de Bonavía] held sway in that *partido*."[54]

The conclusion must be that from 1550 onward most trading activity of any consequence (i.e., of large profit potential) in the Villa Alta district involved the alcaldes mayores. Itinerant peddlers and small shopkeepers with small inventories and limited capital were ever present and for the most part tolerated by the magistrates as relatively harmless, if annoying, elements. Merchants of means with substantial capital to invest met with a chilly reception, however. The degree of friction between alcaldes mayores and merchants increased notably from the midseventeenth through the late eighteenth centuries as the potential for profits increased. The evidence suggests that by the end of the seventeenth century the alcaldes mayores had effectively triumphed over other traders in Villa Alta and that a century later they had driven out competitors from Antequera as well. This left open only one avenue for merchants who wanted to invest in Villa Alta's Indian trade: that of combining business with politics and signing on as an *aviador* (financial backer) of a particular alcalde mayor, with whom profits would be shared.

THE REPARTIMIENTOS DE EFECTOS
OF THE ALCALDES MAYORES

The trading activities of the alcaldes mayores of Villa Alta and other districts of colonial Mexico stemmed in large measure from the government's inability to pay the magistrates adequate salaries. Earnings were not only low, but insufficient to cover even necessary administrative expenditures. While the crown technically forbade political officials from engaging in trade within their districts, this law was routinely contravened by all concerned in the interests of administrative efficiency, colonial control, commercial opportunity, and, in a few large and lucrative districts like Villa Alta, personal enrichment.[55] The commercial transactions were known as *repartimientos de efectos* or *repartimientos de mercancías* (literally, the distribution or dividing up of merchandise; not to be confused with the *repartimiento* system of labor drafts), and amounted to a system of forced production and consumption. Alcaldes mayores would forcibly "sell" commodities to the Indians in their districts at artificially high prices. Cattle, mules, oxen, wheat, tobacco, sugar, cotton, fish, and even corn were often distributed this way.[56] Alternatively, and especially in Villa Alta, repartimientos often consisted of advances of cash or raw materials, such as cotton, to Indian communities and individual households that in turn were obligated to use the money to produce cochineal or other crops or weave the cotton into cloth. Then on a specified date, the alcalde mayor would purchase the harvest or finished textiles at below market prices. Such practices encouraged the widespread custom in the colonial bureaucracy of treating political offices as if they were private property.

While repartimientos de efectos were in evidence in parts of Oaxaca as early as the sixteenth century, they began to flourish in the second half of the colonial period and reached their height during Oaxaca's "boom" years between 1740 and 1790.[57] The practice was regarded in contrasting ways by different sectors of the Hispanic population. Many political officials and merchants, of course, championed the repartimientos as the only reasonable way of providing adequate salaries, ensuring commercial profits (especially in regions with little mining), and persuading the Indians to produce. Others, especially the clergy, condemned repartimientos as a blatant form of exploitation and in some cases a drag on Indian production and exchange. A good many others were simply ambivalent, and periodic excesses by the alcaldes mayores—such as those that brought on the Tehuantepec Rebellion in

1660—provoked episodes of administrative soul searching and fumbling attempts at regulation.

An apt expression of ambivalence came from the crown itself in May 1751. The context was a royal decree establishing commissions in Mexico City, Lima, and Santa Fe to regulate repartimientos by controlling the quantity and price of goods that could be sold to the Indians. The king began by recognizing that the repartimientos were bad for the Indians and that if the current practices continued unchecked they would lead the colonies to "total ruin." But on the other hand, he reasoned, the propensity of the Indians toward laziness, idleness, and drunkenness was well known. Without the repartimientos to force them to produce and consume the necessary items, they would go naked, their fields would sit uncultivated, and the mines would remain unworked.[58] Here we have in a nutshell the essence of the colonial mentality: an admittedly exploitative practice that had become a mainstay of the economy and bureaucracy was rationalized by attributing an inherent moral inferiority and laziness to the colonized population.

Repartimiento trade in Villa Alta did not differ in its essential details from similar enterprises elsewhere in colonial Mexico, but it did stand out considerably in degree. What propelled the district to the top of the "wish lists" of many merchants and would-be alcaldes mayores of New Spain by the midseventeenth century was its large number of Indians and their ability to produce exceptional quantities of cotton cloth (*mantas,* or mantles, as they were called) and cochineal dyestuff. The office of alcalde mayor of Villa Alta retained its preeminent ranking in the colony continuously through the eighteenth century.[59] Even in the best of times,, not all of the alcaldías mayores were profitable. In 1779, with the cochineal boom in full swing, Fiscal Merino of the Audiencia of Mexico noted that

> Only a few Alcaldías Mayores were profitable, and most of these were in Oaxaca. Villa Alta was the best of all, because of the diversity of its trades, which offered a profit in both peace and war. Jicayán, Miahuatlán, and Nejapa also rendered profits in peace-time, but their dye trade suffered in war-time. The other jurisdictions yielding fruitful returns were Teposcolula, the Corregimiento of Oaxaca, Teotitlán del Valle, Chichicapa, Tehuantepec, all dye areas, and the cotton garment and cochineal dye region of Teotitlán del Camino. Apart from those, only three others in New Spain rendered a profit, Tehuacán, Maravitío, and Tulancingo.[60]

The organization and financing of the Spanish side of the repartimientos in various districts of Oaxaca has been studied in detail by Brian Hamnett.[61] The alcaldes mayores normally obtained the goods and cash to be distributed by means of a contract with one or more private merchants in Mexico City or Antequera. The merchant agreed to serve as *aviador* (financial backer) and provide the magistrate's *fianza,* a payment that served as an advance guarantee to the crown that the alcalde mayor would produce the tribute revenue that he was obliged to collect from the Indians. In return, the magistrate contracted to manage his backer's trading activities with the Indians. Profits were split three ways: among the merchants, the alcalde mayor, and the latter's legal lieutenant, the person who actually carried out the trading operations and was usually a nominee of the merchant.

Such a system encouraged commercial monopolies by some of New Spain's leading merchant capitalists at the expense of an especially high degree of exploitation of the Indians. I quote from Hamnett.

> Only the Corregidores and Alcaldes Mayores were able to manage the *reparti-miento*, because only they were endowed with full Royal jurisdiction, which they employed to coerce the Indians to trade in commodities they might not otherwise be inclined to produce in bulk. The Royal power of justice, then, was used to violate the freedom of trading prescribed for the indigenous communities by the Laws of the Indies. By creating commercial monopolies within the locality, and by expelling any intruding merchants, the Alcaldes Mayores sought to keep the local trade confined to their *aviador's* interests.[62]

Despite the heavy concentration on textiles and cochineal, the commodities traded in the Villa Alta district were actually quite diverse. Alcalde Mayor Pedro Fernández de Villaroel in 1660 had a special interest in vanilla, for example. He forced Zapotec villagers in the Partidos of Tanetze and Yae to sell it to him at the rate of twenty-five to thirty pounds per real, then resold it on the market at the going rate of six pounds per real, realizing an enormous profit. According to an inquiry made by Bishop Alonso de Cuevas Dávalos, Indians who had no vanilla to "sell" to the alcalde mayor had to buy it elsewhere at the market rate and then part with it for considerably less than what they paid for it. The bishop's investigation also revealed that Villaroel regularly made repartimientos of clothing, blue woolen cloth, machetes, digging sticks, hatchets, soap, and candles, "all at high prices and with payment due in twenty days." Individuals who did not pay on time were jailed or whipped.[63] Other magistrates traded heavily in animals. Mules were forced on all the Cajonos pueblos in 1764; once in possession of the beasts, the Indians were enlisted at low wages to use them to carry the alcalde mayor's textiles to Antequera![64] By the 1780s it was customary for magistrates to distribute in the district 300–400 oxen each year as well as 250–300 mules. Indians frequently took up to eighteen months to pay for expensive items like oxen.[65]

Much greater profits were made from the cochineal repartimientos. Oaxaca was, after all, the world's greatest producer of the little bug that fed off the nopal cactus cultivated in hundreds of indigenous communities. During the sixteenth century, the market for the dyestuff was modest but growing, and by 1660 *grana*, as it was called, ranked second only to silver among New Spain's exports[66] and was far and away Oaxaca's leading trading commodity. With the lifting of trade restrictions in the eighteenth century, cochineal entered its "golden age" as demand for it increased in France,

Holland, Britain, and Spain.[67] Furthermore, between 1745 and 1954 production was confined almost entirely to the Bishopric of Oaxaca.[68] The boom was over well before independence, however, the peak production years being 1769–78.[69]

Cochineal was cultivated in many parts of Oaxaca, but especially in the Sierra Zapoteca of Villa Alta, the Sierra Juárez, and the districts of Nejapa, Jicayán, and Miahuatlán. Virtually all of it was funneled through the hands of merchants in Antequera, then shipped to northern cities or to Veracruz for export to Europe. It was customary for a government inspector to examine all cochineal in Antequera for signs of adulteration (a common problem), yet in 1756 all dyestuff coming from Villa Alta was declared exempt from inspection by the viceroy, an indication perhaps of the large quantity or the high quality of the grana the district produced.[70]

In Villa Alta in 1660 Alcalde Mayor Villaroel advanced cash to the Indians, then collected the cochineal after the harvest at the rate of 13 to 16 reales per pound, reselling it at the market price of 24 reales (three pesos) per pound. Again, no Indian household was exempt from the repartimiento; those that did not produce their own had to buy it elsewhere, usually at 24 reales per pound.[71] Data are not available to determine to what extent prices paid by the magistrates for cochineal fluctuated in accord with market prices. According to figures published by Dahlgren de Jordán, cochineal prices in Antequera between 1758 and 1790 fluctuated only modestly, hovering close to an average of 17.5 reales per pound except in the peak years 1771 and 1772, when it was valued at 32 and 30 reales.[72] Up in Villa Alta, Alcalde Mayor Joseph de Molina y Sandoval was advancing to the Indians 12 reales per pound for grana in 1770 when the market price was 25 reales.[73] By the 1780s the price had dropped to an average of 16.5 reales, but the 12-real standard was still in effect for the repartimientos.[74] In any case, it is clear that the magistrates' profit margins were substantial and that Indians were forced to surrender much of their crops at one-half to three-fourths of its market value.

While such terms of trade were extremely favorable to the Spaniards, the cochineal business had its risks. Even in years when production was high, alcaldes mayores often had trouble collecting the grana due them at harvest time because of Indian resistance, production problems, or both. Molina y Sandoval, for example, left office in 1770 with twenty-three Cajonos and Rincón pueblos still owing him a substantial amount of cochineal. He lamented that sometimes alcaldes mayores had to wait as long as two or three years for the returns on their cochineal repartimientos.[75]

After 1782 cochineal production suffered a substantial decline, never to be reversed. Hamnett ascribed the downward trend to (1) attempts of the church to raise the tithe (for Spaniards) on cochineal from four percent to ten percent; (2) threat of a reform of the alcabala which would have made transactions more costly; (3) the widespread famine and inflation that plagued New Spain in 1785–87; and (4) the establishment of the intendancy system of 1786 and the prohibition of the repartimiento de efectos. Competition from Guatemala after 1821 and the advent of cheaper chemical dyes after the 1850s brought on the final collapse of cochineal in Oaxaca in the nineteenth century.[76] All these trends were manifest in Villa Alta. When the ban on repartimientos firmly reached the district in 1790, trade in grana had already declined considerably. Subdelegado Bernardo de Bonavía noted that few pueblos cultivated it anymore and that in recent years the alcaldes mayores had only shipped 5–6,000 pounds per year.[77] By comparison, a single load of the dyestuff that sailed from Veracruz in 1779 contained 11,700 pounds of cochineal from Villa Alta.[78] In 1810, Villa Alta was no longer on the roster of major cochineal-producing regions of Oaxaca. Most of the crop by that time came from the Sierras of Miahuatlán, the Pacific coast, Ixtepeji in the Sierra Juárez, and the Chontal region.[79]

But difficult moments in the dye trade had long preceded its final decline. Like all export commodities, cochineal was subject to cyclical price trends that reflected international conditions. One of the low points in the eighteenth century occurred in 1740 when the market price fell to twelve reales with the outbreak of war in Europe and the Atlantic that cut off communications between Spain and its American colonies.[80] In Villa Alta, Alcalde Mayor Juan Francisco de Puertas, working together with his merchant brother in Antequera and his aviador in Mexico City, was planning his repartimientos accordingly. The three in 1739 predicted problems in the cochineal market and were consequently emphasizing the more profitable cotton textiles in their dealings with the Indians. The aviador, in fact, had invested very little in grana in 1739. The market for it was almost entirely in Europe, and it therefore took longer to sell than cotton cloth, which was produced for the internal market and could be sold readily in Mexico City and Guadalajara at surer profits.[81] In fact, it seems that the cotton mantle industry in Villa Alta always held a slight edge over cochineal during the entire second half of the colonial period, except perhaps in the peak dye years of the 1770s. In 1810, when little grain was produced, the textile business in the district proceeded at full steam, its ware continuing to sell at good prices in northern cities. Troops in the independence wars were clothed with cotton material woven in Villa Alta, and the district continued to specialize in weaving more than any other in Oaxaca.[82]

Forced weaving of cotton textiles, a burden borne mainly by the Indian women of the district, had become a mainstay of the local economy as early as the 1540s, as was seen in chapter 2. During the sixteenth century these spoils were shared more or less equally among the alcaldes mayores, corregidores, and encomenderos. The Indians themselves may also have marketed substantial quantities independently. But as was the case with cochineal, in the seventeenth century the alcaldes mayores and their aviadores emerged as by far the dominant figures in the trade. Hamnett describes the procedures firmly established in the midseventeenth century:

> . . . the Alcaldes Mayores . . . were able to commission the Indians to weave the cotton mantles, so much in demand among the lower classes of the Realm, through their control of a large part of the cotton supplies. The raw material they would then issue in lots to the Indians. In Yaguia [Yagila], for example, there would be two *repartimientos* of cotton per month, in which eight pounds of cotton would be issued to each family, deducting the cost from the price of each finished cotton mantle of five yards (varas) in length and one in width. In general, in Villa Alta, one mantle was to be finished in twenty days. This mantle would bring a market price of 16 reales. However, the Indian weavers would receive a price of only 8 reales from the Alcalde Mayor. Besides this abuse, the Indian population, which manufactured its own clothing, would be required to receive imported clothing issued in the *repartimiento*. For such clothing, it was obliged to pay in the products of the region. In such a way, the activities of the Alcaldes Mayores forced the Indians to be both producers and consumers of commodities from which the justices and their financial backers derived a large measure of their wealth.[83]

Most of the cotton used was apparently locally grown in pueblos with access to large stretches of tierra caliente. By the end of the sixteenth century the extensive former lands of deserted Guaspaltepec were ripe for cotton production. All of the cotton-producing communities—Bixanos Latani, Choapan, Yahuive, and Mixe Puxmetacan—bordered on this region.[84] The specific circumstances of cotton production and marketing are not known, but doubtlessly a large portion of it was controlled by the alcaldes mayores. Intendant Antonio de Mora y Peysal in 1790 charged that

> under the former practices, the cotton used in the production of these mantles had been issued among the Indians with the utmost violence in Choapan, Latani, and Puxmetacan. Only 7 pesos would be paid to the cotton growers for a crop of 8 arrobas [200 pounds], the market value of which was really 17 pesos. What had been bought by the *repartidores* at 7 pesos would then be issued to the Indian textile weavers in a further *repartimiento* at 19 or 20 pesos.[85]

There are indications, however, that some cotton was grown and sold independently by the Indians themselves, especially in Latani, where virtually the whole town was involved in its production. Bitter disputes over access to the *algodonales* (cotton lands) of Guaspaltepec in the eighteenth century consumed much time and energy in Latani, Choapan, and Sochiapan. One lawsuit alone lasted from 1736 to 1782.[86]

A distinctive aspect of Indian tribute in the Villa Alta district was that a significant part of it was paid in cotton cloth during virtually the entire colonial era. Even as late as 1790, when all other districts in Oaxaca were paying in money, Villa Alta continued to meet its quotas with cotton mantles, by express order of the viceroy.[87] This was, of course, just what the alcaldes mayores wanted, for by selling the *mantas de tributo* on the open market they could frequently turn a profit above and beyond the cash value of the tribute due the government. Apart from these textiles were the *mantas de compra* or *de rescate* that were sold independently by the justices and their financial backers. In 1739, these were sold in Mexico City for fourteen reales each, while the mantas de tributo commanded a price of fifteen reales. Alcalde Mayor Puerta packaged them in bundles of about 125 and shipped them by mule to his brother in Antequera, who in turn forwarded them to the aviador in the capital. During a four-month period in 1739, the justice sent his brother 11,200 mantles, 5,500 of them *de tributo* and 5,700 *de compra*, telling him that he soon expected to send 2,000 more.[88] The Indians, for their part, often requested permission to pay their tribute in specie but were frequently denied.[89]

By the late eighteenth century, the volume of the textile trade had reached enormous proportions, though available estimates vary. José María Murguía y Galardi in his statistical survey stated that before 1787 Villa Alta produced between fifty and sixty thousand mantles per year. Bishop Bergoza y Jordán, on the other hand, placed the annual rate of production for the same period at two hundred thousand per year.[90] Murguía was probably closer to the truth, but whatever the figure, the alcaldes mayores and their aviadores could expect to share in large profits during the boom years of the eighteenth century. An anonymous document stated that the magistrates were receiving above 40,000 pesos a year from all their activities, considerably more than their actual salary of 2,983 pesos. Another source put the profit of the alcalde mayor in 1784 at 27,840 pesos and in 1785 at 74,645 pesos.[91]

Few, if any, pueblos in the district were exempt from weaving obligations. This meant that most adult women spent large amounts of time at their looms (while their husbands and other family members were either growing cotton or tending to cochineal-producing *nopalitos*). After a visit to Bixanos territory in 1779, the bishop of Oaxaca lamented the plight of the Zapotec woman. When she was not weaving for the alcalde mayor, she produced other goods for sale; but she never received a fair price. She bought the raw cotton she needed for a single mantle in the market at Choapan, spent at least a week of days and nights weaving it, then sold it in the same market, perhaps to a Spanish merchant from Antequera or Puebla, for one-third to one-half its value. Her profit for the week's work would be four or five reales. (By comparison, Indian miners in 1729 were paid two reales a day, a wage they considered low—see this chapter, above). What bothered the bishop most was that the price of cotton was high and still rising. Indians were forced to sell cheap because prices were fixed by the aviadores.[92] According to Intendant Mora in 1790, the weaving that women did for the repartimientos entailed even greater exploitation:

Indian women were expected to weave a cotton mantle (of five yards by one) within ten days. This, however, had been an impossible requirement, for the cotton had arrived in a raw state, unseeded and unspun. If an Indian woman had been unable to produce her work in time, she had been fined 8 or 9 reales, the value of a mantle. Anyone who had been incapable of paying, had been taken from her home and placed in special houses owned by the repartidores.[93]

Indians frequently complained about the abuses of the repartimiento system, and at least nine local rebellions were sparked by the excesses of the alcaldes mayores during the colonial period.[94] Tension was especially high in the early 1660s following the uprising at Tehuantepec in which its alcalde mayor lost his life. According to the naborías of Analco, during several uprisings in the Villa Alta district in 1659–61 as many as four thousand Indians protested the policies of Alcalde Mayor Villaroel.[95] A group of Mixe pueblos also lodged formal complaints against him.[96] Yet, an inquiry led by Oidor Montemayor y Cuenca failed to turn up concrete evidence of any serious threats to the regime in Villa Alta, and although magistrates were changed in Nejapa and Ixtepeji, Villaroel was permitted to finish his term.[97] Criticism of the magistrates was often deflected by their lieutenants and the interpreters who traveled with them. These men were in constant contact with the Indians and served as the most immediate targets for their frustrations.[98]

The year 1787 marked the beginning of the decline of the repartimiento system of Villa Alta. The prohibition enacted the year before with the creation of the intendancy system was beginning to have some effect. Murguía y Galardi estimated that cotton mantle production in the district declined from 50–60,000 units in 1787 to 10–12,000 in 1828. Bishop Bergoza y Jordán spoke of a drop from 200,000 mantles to 60–70,000 in 1810. Though the figures differ, they agree that the decline was to something like one-fifth to one-third of former levels.[99] The first subdelegado of Villa Alta, Bernardo de Bonavía, took office in 1790 and lost no time in trying to convince the viceroy that he should be granted the same trading privileges as the alcaldes mayores before him. He claimed that the ban on repartimientos not only limited the money he could make but also caused the Indians to curtail all their productive activities, to the point that the district was producing less than one-eighth of what it did before. Bonavía's self-serving arguments were effectively countered by his superior, Intendant Mora, however. He noted that Indians of the district continued to produce cotton mantles and were now in a position to sell them themselves at higher profits. He pointed out that Villa Alta Zapotecs had long been coming to Antequera to sell their textiles and predicted that now even more would come. As evidence, he produced a count of 1,543 mantles that entered the city's market on the last three Saturdays of September 1790. Most of these were brought by Indians from Villa Alta in small lots of six, twelve, fifteen, and twenty-five.[100]

Whatever the impact of the reforms on production, repartimientos de efectos sputtered on in Villa Alta and other outlying districts until at least the first decade of the nineteenth century, and in all likelihood until the end of the colonial period.[101] This institution more than any other determined the course of the colonial economy in the Villa Alta district and its mode of integration with the larger colonial and world markets.

THE INDIAN ECONOMY

While taking care of their repartimiento obligations and responding to periodic Spanish demands for foodstuffs, the Indians also maintained their traditional yearly round of subsistence agriculture. This was done for the most part on traditional pueblo lands that existed at the time of the Conquest. Since few Spaniards had any interest in acquiring land in the areas of heavy settlement—except for a handful of miners—few Indian communities had trouble in keeping their lands more or less intact to produce a variety of goods.[102] In addition to basic items such as corn, chiles, beans, and squash, pueblos with access to tierra caliente also took fish (*bobos*) from the rivers and produced honey, fruit (bananas, avocados, *mameyes*, and *chirimoyas*), cotton, and some cacao. Many Mixe villages traded extensively in *ocote* (torch-pine). Irrigation from streams and rivers seems to have been common only in the dry Cajonos zone, rainfall being fairly abundant in the rest of the district. Sources indicate that the Bixanos, Chinantec, and at least parts of the Nexitzo zones regularly harvested two corn crops each year.[103] The pre-Hispanic digging-stick technology did not disappear, but iron hoes were added to the repertoire and the use of the plow and oxen became quite common in the seventeenth and eighteenth centuries. The alcaldes mayores were only too happy to keep households supplied with oxen through their repartimientos, but when these ceased around 1790, the Indians of Villa Alta began making regular trips to Huajuapan in the Mixteca to purchase oxen with cotton mantles.[104]

Viceregal licenses for ranching or herding and grants of land were remarkably few, probably because few pueblos or individuals thought to ask. It is clear that Indians owned many fewer cattle, sheep, and goats than in the Valley of Oaxaca or the Mixteca. Only two records of community land grants have been located for the sixteenth century, both dating from the 1590s, when Mixe Atitlán and Cajonos Yalalag were both granted communal estancias de ganado menor (sheep and goats). An unidentified noblewoman was also given a ranch and four *caballerías* (about 105 acres) of land in a place called Topocantla in 1596.[105] The seventeenth century furnished only four more instances. An estancia de ganado menor went to Tepuxtepec in 1633, another along with an estancia de ganado mayor (cattle and oxen) to a principal of Puxmetacan in 1689, a license to raise pigs to a cacique of Yahuive in 1643, and one for cattle to a cacique of Yalalag in 1694.[106]

Despite the enormous amount of woven cotton goods extracted by the

Spanish in colonial times, the Sierra Zapoteca has never been known to produce many crafts or other manufactured items. There seem to have been few crafts in the area in pre-Hispanic times, and Nader notes that, except for some cotton weaving and leatherwork, highland Zapotec communities have few today. Such basic items as *zarapes* (wool blankets), *petates* (palm mats), *metates* (grinding stones), and pottery are all imported, mainly from the Valley of Oaxaca. The one modern exception is the Cajonos zone, which today is noted for its pottery, *ixtle* work (rope and other goods made from maguey fiber), *huaraches* (sandals), and weaving.[107] In contrast, neither the Mixes nor the Chinantecs today have well-developed craft traditions.

Substantially the same patterns were in evidence during the colonial period, though the documentation is far from abundant. The Chinantec Guatinicamanes were said to make pottery and petates in the midsixteenth century, though these were probably minor industries and only for local consumption.[108] Nexitzo Tepanzacualco was more active; as early as 1579 it was producing considerable quantities of cotton mantles for the market, making petates, and cutting pine beams for sale in other pueblos.[109] For the Bixanos territory there is no record of any crafts except for the ubiquitous cotton weaving, while in the Mixe zone the only nonwoven product on record is pottery, manufactured in the sixteenth century in Chichicaxtepec and Yacochi. These traditions were to continue, for in 1777 some Bixanos Zapotec households were still cooking with Mixe-made pots (others bought pottery from the Valley of Oaxaca in the Choapan market).[110] The Cajonos zone, finally, was already well known for its ixtle products in 1685 and probably earlier; in Lachirioag aguardiente was being distilled from sugar cane in 1716, a number of individuals grinding the cane in their own *trapiches*.[111]

Though craft manufacture in the district was relatively undeveloped, trade was another matter. The Zapotecs were especially active traders, much as they are today, and appear to have dominated "long-distance" exchanges that reached into other regions. Burgoa observed about 1670 that the Cajonos Zapotecs not only excelled in crafts, but in trade and commerce as well. Many of the men worked as *arrieros* (mule drivers) and involved themselves in a greater variety of commercial transactions than members of the district's other ethnic groups.[112] This was partly because the main route from Villa Alta to Antequera passed through Cajonos territory, and Spaniards of all kinds were continually present and in need of a variety of services. The other reason for the Cajonos interest in trade and crafts probably lies in the dry climate in the zone as compared with the rest of the Villa Alta district, which is quite humid. In this respect the Cajonos villagers occupy a niche similar to that of the people of the Tlacolula arm of the Valley of Oaxaca. Both areas seem to have developed active trading and manufacturing interests in part to compensate for the precariousness of farming due to the lack of rainfall.[113] This is not to say that the volume of trade in the Cajonos zone approached the high levels found in the Tlacolula Valley, but only that similar ecological stimuli may be present in both regions.

In addition to trading among themselves, with Villa Alta, and in the Valley of Oaxaca, different Cajonos towns also developed special commercial relationships with particular communities of other ethnic groups. Yalalag, for example, has long carried on extensive trade with neighboring Mixe towns, as did Zoogocho and Yatzachi as well in colonial times.[114] Nearby Betaza, on the other hand, was more involved with Bixanos Choapan, where it used to sell bread in the eighteenth century.[115] The economic dominance of Yalalag in the Cajonos region would appear to date from the early nineteenth century. Before that time the Zoochila and Zoogocho markets were more influential (see below), though by 1800 Yalalteco merchants were going as far afield as the city of Puebla to buy merchandise for resale.[116]

In the Rincón, as early as 1579, people from Tepanzacualco and other communities made frequent journeys to Antequera—a two-day trip by foot—to sell cotton textiles. These trips continued throughout the colonial period, and items sold in the city in the 1690s also included cochineal and some foodstuffs.[117] Economic interchange with Serrano Zapotecs from Ixtlán was also common. In the sixteenth century, Serranos often went to the Rincón for short periods to do wage labor for private households or hired themselves out for public works projects in different communities.[118]

Little is known of the trading activities of the Bixanos Zapotecs, Chinantecs, and Mixes. While today none are nearly as active as the Cajonos and Nexitzo Zapotecs, De la Fuente suggests that more commerce may have taken place in Bixanos territory during colonial times.[119] This was undoubtedly true, but it appears that most of the active traders there were outsiders, particularly Cajonos Zapotecs, peddlers from Tehuantepec, and Spanish merchants.[120] What native Bixanos interregional trade existed was probably more oriented toward the Gulf coastal lowlands than the Valley of Oaxaca, for reasons of proximity. Thus, in the late eighteenth century, Zapotecs from Yovego traveled to Valle Real (now Valle Nacional) in the jurisdiction of Teutila to sell their textiles and buy raw cotton.[121]

The eastern Chinantecs were involved in very little commercial activity. As late as the 1930s, Bernard Bevan remarked that the Chinantecs did not trade or travel very much. The trade routes passing through their territory were used almost exclusively by Zapotec carriers.[122] Likewise, little can be said about Mixe trading patterns other than the marketing of pots in the Choapan area by a few villages and the trading with the Cajonos pueblos that probably involved mainly ocote, corn, beans, and cotton. The only village commercial tradition that can be documented pertains to Mixistlán, which in the mideighteenth century bought petates in Santo Domingo Albarradas (in the district of Teotitlán del Valle) and resold them in Choapan.[123]

An important economic development in the district in the late seventeenth century was the emergence of a group of itinerant Indian merchants, most of them of cacique or principal status. Though Cajonos and Nexitzo Zapotecs predominated, a few Mixes also dedicated themselves to this full-time occupation. In 1694, Gonzalo de Aquino, a cacique of Yalalag, dressed in Spanish clothing and owned cattle and horses. With two mules and a young companion, he regularly made the rounds of all the markets in the district selling salt, soap, plates, bowls, huaraches, chile, and cotton.[124] A contemporary from Betaza, Jacinto de Morales, was in the same business, dealing in chile, salt, shrimp, and "agricultural products permitted to the natives."[125] In the Rincón, a native of Tepanzacualco living in Yotao dealt in *huipiles* (blouses) and cotton mantles in Calpulalpan, Ixtlán, and other Serrano communities in the district of Ixtepeji in 1702.[126] Perhaps most successful of all, however, was don Joseph Luis de Peralta, a cacique of Totontepec, one of the largest and most prosperous Mixe towns. In the 1670s, Peralta dressed as a Spaniard, owned twelve mules, and employed two drivers who accompanied him to the markets to sell salt, chile, corn, soap, cotton, beans, fish, cotton mantles, huipiles, petticoats, hats, huaraches, fruit, and seeds.[127]

Although often opposed by the alcaldes mayores who did not want any trade—Indian or Spanish—competing with their repartimientos, these Indian merchants consistently received the backing of the viceroys and continued to ply their trade. It is impossible to determine how numerous they were, but by the late eighteenth century at least a few individuals were involved in even more far-flung enterprises. Bonifacio de Chávez, a Zapotec from Talea, was living in Antequera in 1776 at the height of the cochineal boom and made a living trading in the dyestuff. Some of it he produced himself in a field near the city, but he also had close ties with a number of Spanish merchants. Chávez regularly visited the markets of the Villa Alta district, buying up what cochineal he could, then returned to Antequera and resold it to the Spanish merchant houses. Some of these employed him to sell their merchandise on his rounds among the Indians, and occasionally even had him make surreptitious repartimientos, distributing money to the Indians in return for their harvests of cochineal (at twelve reales to the pound when the market rate was twenty to twenty-six reales). Chávez did not handle all this work alone, but relied on at least four "lieutenants" in different communities.[128]

These examples show that despite their general poverty, some Indian nobles were willing and able to take advantage of commercial opportunities that were open to them. Some dealt independently and others in concert with Spanish merchants, but all were highly mobile and had a facility for interacting with different Indian groups as well as with the Spanish. In the eighteenth century, cochineal became one of their most important commodities, and they came to serve as indispensable small-time brokers for other Indians who were forced to purchase the dyestuff to fulfill their repartimiento obligations to the alcaldes mayores.

There were two kinds of cochineal, *fina* (cultivated) and wild, and the difference between them was considerable. The cultivated variety was produced only in Oaxaca, Puebla, Tlaxcala, and adjacent regions; wild cochineal came from many parts of the Americas, extending from Jalisco and Chiapas down to Ecuador, Brazil, and Argentina.[129] It was in the Indian communities of Oaxaca where cultivation techniques were most refined and widespread. Dahlgren de Jordán summarizes the process:

> The dye is obtained from the dissected body of the female, whose life cycle and reproduction lasts three months. As the first step in cultivation, the Indians planted a field of *nopal* cactus. After two or three years, when they were well grown and green, the *nopales* were seeded, that is to say, female cochineal bugs ready to multiply were placed on them. These females were kept in the Indians' houses, transplanted from other fields, or more frequently, bought in the markets. For transportation and seeding, they were placed in nests made from various materials, some 15 bugs to a nest, which were later fastened to the leaves of the *nopal*. With the birth of the new generation, the Indians removed the mothers, now dead, with fine brushes improvised from the fur of skunks' tails or other animals. When the offspring in turn reached the end of their cycle, all of them were removed, killed by different methods, and left to dry out. Depending on the climate, seeding was done two or three times a year. It was calculated that 200 females were born for every male and that to make a pound one needed about 70,000 insects.[130]

According to Fray Francisco Ajofrín, a Spaniard who spent some time in Oaxaca during his stay in Mexico between 1763 and 1767, the female bugs were placed on the nopals in April, when they were two months away from maturity. In June, after they had given birth, they were removed. A larger harvest would follow in August when the offspring reached the end of their cycle.[131] In the Villa Alta district one major harvest per year seems to have been the norm in the 1760s, and in the Cajonos zone, at least, nopals were commonly planted in cornfields, interspersed among the stalks.[132]

What remains to be determined is the extent of the independent Indian dye trade. There is little doubt that in the sixteenth century some Indians profited quite a bit from it. Sources are lacking for the Villa Alta area, but in the *Relación geográfica* of 1580 for Ocelotepec (in the southern Zapotec region near Miahuatlán), the town's corregidor provided a vivid description of the local end of the cochineal traffic. After noting the extensive Indian trade in the commodity in the Miahuatlán market, he went on to remark of Ocelotepec:

> They have taken to cultivating *grana* and planting cacti for it, and much is produced for there is no Indian who doesn't produce one, two, or three *arrobas* or so. The price seldom goes below 8 reales per pound, and this pueblo has become

the most fortunate one in the bishopric because so many gold pesos flow into it. . . . [This income is] more than enough to pay their tribute. Among them are some very rich Indians, merchants of cochineal who understand the peso very well and very often even cheat the Spaniards.[133]

An extreme case, perhaps, but it nonetheless illustrates the opportunities and capabilities of the Indians of Oaxaca in the early years of the dye trade. Likewise, if we can believe Burgoa, some Indian fortunes continued to be made in the trade during the seventeenth century, particularly in the Chontal region.[134] While no traces indicate any "rich Indians" in Villa Alta, there was constant buying and selling of the commodity, if for no other reason than to distribute supplies in accord with repartimiento quotas. Clearly, modest profits were to be made here. A cacique of Tepanzacualco was in the habit of buying cochineal in Yatzachi, Zoogocho, Tavehua, and other Cajonos pueblos in 1700, and an over-zealous gobernador of Lachichina was charged in 1705 with trying to pass off wild cochineal from Chiapas as *grana fina* in neighboring Yagallo.[135]

But in the eighteenth century things changed. Dahlgren de Jordán notes that sources from this period indicate that the Indians were highly exploited and earned little from cochineal.[136] Such was the case in Villa Alta, where the evidence tends to confirm the observation made earlier that the repartimientos of the alcaldes mayores became ever more monopolistic as the century wore on. Spaniards with their own particular axes to grind occasionally suggested this was not the case. Bishop Maldonado, for example, remarked in 1702 that the Indians of the bishopric knew that considerable foreign demand for cochineal persisted and that New Spain was the only producer. He further pointed to a shortage of corn in the province because the Indians "have left the major part of their fields uncultivated. They are no longer interested in foodstuffs and only look for places where cochineal can be raised. More than two-thirds of the farmers in this province produce it."[137]

The bishop may have been generally correct, but Hamnett has since demonstrated fairly conclusively that the reason for the neglect of the cornfields was not Indian trade on an "open market" but the repartimientos of the alcaldes mayores. This was true even in times of famine and epidemics that struck Oaxaca in 1739, 1766, 1780, and 1785−87.[138] During the food shortage in 1785, for example, Hamnett claims that the Valley of Oaxaca was supplying food to the jurisdictions of Villa Alta, Ixtepeji, Miahuatlán, Peñoles, Teojomulco, and much of the Mixteca, "for those territories did not cultivate maize. Their chief occupation was the production of the cochineal dye. The demand for that dye was so great that the indigenous population there even neglected their own subsistence maize crops, in order to produce it. As a result, in times of food shortage, there would generally be competition between them and the public granary of Oaxaca City."[139] This statement is probably an exaggeration, and the peak cochineal years were not representative of village subsistence strategies in the eighteenth century generally. Nevertheless, it is illustrative of the power of the political officials and merchants and the thriving world market for the scarlet dye.

INDIAN MARKETS

Just as they shaped relationships between Spaniards and Indians in the cochineal trade, colonial circumstances were important determinants of the structure of the indigenous market system in the Villa Alta region. It goes without saying that there was no *Spanish* market *system* as such in the jurisdiction. Villa Alta itself had no marketplace at all until the 1720s, and while it continued for the rest of the century, it was never large. Even finding a vecino who would contract to supply the town with meat was a perennial problem.[140] All the other marketplaces were located in Indian communities and, with the partial exception of those in Choapan and Zoochila, served a predominantly Indian clientele.

Unlike the Valley of Oaxaca, where the thriving rotating market system was an indigenous creation that long preceded the Spanish Conquest, colonial markets in the Villa Alta region appear to have sprung up in response to distinctively colonial economic pressures. This is not to say that there were no markets in pre-Hispanic times; a few marketplaces surely existed, but they probably shared few systemic qualities and were smaller than in the Valley, where craft specialization and trading in general were much more developed. At any rate, no references exist to markets in the Sierra Zapoteca during the pre-Hispanic period or in the sixteenth and most of the seventeenth centuries.

Indian markets enter the written record at precisely the same time that the traveling Indian merchants made their appearance—in the 1690s. By this time the native population was on a slow but steady course of recovery. At the same time, the repartimientos of the alcaldes mayores were becoming increasingly onerous, and many Indian households were hard-pressed to maintain their previous level of self-sufficiency. Having been forced to specialize more than they wished in the production of textiles and cochineal, the Indians of the district had a growing need for a system of marketplaces where foodstuffs, especially, could be bought and sold. The endless series of disputes and intervillage rivalries that accompanied the emergence of such a system in the eighteenth century suggests either that the markets had no firm pre-Hispanic basis or that if they did, it was being systematically ignored.

While many markets did not come into existence until several decades later, a large and important market developed in the Bixanos community of Choapan as early as the midseventeenth century. Unlike others that followed, the Choapan market was held twice a week—on Tuesdays and Saturdays—and attracted Indians from all over the district and others from as far away as Tehuantepec who came to sell textiles, cotton, fruit, fish, and other items. It also attracted more Spanish merchants than any other market in the jurisdiction, due to Choapan's proximity to the cotton fields and the possibilities it offered for buying textiles close to their source at low prices. In fact, the first mention of the Choapan tianguis was a complaint lodged in 1635 against Spanish merchants who were forcibly buying goods from the Indians at unfair prices. In 1693, merchants from Antequera and Puebla journeyed to Choapan to purchase textiles whenever they could evade the watchful eye of the alcalde mayor. In the eighteenth century pottery from both cities had become a common and popular item in the Choapan market.[141]

By the 1740s, a Friday tianguis was also held at nearby San Juan Comaltepec. This was the only other market in Bixanos territory, and in 1758 Isthmus Zapotec traders came to sell *tasajo* (beef jerky), salt, shrimp, sugar, hats, shoes, and rosaries.[142] Choapan was always the more important of the two, however, and served as an important trading place for the eastern Chinantecs and the Villa Alta Mixes. There is no mention of markets in Chinantec towns, and the first request for viceregal permission to hold a tianguis in the Mixe zone came from Tepuxtepec in 1773, though it was apparently never approved. It was not until 1794 that a regular Mixe market got underway at Totontepec, serving the people of the doctrinas of Ayutla, Atitlán, Chichicaxtepec, and Puxmetacan.[143]

The earliest mention of a weekly Cajonos tianguis, probably located at Zoochina, is in 1700.[144] In 1715 it was moved to nearby Zoochila, where it continued to be held every Thursday for the next hundred years. It began to decline in 1807, when the viceroy approved a new market at Zoogocho. After several years of acrimonious dispute, Zoochila was forced to give up its market in 1815, while the one at Zoogocho continued to thrive. Today Zoogocho has the largest tianguis in the modern Villa Alta district.[145]

Other markets held concurrently (on different days) in Cajonos territory in the latter half of the eighteenth century were at Yojovi (Wednesday), Tabaa (Saturday), and Yalalag (Tuesday). San Francisco Cajonos in 1745 asked for permission to hold a Tuesday tianguis, but apparently lost out to Yalalag.[146] As we have seen, Zoochila had a small Spanish community in the late eighteenth century that served as a stimulus for trade. Perhaps this influence carried over to the Zoogocho market after 1815, though the nineteenth century in this region awaits further investigation. Mixes were doubtless important participants in all the Cajonos markets, for they didn't begin holding their own in Totontepec until 1794. Rincón Zapotecs were also regularly in attendance at the Zoochina and Zoochila markets. One interesting episode that attests to some Spanish involvement in the Indian economy occurred in 1778. Bids were sought for the job of supplying meat for a period of two years to the markets in Villa Alta, Zoochila, Yalalag, Yojovi, Tabaa, and Tanetze and Yae in the Rincón. The first announcement met with no takers at all, but finally two peninsular merchants, don Antonio de la Puente and don Francisco Gordon, agreed to do it, noting that they would have to import cattle into the district to meet the demand.[147]

The weekly markets, especially the larger ones, were of great political as well as economic significance. Nowhere was this truer than in the Rincón, where two protracted disputes over markets and cabecera status filled much of the eighteenth century, the protagonists being Tanetze versus Yae and Yagavila versus Yagila. A tianguis at San Juan Yae began to function, with the blessings of the alcalde mayor, in 1696. It was not held in the town itself, but at an uninhabited site nearby, to be more accessible to people from other pueblos. Both the location and the organization of the market appear to have been designed by Spanish political and ecclesiastical officials acting together in a rather innovative fashion. An *ermita* (hermitage) was constructed at the site of a cofradía founded to carry out religious observances (whether these were the idea of Indians or Spaniards is not known). Membership in the cofradía was restricted to the gobernadores and alcaldes from six Rincón communities: Yae, Lachichina, Yagallo, Yaviche, Yatoni, and Lahoya. The cofradía also doubled as a "board of governors" for the tianguis, which was held each Saturday at 11:00 A.M. The members had both police and judicial authority in the marketplace, though the final word rested with the alcalde mayor.[148]

Within a decade another similar weekly marketplace—also meeting on Saturday—had been established just outside Yaviche, serving primarily the pueblos of Yaviche, Tanetze, Cacalotepec, Yotao, Juquila, Talea, Lahoya, Lalopa, Yagallo, and Yatoni. This market had apparently been established to avoid problems that had cropped up in Yae, but the one at Yaviche, too, proved difficult to control, and in 1709 the alcalde mayor moved it into the pueblo proper.[149] Soon thereafter the tianguis was moved back to Yae, while at roughly the same time other pueblos in the region, not wanting to be left out, sometimes attempted to sponsor their own markets. Two of the successful ones were in Tiltepec (licensed by the viceroy in 1696) and Lachichina (already under way in 1709).[150]

The tianguis at Yae continued as the major one in the Rincón, however, and other communities began to grumble that Yae wanted to dominate all marketing activity in the region and that prices in its tianguis were too high. A related problem was that not all towns in the area recognized Yae's claim to be a "cabecera." As was seen in chapter 3, Tanetze (formerly Ixcuintepec) was in the early seventeenth century by far the largest town in the area and the seat of a Dominican doctrina. The friars' subsequent decision to make Yae head of a doctrina of its own was not well received in most communities, and this lingering discontent proved to be a factor in the market dispute a full century later.

Things came to a head in 1744, when Tanetze, with the support of Lalopa, Yagallo, Lachichina, Yaviche, Lahoya, Yatoni, Talea, Juquila, Yotao, Cacalotepec, and Roavela filed suit to have the market moved. They argued that Tanetze was not only more conveniently located for a tianguis but that since the "time of the Dominicans" of the early seventeenth century it had been an important cabecera and deserved to have its own market. The audiencia disagreed, however, and the Saturday tianguis continued at Yae.[151] The dispute dragged on until April 1772, when the viceroy finally gave permission for a market in Tanetze. Then a new round of negotiations began as to the proper day. The viceroy had initially indicated Monday, but when Yae protested that this was too close to Saturday (the day of its tianguis), Tanetze was then assigned Wednesday. But the latter was still not satisfied and asked for Friday or Sunday instead. After lengthy deliberations during 1773 involving both civil and church officials, it was decided that Tanetze would stick with Wednesday (an arrangement that lasted at least through 1778) while the Yae tianguis would continue on Saturday (still in effect in 1799).[152]

Though seemingly trivial on the surface, this 29-year wrangle over market sites and days stemmed from two fundamental concerns of the villagers, one of them political, the other economic. The political problem, mentioned above, was that Spaniards and Indians had different ideas about which pueblos in the region should function as cabeceras. Alcaldes mayores and the clergy were thinking primarily of administrative and transportational convenience when they authorized the Yae tianguis, while the natives saw things in accord with colonial Nexitzo culture and older patterns of intercommunity relations. In 1744 most of its neighbors viewed Yae as an upstart that could not compete for power and prestige with Tanetze; Yae was a cabecera with a market only because the colonizers found such an arrangement convenient.

Another equally important concern, which shows how dependent on their small market system many villagers had become, emerged in the court testimony. The dispute over market *days* was not just a matter of jealousy and local ethnocentrism. Rather, there were very real fears that if two nearby towns held markets on days that were too close together, not all the traveling Indian merchants would feel compelled to visit each tianguis, causing some people to go without needed goods that only these merchants offered for sale.

Similar problems were behind the other Rincón market dispute between Yagavila and Yagila. Yagavila, a Dominican cabecera de doctrina, was already holding a weekly Wednesday market when Yagila, of the same doctrina, received permission for a Sunday tianguis in 1719. Yagavila filed a complaint with the viceroy in 1724, arguing that as a cabecera de doctrina it should be allowed to have its tianguis on Sunday as well. It got nowhere at first, but the request was finally granted in 1734, only to be revoked a few months later when Yagila complained. Rivalry between the two was still smoldering after a lapse of forty years when the bishop of Oaxaca in 1775 forbade Sunday markets in Yagila and all other pueblos on religious grounds. Yagila, of course, protested that this was unfair and that its people did not like having to travel to the Yae market on Saturday or to Zoochila in the Cajonos on Thursday (Yagavila's Wednesday tianguis, by far the closest, was not mentioned). When the alcalde mayor also backed Yagila, noting that its women needed to sell the mantles they wove each week to buy food, the viceroy finally restored the Sunday date, over the bishop's protest, in 1780.[153]

It thus appears that an actual market *system* arrived late in the Rincón and other subregions of the Villa Alta district, not emerging until the early eighteenth century. But while its dimensions were always modest, the system played an increasingly important role in the provisioning of Indian households as the century unfolded. The alcalde mayor's comment that women needed a market where they could exchange textiles for food was an astute observation on the state of the district's economy in the late eighteenth century. The nearly self-sufficient village-centered economy of pre-Hispanic times and the sixteenth century had long since disappeared, giving way to much more active market exchange as the burdens of the repartimientos de efectos increased.

CONCLUSION

The colonial economies of the Sierra Zapoteca, the Valley of Oaxaca, and other parts of the province of Oaxaca shared one important characteristic that made them different from many other Indian regions of New Spain. Unlike many areas to the north where it was not uncommon for whole villages and their populations to be swallowed up in the late colonial period by mining and hacienda enterprises, in Oaxaca most Indian households became integrated into expanding markets while at the same time retaining considerable control over the means of production. In both the Valley and the Sierra, Indian communities succeeded in holding on to most of their traditional lands and many of their traditional subsistence activities.[154]

In the Sierra, however, every village also had to contend with especially heavy repartimientos of cochineal and cotton textiles. These were real burdens, but the important point is that most of the time they did not totally replace subsistence activities, but came to coexist alongside them.[155] As Marcello Carmagnani has recognized, cochineal cultivation by itself had few disruptive aspects. It did not demand inputs from outside the pueblo and had the potential for utilizing labor from all members of the household, including men, women, children, and the elderly.[156] Likewise, the burden of weaving, though it fell disproportionately on the women, was similar in that it could be integrated with other traditional economic activities. The alcaldes mayores supplied the cotton, and all the work was done in Indian homes interspersed with household chores. Thus both cochineal and textile production benefited the Spanish economy, primarily through the repartimiento mechanism, while keeping Indian pueblos intact, though certainly not unchanged.

The only way such an economic system could be maintained, of course, was by force. In the eighteenth century, long after the direct use of force in the Valley of Oaxaca had largely given way to the more impersonal mechanism of the market system, in the Sierra Zapoteca threats, monopoly, and coercion were still very much the order of the day. Bishop Ortigoza stated in the late 1770s that when it was time for the alcaldes mayores to collect repartimiento debts, Indians unable to repay the finished product would flee to the hills and hide for fear of arbitrary arrest. Likewise, a priest in Ixtlán reported that many Indians had stopped attending mass, for it was common for debtors to be arrested as they were leaving the church.[157] The point is not that there were no repartimientos in the Valley and elsewhere, but that they weighed much more heavily on the pueblos in the Sierra where the market system was much weaker.

The effect of the repartimiento monopolies in the Villa Alta district was that the indigenous population became integrated into expanding colonial and world markets through political coercion. The Indian market system of the region, never large, existed apart from the colonial and world markets as a purely local mechanism for the distribution of food staples. Integration into wider systems was effected not through the marketplace but through the direct intervention and coercion of the alcaldes mayores, their lieutenants, and their merchant backers in Antequera and Mexico City.

CHAPTER 5

INDIAN COMMUNITY ORGANIZATION

ONE OF THE MANY challenges facing the ethnohistorian of colonial Meso-america is to find ways to study the internal social and political organization of Indian communities on the basis of documentation written primarily, if not entirely, in Spanish by Spaniards. Even when the original purpose of the documents was to describe some aspect of indigenous affairs, a powerful filtering process selected out certain kinds of information and presented it in accordance with reigning Spanish ideals concerning interpersonal relations and municipal government. A number of research strategies have been used to partially overcome this handicap. The most obvious is to utilize native sources whenever possible. Codices painted in the native tradition are some-times available for the sixteenth century, and written documents in a variety of indigenous languages adapted to the Roman alphabet also exist.[1] Criminal court records constitute another type of source that often provides penetrat-ing insight into the vicissitudes of daily life in colonial Indian communities, as a recent study by William Taylor has shown, and much the same can be said for the proceedings of Inquisition trials, used effectively by Ronald Spores and others.[2] Still other possibilities are afforded by quantitative sources such as census counts and parish church records. While numerical forms of evidence are of course far from unbiased, they often allow the investigator to get closer to peoples' actual behavior than is often the case with narrative accounts, which on the whole tend to be more normative in character.[3]

It has not been possible to make use of any of these types of sources to a great extent in this book,[4] but the materials on which much of this chapter is based do have one point in their favor. Most of the key sources consist of civil disputes that Indians of the district took to the alcaldes mayores for adjudication. These were regarded as minor, even petty matters by many administrators, and only rarely did such cases rise to higher levels of the judicial hierarchy. But for the Indian communities, the matters under litiga-tion lay at the very heart of their social and political structure and these cases are of extraordinary value for the ethnohistorian. Taken as a whole, they provide insights into colonial Indian society that only local archives like the one in Villa Alta can produce.[5] Once again, it is the late colonial period that provides the most abundant documentation, though some information is also available for the earlier years. Certain topics, such as family and household structure, kinship relations, and fictive kinship still remain largely beyond our grasp for lack of adequate information. The focus of this chapter is on social stratification, the position of the caciques, the nature of town government, and the impact on all of these of the Spanish alcaldes mayores.

A NOTE ON LANGUAGE AND ETHNICITY

In general, my findings in the Villa Alta jurisdiction support William Taylor's contention that the landholding village—the pueblo—gained importance in the colonial period at the expense of ethnic and regional ties.[6] The district's five basic ethnolinguistic groups have of course persisted until the present time, but only as rather vague, language-based reference groups as far as the people themselves are concerned. De la Fuente's ethnographic observation that the most important unit of identification is the pueblo applies equally well to colonial times as it does to the modern scene.[7] In addition to abundant contextual information in much of the documentation on which this book is based, parish marriage records for seven Nexitzo and Cajonos Zapotec towns in the vicinity of Villa Alta are also revealing. They show that community endogamy was quite high in the late seventeenth and eighteenth centuries, in a few cases even approaching 100 percent in some periods. Likewise, *padrinos* of baptism (i.e., one's *compadres*, or co-parents) were also usually sought in one's own community.[8] Aside from the Cajonos uprising of 1700 (see chapter 6) and possibly the earlier Mixe rebellion of 1570, episodes of any kind that united people on a supra-communal regional or ethnic basis were few and not well organized.

Data on language use suggest real differences between regions in degrees of acculturation. No Indian community in the district could be characterized as "Spanish speaking" by the end of the colonial period—or perhaps even today—but more people spoke Spanish in Nexitzo, and perhaps Cajonos, pueblos than in any others by the eighteenth century. This phenomenon was restricted to the *principal* and cacique strata, but since these often comprised as much as one-third to one-half of a town's population (see table 18) the numbers were not insignificant. In Yae, for example, most principales in 1742 knew Spanish and dressed in Spanish clothes. The community's twenty-one caciques in 1776 were all conversant in Spanish, as were the town officials in that year.[9] Outside the Rincón, however, indigenous languages still held sway and interpreters for Bixanos Zapotec and Mixe remained indispensable.[10] None were needed for Chinantec, for people in that region both spoke and wrote Bixanos Zapotec (continuing a pre-Hispanic tradition).[11] Mixe was always a difficult language for Spaniards, and a method for writing it in the Roman alphabet was apparently not introduced by the friars until the eighteenth century. Before that time most legal documents drawn up in Mixe pueblos were in Nahuatl, which continued to be spoken by most caciques and principales.[12] Nahuatl was also in use in the Cajonos Zapotec town San Andrés Yaa as late as the 1690s, and probably in other Cajonos communities as well.[13]

We cannot be sure which languages were used for communication among the different ethnic groups themselves, though surely Nahuatl would have been an ideal lingua franca for Mixe-Zapotec contacts, especially given the bitter wars between the two before the Spanish Conquest. Since this region was never part of the Aztec sphere of influence, however, it is quite possible that Nahuatl was a post-Conquest introduction of the Dominicans and the Tlaxcalans who settled in Analco. An interesting indicator of the local language policy of the conquerors dates from 1774, when a viceregal decree was translated for the benefit of all Indian communities in the district.[14] One of the translations is in Mixe—the earliest and perhaps only document in this language in the Villa Alta Juzgado archive. Separate translations were also prepared for the Cajonos, Nexitzo, and Bixanos Zapotec peoples, yet all three renderings turn out to be identical. Clearly, some effort had been directed by the friars toward establishing a standardized form of written Zapotec.[15] No translation was prepared in Chinantec.

THE COLONIAL CACIQUES

As we saw in chapter 1, the social hierarchy present in the Sierra Zapoteca at the time of the Spanish Conquest was far less developed than in other parts of Oaxaca and central Mexico. Slaves and mayeques did not form important categories, and the commoner or macehual group was minimally differentiated. The caciques were distinguished more for their leadership in warfare than for their landholdings or other kinds of wealth and probably lived no better than the principales, the second tier of the nobility. The weakness of the native nobility was especially apparent during the Conquest years. In chapter 2 it was noted that many caciques and principales were indiscriminantly killed by the conquistadores whenever they got in the way. They were frequently viewed as little more than nuisances to be eliminated. Class stratification in indigenous society, if not totally absent, is best regarded as only incipiently developed.

A group of midsixteenth-century documents apparently prepared from lienzos in five Zapotec pueblos provides some details on the initial Spanish recognition of the caciques of the region.[16] These sources also suggest that the title of cacique (or *abuelo*, grandfather, as it was translated in Villa Alta) was used and understood differently in the Sierra than in many other parts of New Spain. Most of the extant studies of colonial Indian societies in Oaxaca and central Mexico imply that a given community had only one cacique (or a married couple) at a time. Close kin of the cacique shared in the perquisites and special status of royalty, but there was nonetheless a throne to which only one person would succeed, and usually a landed estate—the *cacicazgo*—that went along with it. Such an arrangement is amply documented for the Valley of Oaxaca, the Mixteca Alta, and elsewhere. In the Sierra Zapoteca, however, each community—or cacicazgo—had several caciques,[17] and no clear-cut legal distinction between pueblo common lands and cacicazgo lands is apparent.

We are told that three caciques from Talea (of a total of six), five from Lahoya, three from Juquila, and others from ten other Zapotec communities accompanied two Spaniards from Villa Alta on a trip to Mexico City to request that Dominicans be sent to the Sierra Zapoteca to convert the Indians to Christianity.[18] When the friars eventually arrived, a series of mass baptisms of caciques was held in various places. Many Zapotec Serrano and Nexitzo lords were baptized at San Pedro Nexicho (today a rancho of Ixtepeji). Five caciques from Yatzona, two from Temaxcalapan, and five from Lachichina were baptized on another occasion, and separate ceremonies were also held for the Chinantecs and Mixes (brought together in another place) and the Cajonos Zapotecs. Legal confirmation and boundary marking of community lands was carried out by Alcalde Mayor Juan de Salinas between 1556 and 1560 in the Nexitzo towns of Talea, Juquila, and Lahoya, the Cajonos towns of Solaga and Yatzachi, and almost certainly many others in the district.

Not until 1575 were the first of the viceregal recognitions of noble status issued, however. In that year and the one following the customary licenses for use of a sword and a mount were issued to a Mixe in Mixistlán, three Zapotecs in Juquila, and five others in unknown pueblos.[19] Interestingly, none of these individuals was identified as a cacique; some were described as principales. The only named caciques to receive such licenses in the sixteenth century—again in 1575—were two Chinantecs, one of whom was from Lalana.[20] The one other recorded privilege of the century, also for a sword and a mount, was given to a Mixe principal of Totontepec in 1591.[21] Viceregal licenses in subsequent years were similar, but with two important differences: they often included approval to dress in Spanish clothes (a right that had been requested by the Indians), and they were invariably granted to individuals described as caciques. Five of these were issued in 1618, three in 1635, and nine in various years from 1642 to 1719. These favors were bestowed upon caciques of all five ethnic groups, though those of Bixanos Choapan received a disproportionate share.[22]

Intermarriage among cacique families of different communities—but within the same ethnolinguistic group—was probably common as it was elsewhere in colonial Mexico, though remarkably few traces of it emerge in the documentation. In only one known case did formerly independent communities become part of a single cacicazgo through royal marriage ties. Certainly the presence of multiple cacique families in a single town would make it easier for one to find a suitable mate in one's own community, provided that kinship ties did not get in the way.

Communities could be knit together by noble prerogatives in different ways. Miguel Fernández de Chávez was a fairly well-to-do cacique in three towns in the early eighteenth century, spoke Spanish, and dressed in Spanish clothes. A native of Tiltepec, he could also claim cacique status in La-chichina, perhaps by marriage. Later, Fernández was also recognized as a cacique of the Serrano town of San Pedro Nexicho, where he was residing in 1709, though the nature of his ties there is not known.[23] Fernández was not typical of the Rincón or of the district, however, and most intervillage caci-que marriages, such as the one between Yalahui and Temaxcalapan in 1672, did not lead to any great consolidation of land or political power in the hands of particular individuals or families.[24] Only in the Bixanos Zapotec zone is there evidence that colonial caciques retained inherited jurisdiction over multiple communities. Thus in 1643 don Miguel de los Angeles was a caci-que in both Santa María Yahuive and San Jacinto Yaveloxi. He claimed to occupy his position by direct descent from pre-Hispanic forebears and noted that the people of the two pueblos had traditionally paid rent (*terrasgo*) for their corn and cotton fields to him and his brothers and sustained them through personal service.[25] In 1715, two cousins, don Diego de Santiago y Mendoza and don Gerónimo de Santiago were both caciques in Choapan with special joint rights in the two sujetos of San Bartolomé Lachixova and San Juan Lealao. They argued that all of the lands in these two settlements were part of their cacicazgos and that they had always received rent from the inhabitants.[26]

These cases from the Choapan area pose the question of what sort of prop-erty rights were attached to Sierra cacicazgos. The documentation is thin but does permit some insights. Only two sixteenth-century references to inherited cacique property remain. A widow of a cacique in Chinantec Teotalcingo in 1551 complained that another cacique of the pueblo had wrongfully appropriated some cacao groves, slaves, and other items after the death of her husband.[27] In Mixe Chichicaxtepec in 1591 the viceroy gave official confirmation of the patrimonial lands of two individual nobles and three groups of relatives. This is the only viceregal acknowledgment of noble lands that has been located, and in these cases the individuals are not even explicitly identified as caciques.[28] As early as the 1570s some caciques had already lost whatever special access to property they once held. Don Di-ego de Guzmán of Nexitzo Tiltepec, for example, was eking out a living from a small amount of excess tribute and a small community-worked corn-field granted him by the viceroy.[29] In 1591 don Juan de Mendoza from the same community requested an official title of cacique, but offered little evi-dence of his status besides the testimony of a few sympathetic villagers.[30]

Significantly, the only seventeenth-century references to substantial in-herited cacicazgo lands come from the Bixanos Zapotec and Chinantec low-lands, and even these were subject to dispute. The above-mentioned don Miguel de los Angeles of Yahuive and Yaveloxi encountered stiff resistance from the macehuales of the latter town, who argued that he did not own the patrimonial lands which he claimed.[31] In Teotalcingo the death of a cacique about 1663 set off a tremendous inheritance squabble over land among his several sons and daughters.[32] Caciques in other places were also suffering declining fortunes. Don Joseph de Celis of Yatzona, who in 1688 claimed ownership of twenty-nine parcels of land, lost many of them to two mace-huales a decade later in a dispute that was adjudicated by the audiencia.[33] In Mixe Tonaguia the cacique don Luis Pérez died in 1644, leaving only eleven pieces of land to be distributed equally between his two sons. In his will he was quite emphatic that the land, which he had inherited from a grandfather and grandmother, was all he had: "I don't have any property of my own, money, or clothes; I am poor, I have no occupation, and have no property at all."[34]

The decline in cacique property bottomed out in the early eighteenth century, when evidence of it all but vanished. Don Miguel Fernández de Chávez of Tiltepec stands out as the only cacique in the Rincón who had much economic clout, and as late as 1727 the contentious De los Angeles family was still in possession of its cacicazgo in Yahuive, though it was locked in a dispute over part of it with the Mixe town of Metaltepec.[35] After this point all mention of cacicazgo property ceases for all parts of the Villa Alta district.

The form of land tenure associated with Sierra cacicazgos before their demise differed from that found in other parts of colonial Oaxaca and throws some light on the kinship patterns of the nobility and the phenomenon of multiple caciques. In the post-Conquest Valley of Oaxaca and the Mixteca Alta, private ownership of cacicazgo lands was well established, and such estates were modeled after the entailed Spanish *mayorazgos*, with succession usually following the rule of primogeniture. Cacicazgo rights and other lands were granted to Indian nobles by the Spanish king in the early sixteenth century, long before Spaniards became interested in land-holding. These estates were sometimes of considerable size, especially in the Valley of Oaxaca, and many of them survived intact well into the eighteenth century. In all, they were an important factor in maintaining the status and wealth of the Zapotec and Mixtec nobilities in these areas.[36]

In the Sierra Zapoteca, however, we confront a very different pattern. Though they were recognized locally and occasionally confirmed by the al-caldes mayores, few if any of the cacicazgos in this region ever received official recognition from the viceroy or the crown. This was due in part to their small size and relative poverty, but there was another reason for this lack of legal confirmation: the Indians' insistence that ownership of the estates continue to be vested in kinship groups, rather than individuals. In each kin group, several members (if not all) carried the title of cacique and appear to have had joint access to cacicazgo lands. This concept of land tenure ran counter to trends elsewhere in Oaxaca and was also foreign to Spanish custom, which provided for holdings by individuals and communities, but not joint ownership by corporate kin groups.[37]

In the only known case of viceregal confirmation of noble lands, a man and his "sister" in Mixe Chichicaxtepec were given title to nine parcels of land that were "part of their patrimony" in 1591.[38] While such an arrangement may have puzzled Spanish officials, it continued to be characteristic of cacicazgo holdings throughout the district in the seventeenth and early eighteenth centuries. In Chinantec Teotalcingo up until at least 1664, cacique groups composed of "brothers and sisters" held land jointly, each individual receiving a portion for his or her own use.[39] Similarly, in a dispute with the communities of Yovego and Lachixila in 1709, Rincón cacique Miguel Fernández de Chávez claimed that the property in question belonged to him and his "brothers."[40] In Nexitzo Yatzona in 1614 doña María de la Cruz (whose husband was still living) bequeathed fifteen pieces of land to her two sons, forbidding them to ever sell it because it was part of their cacicazgo. Should they leave no heirs, she said, they should give the land to the church (meaning, in effect, the community; see below). Heirs were provided, however, and by the end of the century the lands were being farmed by several "brothers."[41]

Other examples from the Mixe, Bixanos and Nexitzo regions mention corporate kin groups. In the Mixe town of Huitepec, a group of unspecified relatives referred to as a *parentela* owned land in 1725. The fact that some of them had left to live in other pueblos did not affect their ownership rights, which were determined by common descent. Even if absent, members of the group alternated each year in planting and harvesting the fields.[42] According to one account in 1715, the cacicazgo in Lachixova and Lealao, both sujetos of Choapan, was shared by a group of *primos* (cousins), all of whom received rent from macehuales who farmed part of the land.[43]

A final case from the Nexitzo town of Yae reveals both traditional practice and the problems that had grown up around it. One of the many legal free-for-alls to develop in this community (more will be discussed below) occurred in 1697 when the ownership of two parcels of land was disputed. A contingent of fourteen cousins stated that it had been working the land, which it owned by inheritance. All the cousins were "descendants of the same trunk" and took turns in cultivating the plots every six years. The town officials, on the other hand, argued that the lands were communal and subject to the management of the cabildo. When the case arrived at the desk of the alcalde mayor for adjudication, two additional viewpoints were furnished by the Indian witnesses. One witness presented by the cabildo failed to confirm the land's communal status, stating instead that one of the two parcels was the private property of one of the fourteen cousins, though he permitted many of his relatives to farm the land on a yearly rotating basis. A rival cacique from the town did confirm that the lands were communal property and, getting to what must have been the crux of the dispute, said that any member of the community who planted on common lands must pay rent to the cabildo. (In 1663 the town had thirty-two pieces of common land that, although controlled by the cabildo, were euphemistically described as lands of the church that had no inheritor.) Interestingly, the alcalde mayor ruled in favor of the fourteen cousins, a decision that was contrary to the growing trend in other parts of Oaxaca toward either private or communal land tenure.[44]

Without further information, it is difficult to determine just what sort of kinship groups existed among the nobility of the Sierra Zapoteca. Modern ethnography in the region has turned up no explicit statements about functions these groups exercised apart from land ownership. The cases of joint tenure by brothers and sisters, if these terms are taken literally, suggest that extended families were the landowning units, while the others that speak of "cousins" are sufficiently vague to allow for corporate stem kindreds based on bilateral kinship or cognatic lineages, perhaps with a patrilineal bias.[45] However, a consideration of indigenous kin terms in use in the region today makes the latter possibility the most likely. In conservative Zapotec, Mixe, and Chinantec communities, sibling terms are frequently extended to consanguineal-collateral relatives in all generations.[46] Assuming this was the norm throughout the district in pre-Hispanic and colonial times, the cases of landowning "brothers and sisters" and "cousins" most likely referred to cognatic descent groups in which no terminological distinction was made between one's siblings and cousins.

The fragmentary data on the inheritance of cacique *status* in the eighteenth century, all of it from the Rincón, lend qualified support to this hypothesis. Hearings on cacique status in Yagallo and Yaviche seem to stress bilateral kinship, while in Yae patrilineal descent was invoked.[47] It is possible to argue, as I have previously done, that a bilateral ideology would have permitted maximum flexibility in an already clouded genealogical atmosphere.[48] On the other hand, several Nexitzo pueblos contained various large *familias* of cacique rank that were distinguished by particular Spanish surnames, an arrangement reminiscent of a patrilineal or cognatic descent rule. For example, in Yae in 1776, twenty-one men of the "families" (or lineages) López Flores, Santiago, Tarifa, Mendoza, and Yllescas claimed cacique status.[49] In the previous year, a similar claim was made by twenty-six men with the surnames López Flores and Velasco Yllescas.[50] In Lalopa in the late colonial period possession of any of six surnames conferred cacique status, while in Yaviche there were only three.[51] While the matter clearly deserves further study, I would hypothesize on the basis of these data that the nobility throughout the Sierra Zapoteca was organized aboriginally in corporate, landholding descent groups or lineages. Since women could inherit and bequeath as well as men, the descent rule was probably cognatic (ambilineal), meaning that one could trace descent from a founding ancestor through any combination of male or female links. Such a system would also allow for a patrilineal bias or preference as well. If the case discussed from Yae is typical, it would indicate that these cacique lineage groups had begun to fragment under colonial pressures by the late seventeenth century. After 1730 they lost their corporate character altogether and were reduced to sur-name groups.

Assuming that such lineages were indeed widespread among the nobility in the early years, ranking within and among them appears to have been limited. Each group had a "head cacique," though he was more of a "first among equals" who shared status and privilege with his lineage mates. Much the same can be said for relations among the heads of different lin-eages. It can be argued that strong, lasting noble hierarchies headed by indi-vidual chieftains remained truncated in the colonial Sierra Zapoteca because of (1) the general impoverishment of the region as compared with other parts of Oaxaca and (2) the reluctance to accept the Spanish concept of pri-vate property that could have aided the preservation of the cacicazgos.[52] Leadership in warfare in pre-Hispanic times led to the ascendancy of par-ticular communities and, within them, of particular lineages and chieftains, but by the 1550s all this was gone and no other completely successful means of maintaining inherited, pre-Conquest noble status ever took its place.

In the absence of a concept of private ownership, each community prob-ably reserved a portion of its lands for support of the local noble lineages and the offices of rule. In the Sierra, as throughout much of Mesoamerica, it was common practice to identify community interests with the interests of particular caciques and principales. But as the above-mentioned cases of Yatzona and Yae suggest, the changes brought by the Spanish Conquest caused the modest cacicazgos to be gradually whittled down by rival village cabildos. Instead of becoming the private entailed estates of colonial noble families, the land became communal property under the control of others as the caciques lost most of the power and influence they had once enjoyed.

Evidence of the caciques' weak political position in the late sixteenth and seventeenth centuries abounds. Disputes between caciques and the elected gobernadores and cabildos were frequent and rarely were resolved to the nobles' advantage in this period. Thus a cacique of Mixe Moctum in 1591 complained that other cabildo officers routinely ignored him, even though he himself occupied the office of gobernador.[53] In Choapan in the 1640s town officials were even successful in persuading the alcalde mayor to banish four caciques from the district for two years, as punishment for certain al-leged crimes.[54] Another cacique of Yahuive complained of persecution by the gobernador of Yaveo in 1664.[55]

Nor was the weakening of the caciques' position confined to relations with their Indian peers. Most Spaniards held them in even less esteem, continu-ing the tradition of violent exploitation that began with the Conquest. A cacique of Nexitzo Cacalotepec paid dearly in 1638 for voicing complaints about his parish priest. As punishment, the alcalde mayor ordered him to perform certain services for a local Spanish teacher, but when the cacique balked at this the priest had him whipped and confiscated all his property.[56] Such an instance contrasts sharply with Burgoa's remark that many cacique boys of this period "dressed in Spanish silks, with swords, and with nice mules with good saddles."[57] Whether numerous or few, the fate of such young men was a tragic one. They were encouraged to separate themselves from the rank and file of their fellow villagers who no longer respected their position and, even though they could ill afford it, to mimic the customs of the Spanish, whose esteem for them was scarcely any higher. By the opening decades of the eighteenth century these caciques, now mature adults and bereft of any cacicazgo estates, were relegated to a curious status group of impoverished holders of noble titles that no longer commanded special respect or singular treatment.

COMMUNITY GOVERNMENT

In direct competition with the cacique lineages for power and control of local resources were the cabildos and their titular heads, the gobernadores. Both of these were Spanish introductions based on a concept of local government that was alien to the indigenous cultures of the Sierra Zapoteca. There was no pre-Hispanic precedent for a local council of officials, as we saw in chapter 1.

Before 1550 the Spanish meddled little, if at all, in the internal civic affairs of Sierra villages. Indeed, the concept of the "town" itself was lacking in some parts of the region at this time, particularly among the Mixes. The conquerors were so few and their hold on the region so tenuous that most of their energy was directed toward extinguishing indigenous warfare, extracting booty, searching for mines, and ensuring an adequate food supply for the town of Villa Alta. It was not until Luis de León Romano arrived as juez de comisión in 1550 that the first step was taken toward the political transformation of Indian communities. By order of the viceroy, León Romano appointed Indian *alguaciles* (constables) in twenty-four towns scattered throughout the five ethnic zones of the Villa Alta district and the adjacent Serrano Zapotec region in the vicinity of Ixtlán. The alcalde mayor of Villa Alta was to give each alguacil a copy of the viceregal order (though surely it would have been unintelligible to them, even if translated), and he was instructed "not to give the said Indians too much authority, no more than is given to the Indians who by general order serve as alguaciles in the villages of New Spain." The appointment of all twenty-four constables was for one year.[58]

There things lay until the advent of the Salinas administration of 1556–60, when full cabildos were appointed in Indian communities for the first time by the alcalde mayor. Information is available only for three Rincón villages (Talea, Lahoya, and Juquila) and two Cajonos towns (Solaga and Yatzachi), but it is clear that these were not isolated incidents and that Salinas probably made similar appointments throughout the district, with the possible exception of some Mixe settlements. In the cases documented, Salinas appointed a *gobernador*, one *regidor* (councilman), one *alcalde* (judge), one *mayor* (a police chief who functioned much as the previous alguaciles), an *escribano* (scribe), and a *fiscal* (a servant of the church who was responsible to the local priest). These officers were sworn in at mass ceremonies in Villa Alta, then returned to their communities to take up their posts.[59] In later years the number of regidores was augmented to two or more, an additional alcalde was added, and some lower, menial positions appeared, but the offices introduced by Alcalde Mayor Salinas were the standard ones found in both Indian and Spanish communities throughout New Spain and would form the core of village cabildos in the Sierra until the end of the colonial period.

After these initial appointments, all cabildo offices, including the top post of gobernador, were filled by election on an annual basis, the change in personnel occurring in early January. Each election had to be ratified by the alcalde mayor, from whom all Indian officials received their authority, and in the sixteenth century the gobernadores were in addition confirmed by the viceroy. The first of such confirmations occurred in 1563, three years after Alcalde Mayor Salinas left office. The viceroy approved one-year terms for gobernadores in four Nexitzo, three Cajonos, and one Chinantec town (most likely there were others as well), granting all of them the nominal right to collect from the villagers twenty *fanegas* of corn and fifteen turkeys each year, eight hundred cacao beans every three months, and two personal servants on a continuing basis.[60] Additional confirmations were recorded in the 1570s, though "salaries" were reduced to seven or eight pesos a year and the right to roof repairs on the officials' houses. Alcaldes received only two pesos a year, the rest of the cabildo officials—now including a small number of *cantores* for the church—receiving one peso.[61] The documentation is most plentiful for the Nexitzo Zapotec towns; significantly, only one Mixe community (Tonaguia) was represented.[62]

The colonial administration made no effort to place a gobernador and full cabildo in every Sierra community. Many villages were too small to support such a bureaucracy and some partial accommodations were also made to indigenous cabecera-sujeto relationships, though the evidence is too sparse to permit a systematic examination of which towns supported gobernadores and which did not. Chinantec Toavela and Petlapa shared a gobernador in 1595, while the other two Guatinicamanes towns—Lobani and Jocotepec— apparently each had its own.[63] Tagui's status as a sujeto of Yalahui was also recognized from the beginning and the two were under one gobernador until the midseventeenth century, when Tagui asserted its independence.[64] Some configurations originated with the congregaciones of 1600, as in the case of Mixe Tlahuitoltepec, which began to elect a gobernador after it was recognized as a cabecera. This official had authority in the four sujeto communities of Tamazulapan, Ayutla, Tepuxtepec, and Tepantlali, though each of these elected its own cabildo.[65] A similar arrangement existed in the Cajonos pueblos, where the gobernador of San Francisco had authority in the other five during most of the colonial period.[66] In Mixe country in the late 1600s, Tepitongo and Amatepec both had cabildos but were subject to the gobernador of Totontepec, and Moctum stood in a similar relationship to its cabecera Ocotepec.[67]

Gobernadores and cabildos were not always distributed to everyone's satisfaction, however. Even before the population began to recover in the second half of the colonial period, it was not uncommon for communities to assert their independence and challenge colonial authority by electing their own officials. Thus Latani, a sujeto of Choapan in 1643, tried to elect its own gobernador and cabildo but was blocked by the viceroy.[68] A decade earlier in the Zapotec Rincón, Teotlaxco and Yaneri complained of the services they were forced to provide for the gobernador of Yagavila, arguing that since they both had their own churches and cabildos, they should be independent cabeceras.[69]

Not surprisingly, Spanish attempts to impose Iberian concepts of community government were least successful in the Mixe zone. The Mixes were the last of the district's five ethnic groups to adopt the Spanish model in the sixteenth century, and the sparse documentation from Mixe pueblos suggests that cabildos and gobernadores were sometimes mere figureheads with little to do. In fact, by the 1790s it was official policy that no gobernadores were to be elected in any Mixe pueblo in the district.[70] Cabildos continued to exist, but even some of these were weak. In 1789, the alcaldes of Ayutla, Tamazulapan, and Tepantlali went so far as to ask the alcalde mayor for a special agent to collect the royal tribute in their communities, "because if we don't take an agent with us the tribute will not be collected, for the sons of the pueblo no longer pay any attention to us officials."[71]

Municipal councils were considerably more influential in town affairs in the rest of the district, however, above all in the Rincón. The declining power of the caciques in the late sixteenth and seventeenth centuries converted the cabildos of many pueblos into arenas of conflict and social climbing in which principales and macehuales competed for prestige and political control. In most communities, only the caciques, principales, and outgoing officers were permitted to vote, though elections were often held with the entire pueblo present.[72] The number of nobles eligible to vote could be large, however. In 1816 it ranged from lows of seventeen and eighteen in Yojovi and Yaviche to highs of fifty to fifty-nine in Choapan and Yovego.[73]

In the early colonial period it was not unusual for the Indians themselves to devise electoral mechanisms to ensure proportional representation in the cabildo of different constituent groups. For example, in 1595 Mixe Totontepec and its sujetos Huitepec and Yacochi agreed that nobles from all three towns would meet each year to elect officials to the cabildo of the cabecera. A regidor would be chosen from each pueblo, but because only two alcaldes and one alguacil mayor were permitted, it was decided that the alguacil would come from a pueblo that did not furnish an alcalde in a given year.[74]

By the eighteenth century, however, all such cooperative schemes had long since been replaced by conflict and factionalism. In Choapan in 1742, the town protested when an election took place in which only 15 of 107 electors voted, and a new election was subsequently held.[75] Two factions in Cajonos Tabaa were at loggerheads in 1789, one claiming that the outgoing cabildo should propose candidates for election (by the principales), the other arguing that an open town meeting was required before candidates were proposed. The alcalde mayor eventually agreed, reluctantly, to arbitrate the dispute.[76] It had once been the custom in Nexitzo Talea that cabildo officers were elected alternately from different barrios or *parcialidades* of the town, but previous understandings had broken down in 1770 and the alcalde mayor was forced to order a new election.[77] All these examples are symptomatic of a late colonial trend of increased assertiveness on the part of the macehuales. Commoners often demanded the right to vote, though they would not succeed until after independence, when the noble/commoner distinction was dismantled.[78]

Other sorts of conflict and abuses of power were also common. Several individuals had gained control of the cabildo of Choapan in the 1640s and proceeded to reelect themselves to office year after year, much to the consternation of many villagers.[79] Factionalism in Yatzona confounded the Spanish regime in 1696 when two separate elections were held, the alcalde mayor confirming one of them and the viceroy the other.[80] Dissension reached such a high level in Cajonos Yojovi in 1767 that the alcalde mayor decided to reinstate the office of gobernador, which had been allowed to lapse many years before. But when the town was unable to settle on a candidate for the office, only a threat from the magistrate to impose a Nahua gobernador from Analco succeeded in persuading the villagers to find a workable solution.[81]

Many of the conflicts focused on the gobernadores and their differences with the caciques on the one hand and the macehuales on the other. Frequently the most powerful individuals in their communities, gobernadores also acted as brokers with outside Spaniards, particularly the alcaldes mayores and merchants. They were thus often in a position to exploit their fellow villages for personal gain, and this rapidly became a common occurrence. Complaints about unscrupulous officers go back as far as 1580, when the gobernador of (pre-congregación) Ayutla was accused of levying excessive *derramas* (collections) and demanding more than his share of tribute and personal service.[82] Other charges leveled at gobernadores in different communities over the years included harsh treatment, personal use of community property, appropriation of clothing and other goods, and holding secret meetings.[83] Interestingly, only one gobernador—in Tabaa in 1708—

was ever accused of being a macehual, and only one—in Atitlán in 1687—was denounced as a mestizo.[84]

While the Spanish magistrates were often loathe to intervene in internal pueblo politics, on numerous other occasions they interfered much more actively to safeguard their own interests. Alcalde Mayor Bernardo de Quiroz, for example, imposed his own choices in cabildos throughout the district in 1687–89, provoking ninety pueblos (the vast majority) to lobby the viceroy for their right to free elections.[85] Another problem was the magistrates' long-standing practice of stationing a special lieutenant in Choapan, an important trading center but too far from Villa Alta for frequent personal visits. Sometimes these lieutenants were more exploitative than the justices themselves, and it was not unusual for them to interfere with local elections.[86] The only time Spanish officials had a legal right to impose on the electoral process was in cases of uprisings or other emergencies; in these cases special Indian gobernadores could be appointed, and elections postponed until the crisis was over. This law was invoked successfully at least once in 1685, when an uprising in Yaveo and Latani caused the alcalde mayor to temporarily appoint two gobernadores.[87]

Indians resented that their elections frequently had to be approved by local priests if the alcaldes mayores were to confirm them. They were also wronged by the *jueces de residencia*, who on arriving to inquire into the magistrates' behavior were in the habit of extorting twenty to fifty pesos from the cabildos when they made their rounds.[88] But what rankled cabildo officers most was the fee they had to pay to be installed in office. Every January all new elected officials journeyed to Villa Alta, where the alcalde mayor formally presented them with their *varas* (staffs of office). In 1618 each vara carried the price of five pesos plus quantities of mantles, turkeys, and other items. A century later in 1732, the alcalde mayor was charging six pesos when two hundred Indians from twelve Cajonos pueblos rioted in Villa Alta to express their opposition.[89] But things got worse for the Indians instead of better. Tabaa complained in 1752 that elected officials now had to pay thirty-four pesos to receive their varas, six pesos to present any written request to the magistrates, and twelve pesos per witness to the interpreter whenever legal business was initiated.[90]

Pressures such as these placed sharp limits on the powers of independent-minded gobernadores and cabildos. Further, as the fortunes of the caciques declined, those of the lower-ranked principales and macehuales brightened, and it eventually became possible for individuals of commoner background to play major roles in pueblo politics. Lacking any strong power bases or economic resources of their own, pueblo officers soon found that they could best advance their own personal interests by cooperating with Spanish authorities. As the repartimientos de efectos increased in volume during the eighteenth century, to refuse to cooperate with the alcalde mayor meant one had to remain forever at the bottom of the political hierarchy, for one of the key duties of the regidores, alcaldes, and gobernadores was the administration of the repartimientos. With the cacique lineages in disarray after 1730, the importance of the cabildo and its hierarchy of civil *cargos* (offices) was enhanced as it became the chief mechanism for validating rank within the community and for interface with the external world.

STRATIFICATION AND THE LATE
COLONIAL CARGO SYSTEM

While the cabildo with its ranked hierarchy of offices became firmly entrenched in the Sierra Zapoteca in the latter half of the sixteenth century, as time wore on it steadily extended its authority over community affairs and was increasingly relied upon by Spanish officials for purposes of commercial exploitation. At the same time, the cabildo was becoming more important to the status aspirations of individual caciques, their families, and the principales. In earlier years, the caciques had fought, unsuccessfully, to hold on to their cacicazgos and special services allowed them by the Spanish regime. By the opening decades of the eighteenth century, however, this battle had been lost and the native nobility embarked upon a different sort of struggle. They were now faced with the problem of how to keep what little prestige and political power they still had, in the absence of any significant accumulation of wealth to buttress their position. Simultaneously, the macehuales, no longer content with their inferior status and perceiving the vulnerability of the nobles' position, sought a greater voice in community politics.

Both sides could claim some support from the Spanish regime. On the one hand, it still bestowed a limited form of recognition on those Indians who could demonstrate hereditary noble rank. On the other, the cabildo form of village government, based as it was on electoral principles, opened the door to an egalitarian ideology and legitimized the political aspirations of the macehuales. Given these conditions, it is not surprising that nobles and commoners alike sought to use the municipal councils to advance their interests. The conflict began in the sixteenth century, but local conditions in the Villa Alta district caused the struggle to heat up greatly in the eighteenth century, especially the period between 1760 and 1820. In many villages the cabildos were converted into battlegrounds as contending factions and status groups vied for power and privilege. In harmonious and contentious pueblos alike, this period saw the final flowering of the colonial civil cargo system, the ranked pyramid of municipal offices based on the opposing principles of hierarchy and egalitarianism.[91]

Beginning as early as 1717, a number of disputes over noble status and cargo office holding began to emanate from pueblos in the district, increasing in frequency as the century unfolded. A growing number of families and individuals, unable to resolve their problems within the confines of their villages, sought the arbitration and support of the alcaldes mayores and subdelegados in Villa Alta and occasionally even the intendente of Oaxaca and the viceroy. Thirty-six such cases have been located, all of them remarkably similar in their content and manner of resolution. Almost all were initiated by individuals who had been elected by ruling village officials and other principales to low-ranking cargos in the civil hierarchies of their respective communities. Believing such cargos to be beneath their dignity, the designated individuals asked the alcaldes mayores in Villa Alta to grant them exemptions on the grounds that they were principales or caciques and, therefore, should not have to perform such lowly duties. All the petitioners were males. Some of the suits were initiated by individuals, others by groups of relatives (frequently "brothers"), but all were similar in that they pitted these claimants of noble status against their rivals, officials who held high cargos in the local village governments. As part of the legal proceedings, the plaintiffs had to present evidence of their noble status—in the form of written documents, testimony from witnesses, or both—and the town officials were frequently asked to state the local customs for serving cargos.

By the end of the century, these disputes had become so lengthy and voluminous that exasperated Spanish officials often despaired of the mountains of paper they were called upon to sift through. One attorney for the audiencia, who often gave legal advice to bewildered magistrates in Villa Alta, noted in 1796 that lawsuits over noble status were "much too common in that jurisdiction."[92] The following year an assessor in the office of the intendente of Oaxaca erupted in anger while reviewing a case from the Bixanos community of Yovego. A carefully arranged agreement between the cabildo and three cacique families had broken down, and village officials insisted upon more documentary proof of cacique rank. The families were only too happy to comply and submitted forty-seven baptismal and marriage certificates along with the testimony of eighteen witnesses. When called upon to review the entire file of three hundred folios—nearly six hundred pages—of what was very slim evidence of hereditary cacique status, the assessor exploded and wrote that the town of Yovego should be officially condemned "for the manifest temerity with which it has litigated."[93]

The Yovego case was not exceptional, and in fact other communities produced much greater numbers of similar disputes. Two are recorded for another Bixanos town, Santiago Camotlán, in 1789 and 1798; two for Mixe Tonaguia in 1728 and 1832; and one for Cajonos Tabaa in 1789.[94] That such disputes were not confined to the Villa Alta region is shown by two similar cases from Zapotec towns in the Valley of Tlacolula, in which men from Macuilxóchitl and San Juan Guelavía protested that the low-ranking cargos to which they had been elected (*tequitlato* and *topil de fiscal*) were beneath their dignity as principales.[95]

The vast majority of the cases produced in the Villa Alta district, however, came from six pueblos in the Zapotec Rincón, as shown in table 17. As was seen in previous chapters, many of these same communities—especially

Yae—were involved in extensive legal battles over cabecera status and marketplaces. The Rincón pueblos were by far the most litigious of the district, and their greater number of internal conflicts over cargos must be understood in this context. But why, we must ask, was the Rincón especially conflict-prone? There are at least two reasons. First, since the initial battles of conquest at Tiltepec, the Rincón was always a major area of Spanish exploitation in the Sierra Zapoteca. It contained more than its fair share of encomiendas and corregimientos in the early years (see tables 1 and 2) and in the eighteenth century was also the site of the extensive Santa Gertrudis mines, which took their toll on the laboring population of all Nexitzo communities. The cochineal and textile repartimiento demands of the alcaldes mayores may also have been especially onerous in the Rincón. Over time, these heavy demands had the effect of keeping Nexitzo communities divided. Those who could sought exemptions from the various burdens, and the late colonial disputes discussed here represent a final culmination of a long history of colonial oppression. The second major reason for the litigiousness of the Rincón pueblos is that as a group they were the most highly acculturated in the district. By the mideighteenth century many nobles in the Rincón were fluent in Spanish and dressing (at least occasionally) in European fashion at a time when pueblos in the other four ethnic zones remained much more conservative and monolingual. Nexitzo Zapotecs had a greater knowledge of and access to Spanish institutions, and this was most evident in their use of the Spanish judicial system to settle their differences.

The cabildos or civil cargo systems in the Rincón varied somewhat from village to village, but they were all fundamentally alike in that they encompassed the formal political offices introduced by the Spanish, as well as the more lowly duties of policeman, messenger, and general municipal servant. All adult males were expected to serve throughout their lifetimes, or until the age of fifty, and the cargos had to be fulfilled in ascending order. A typical system was that of Yaviche in 1760, which included the following positions:

gobernador	governor
alcalde	judge
regidor (2)	councilman
mayor	police chief
topil de común	policeman and messenger
topil de iglesia	church-keeper
gobaz	general servant

Significantly, all but the last were always referred to with Spanish terms, even in documents written in Zapotec.

Rinconeros made a clear distinction between the top three positions, the so-called *cargos honoríficos*, all of them of Spanish origin, and the bottom three, frequently referred to with disdain as *servicios bajos*, which had a

TABLE 17.   Disputes over Noble Status and Cargos in Rincón Villages

Town	Date	Source
Santa María Lachichina	1717	AJVA Civil y Criminal 1697–1797, *28*
	1789	AJVA Civil 1779–1802, *31*
	1793	AJVA Civil 1639–1843, *4*
	1794	AJVA Civil 1734–97, *27*
	1796	AJVA Civil 1759–97, *55*, cuarta parte
	1797	AJVA Civil 1635–1803, *56, 57*
	1803	AJVA Civil 1793–1840, *44*
	1805	AJVA Civil 1793–1840, *73*
Santiago Lalopa	1750	AJVA Civil 1579–1825, *23*
	1797	AJVA Civil 1759–97, *34*
	1801	AJVA Criminal 1682–1816, *61*
	1802	AJVA Civil y Criminal 1682–1831, *9*
	1814	AJVA Civil 1807–17, *65*
	1815	AJVA Civil 1807–17, *48*
	1816	AJVA Civil 1807–17, *17*
San Juan Yae	1723	AGN Indios 66, *48*
	1764	AJVA Civil 1697–1796, *26*
	1766	AJVA Civil 1697–1796, *20*
	1768	AJVA Civil 1697–1796, *9*
	1773	AGN Civil 374, *3*
	1774	AJVA Civil 1753–82, *33*
	1775	AJVA Civil 1753–82, *18*
	1811	AJVA Civil 1807–17, *81*
Santiago Yagallo	1706	AJVA Civil 1584–1793, *29*
	1725	AJVA Civil y Criminal 1701–50, *28*
	1802	AJVA Civil 1793–1840, *61*
San Juan Yagila	1721	AGN Indios 44, *135*
	1795	AJVA 1759–97, *55*, segunda parte
Santa María Yaviche	1760	AJVA Civil 1759–97, *8*
	1796	AJVA Civil 1759–97, *55*, primera parte

more indigenous character. The cargo of *gobaz* was often held by youths
between the ages of twelve and eighteen who were just entering the system,
though older men sometimes served as well. The gobaces were general servants for the higher officials, and ran errands and hauled fodder and fire-
wood as needed. The topiles often assisted them and doubled as village
policemen. In reality, these cargos were viewed by many as a form of personal service for the regidores, alcaldes, gobernador, and the Spanish priest.
The office of *mayor* occupied an ambiguous middle position because it was
not one of the honorific cargos, but neither was it classified as a form of
personal service. But it was sometimes grouped with the servicios bajos that
many aspiring nobles sought to avoid.

While it rarely works out this way in practice, modern Mesoamerican villages with functioning cargo systems usually cling to the ideal that every adult male should serve the same cargos in the same order.[96] This belief is associated with a distinctly egalitarian ethic; all "sons of the pueblo" are in theory equals and should serve their communities equally. In the eighteenth-century Rincón, however, this was not the case. Very different requirements and expectations applied to caciques and principales on the one hand and macehuales on the other. The former were permitted to enter the hierarchy in the middle—frequently at the level of mayor or regidor—without having to perform any of the servicios bajos, while the latter had to start at the bottom.

As always, there was variation among villages. In Yaviche in 1760, for example, sons of the nobility did not have to serve as gobaz, topil, or mayor but began as *sacristán* in the church, then went on to regidor, alcalde, and gobernador. Although it took them longer to get there, some macehuales eventually became gobernador in most pueblos. This was due in part to demographic factors, for elections were held annually and the small size of many villages virtually guaranteed that macehuales would have to serve in the honorific cargos. But this was not universally the case. San Juan Yae, the most rigidly stratified Rincón community, differed in important ways from its neighbors. In 1768, one of the town officials described the cargo system in this way: "The difference between principales and *plebeyos* [plebians] is that the former begin as mayores, then serve as alcaldes and gobernadores, while the latter begin as topiles and can rise no higher than regidores." This pattern was still prevalent in Yae as late as 1811, when it was not uncommon for macehuales to serve permanently as gobaces until the age of fifty when they were relieved of all communal duties and levies. Conflicts seldom arose over the definition of the offices themselves or the order in which they were ranked. Rather, the point of contention was *who* was eligible for exemption from servicios bajos; in other words, who were the caciques and principales.

As the preceding discussion indicates, status in the Rincón was related to the cargos occupied by male household heads. While this was a common pattern throughout central Mexico in this period, office holding seems to have assumed special significance in these small mountain communities where the native nobility possessed neither wealth nor genealogies to bolster its position. But the question remained: Did one have to actually pass through the cargo system to become a principal, or could this status be inherited from one's forebears? If it could be inherited, what served to distinguish between the statuses of cacique and principal? The documents provide no clear-cut answers to these questions, but rather indicate that two opposing views of social status prevailed—among Indians and Spaniards alike—and that they were never fully reconciled during the colonial years. In a word, we are presented with a classic case of conflict between the principles of ascribed versus achieved social status. It is frequently claimed that one effect of Spanish colonialism in the Indian communities was the steady erosion of inherited status and a corresponding emphasis placed on achievement, via cargo service. For the Rincón, however, this is but a half-truth, for ascribed status continued to be significant well into the nineteenth century.

To begin with the position of cacique, there was no question that this highest status could come only through inheritance. We have seen that Nexitzo Zapotec pueblos of this period contained certain *familias*—really remnants of the old noble lineages—with particular Spanish surnames that entitled their bearers to cacique rank. Theoretically, every cacique family was supposed to have a written title, but when called upon to present evidence in court, most could do little more than provide copies of old wills and baptism certificates. Extensive intermarriage persisted among the cacique families of the Rincón in the eighteenth century, but since few nobles could present proof of ancestry that extended back more than three generations, it is likely that many remote kinship links had been forgotten. A notable exception is provided by the four Pérez de Mendoza brothers of Yagallo, who in 1725 were able to document their descent back to the cacique Juan Pérez of Tepanzacualco, who was living in 1565.[97] But this is the only known case that furnishes such time depth. Further, in no instance was inheritance of cacicazgo property even mentioned, nor was any special descent rule explicitly invoked.

Even if clearly established, however, cacique status was mainly honorific and was certainly no guarantee of power or privilege by the late eighteenth century. In practical terms, it carried three benefits: exemption from royal tribute, exemption from the low community cargos, and exemption from labor service in the mines.[98] Political power in the community was not part of the package. In this sphere the elected gobernadores were clearly more influential, and very frequently they were not chosen from the cacique families. The volume of cases accumulated from these few villages attests that many caciques and principales alike were frequently on the defensive and felt persecuted by the egalitarian rhetoric of village officials of commoner extraction. Sometimes compromise solutions were hammered out to provide cacique families with a permanent place in local government, but they were rarely successful for long. In Yaviche in 1791, it was agreed that the office of gobernador would go to a member of one of the three cacique families every other year, but the pact lasted only five years.[99] The caciques of Yae also encountered problems. In 1774, the pueblo seemed united when it drew up a list of rules specifying the roles of the macehuales, principales, and caciques in community fiestas and the cargos to be held by each group. Sons of caciques were to enter the cargo system at the level of regidor, while sons of principales would start one rung below, at alguacil mayor.[100] Just one year later, however, the alcalde mayor was forced to order new elections in

Yae because twenty-six caciques had illegally been prevented from voting and not one cacique had been elected to any municipal office.[101]

With its tenuous hold on status and privilege, the cacique stratum was often merged conceptually with the principales. Where this occurred it was often said that there were two different kinds of principales. In Lachichina in 1803, for example, different sequences of cargos were prescribed for *principales menores* and *mayores*, and the subdelegado of Villa Alta concluded one dispute by ordering that the plaintiffs be regarded as "*principales de segundo grado y calidad.*" Another distinction frequently made was between *principales de nacimiento* (by birth) and *principales de oficio* (by office). Of the two ways of subdividing the principales, this was the more common and brought to the fore the opposition between ascribed and achieved status. The principales de nacimiento seem to have occupied a rank nearly identical to that of the cacique families in other villages, though they were presumably not exempt from tribute. In Lachichina in 1797, the principales de nacimiento consisted solely of the members of the López Osorio family. These individuals were exempt from the lower cargos and were not obligated to participate in repairing the church, working the community cornfield, decorating the road for fiestas, or laboring in village *tequios* (communal labor service). The more numerous principales de oficio, however, had to perform all of these and attained their rank only on completion of the cargo of regidor.[102]

Up to this point I have been discussing distinctions drawn by the Zapotecs themselves, but it is evident that similar principles—and similar contradictions—were present in Spanish legal thought of the time. In some ways the dilemma of the alcaldes mayores and subdelegados, who had to decide these cases, was even greater. They customarily arrived in Villa Alta directly from Spain, with virtually no knowledge of the peoples and cultures in their jurisdiction. Often they were frankly bewildered when first called upon to adjudicate the internal affairs of Indian communities. From the Spanish point of view, these squabbles over noble status could be regarded in two ways. If they were viewed primarily as disputes over municipal *offices*, the magistrate could hypothetically choose to impose the Spanish cabildo model, which was familiar to him and excluded inherited status; or he might simply accept the status quo in the village and deliver a ruling that took local custom into account. On the other hand, and this seems to have been the case in practice, the Spanish official could regard these cases as fundamentally disputes over the issue of noble *privileges*, the cargos being merely a means to this end. Looking at the lawsuits in this light caused less confusion, since both Zapotec and Spanish cultures had well-defined concepts of hereditary nobility. Most of the alcaldes mayores themselves held noble titles, and this was something they could readily understand.

Nonetheless, some magistrates solicited legal opinions from attorneys when they were first presented with these problems of Zapotec custom. One subdelegado, Bernardo Ruiz de Conejares (1796–1801), twice sought advice from Oaxaca lawyers and got conflicting replies. Don Luis de Acosta, an abogado of the audiencia, advised him to follow the Spanish cabildo model and recognize as principales only those Indians who had served as gobernador; no prerogatives should be passed on through inheritance. In contrast, Licenciado José Mariano Ynduciaga argued that these were mainly disputes over social rank and that the subdelegado should ground his decision in native custom. He went on to expound on the nature of *principalidad* among the Indians in general, noting three types that must be recognized: (1) by virtue of cacicazgo, (2) by virtue of completing one's cargos, and (3) by virtue of ancestry, i.e., one enters the system at the same level as his ancestors.[103] In the end, the subdelegado, like many of his predecessors, opted to resolve his cases within the framework of village custom. "Keeping the Indians happy" was more important—and less troublesome—than imposing a Spanish cabildo model that did not fit the colonial circumstances. Of the thirty cases listed in table 17, only half contain the final decisions by the Spanish magistrates. But of these fifteen, only four ruled against the nobility; the remaining eleven confirmed the cacique or *principal* status of the plaintiffs even when the supporting evidence was nearly nonexistent. Simply producing a few witnesses or showing that one's father and grandfather had not held the lower cargos was usually sufficient.

One inevitable result of this constant reinforcement of the native nobility—both by ascription and by achievement—was a vast increase in the size of the *principal* stratum and a corresponding decrease in the number of macehuales. Table 18 gives some rough figures for the size of the cacique and *principal* groups in ten villages in the late colonial period. The ratios calculated for nobles to tributaries are only approximate, for principales were themselves tribute payers. The general trend is clear, however: caciques and principales together comprised well over one-third of the population in most villages. In a few they accounted for over half!

Two sets of problems stemmed from this top-heavy system. First, since only caciques and principales could vote in the annual municipal elections, their larger numbers tended to foster increased factionalism and rising discontent among the macehuales. Second, an even more serious problem was a shortage of macehuales to fill the lower municipal cargos, especially in the smaller villages. This was, of course, inevitable in a system that involved so few people and where exemptions were granted on the basis of both birth *and* achievement. Indeed, this sheer lack of personnel caused many town officials to press otherwise exempt principales into serving the lower cargos. If the nobles refused, or if they went to court to seek redress, the only alternatives were leaving the positions unfilled or revamping the system.

The latter option was frequently chosen, and there was a considerable amount of adjustment and "fine tuning" of cargo systems in the Rincón during this period. The officials of Lachichina in 1797 noted that if every man

TABLE 18. Proportion of Caciques and Principales in Ten Towns in the Villa Alta District

Towns	Date	Caciques and Prin- cipales	Tributaries, Casados or Familias		Ratio
Rincón Towns					
Santiago Lalopa	1814	31	112	tributaries	1 : 3.6
Santa María Temaxcalapan	1798	25	63	tributaries	1 : 2.5
San Miguel Tiltepec	1819	28	102.5	tributaries	1 : 3.6
San Juan Yae	1772	108	210	adult males	1 : 1.9
Santa María Yaviche	1816	18	33	tributaries	1 : 1.8
Other Zapotec Towns					
Santiago Choapan	1742	107	412	familias	1 : 3.8
San Juan Tabaa	1789	39	153.5	tributaries	1 : 3.9
San Gaspar Xagalasi	1816	37	140	tributaries	1 : 3.8
Santo Domingo Yojovi	1816	17	75	tributaries	1 : 4.4
San Francisco Yovego	1816	59	130	tributaries	1 : 2.2

Sources for Caciques and Principales: AJVA Civil 1807–17, *4, 20, 65* (Lalopa, Yaviche, Xagalasi, Yojovi, Yovego); Civil 1779–1802, *21* (Tabaa); Civil y Criminal 1698–1865, *1* (Temaxcalapan); Civil y Criminal 1682–1882, *27* (Choapan); Criminal 1735–1821, *94* (Tiltepec); AGN Civil 374, *3* (Yae).
Sources for Population: AGN Tributos 25, *19* (1789); Villaseñor y Sánchez, *Theatro americano* (1742); AJVA Civil 1819–21, *8* (1820); AGI México 881, *12* (1703); AGI México 2589, *50* (1777).

whose father had passed the cargo of regidor was entitled to be a principal, eventually no one would be left to fill the oficios bajos.[104] In a similar vein, the officials of Yaviche in 1760 stated their position:

> Because our *pueblo* is small, with only fifty married men, and because most of these are *caciques* and *principales*, it is necessary for all of us to serve and fulfill our customary obligations. We cannot accept any excuses, for if each one of us were to argue his privileges, we would all be reduced to misery. It is the custom that all the principales must serve in *oficios bajos* until completion of the cargo of regidor.[105]

A similar situation obtained in the Bixanos community of Camotlán, which in 1798 had only twenty-five families. To keep their cargo system going with so few people, the community extended the period of service for the lower cargos to as many as four or five years, and the positions of mayor, regidor, and alcalde had to be served twice before one became eligible for gobernador.[106]

Adjustments such as these inevitably threatened the prerogatives of many nobles, but no other solution seemed feasible. The truth of the matter was that these small mountain villages had become saddled—through a long process of colonialism and cultural syncretism—with a sociopolitical system that was really designed for much larger aggregations. The resulting conflicts never abated as long as the Spanish regime continued, for villages remained small and the Spanish magistrates in their legal decisions tended to reinforce the status quo instead of effecting social change. Not until after independence when the Spanish administrative apparatus had been dismantled could Rinconeros begin to redefine themselves on a more egalitarian basis. Eventually, the cacique stratum disappeared altogether, as did the principales de nacimiento (at least as a formally constituted group). Increasingly, every male was expected to serve his village equally, and one could become a principal only through serving in at least some of the higher cargos. In this fashion, yesterday's large social stratum or "status group" of principales was transformed into today's small contingent of village elders and political advisors that carries the same name.

THE ROLE OF THE REPARTIMIENTOS DE EFECTOS

Now that the general pattern of late colonial stratification and cargo politics in the Rincón has been described, a discussion of precipitating factors is in order. We have already seen that this region was characterized by a higher degree of acculturation and Spanish exploitation than other parts of the Villa Alta district, but we still lack a satisfactory explanation of why status seeking in these villages was so intense. Furthermore, we must also consider the logic behind the legal decisions of the alcaldes mayores. Why, indeed, did these Spanish officials routinely confirm the nobility of so many Indians when the supporting evidence of descent was almost always weak? I believe that a compelling case can be made for the pivotal importance of the magistrates' commercial interests, in particular the administration of the ubiquitous repartimientos de efectos. It is not coincidental that the lawsuits over cargos and the demands of the repartimientos both reached their height at roughly the same point in time.

The trading monopolies of the alcaldes mayores and the requirements of textile manufacture and cochineal cultivation together kept the indigenous communities intact, as we have seen, but far from unchanged. The repartimientos had a substantial impact on community political organization and were a key factor behind the transformations that occurred in the indigenous stratification system and the position of the native nobility. In the Villa Alta district, as in others, repartimientos were administered with the aid of the top town officials, all of whom usually served one-year terms.[107] These individuals were in the position of mediating between the alcaldes mayores and their fellow villagers, and without their cooperation the distribution and collection of money and goods would have been an impossible task. We know little about the actual operations involved, but the following brief account by the curate of Santa María Ecatepec about Indian participation in the cochineal repartimientos in the adjoining jurisdiction of Nejapa in the 1770s is revealing:

The republics [officials] of all the villages, in the four months of April, May, June, and July when collections are held, are maintained [by the alcalde mayor] with provisions for themselves and their families, together with mules and servants for transport from village to village. They are only paid for the sacks [of cochineal] which they deliver to the head town of the alcalde mayor, where everything is brought together. These officials, the gobernadores, alcaldes, and other ministers, remain in the town hall while they make their collections. The debtors must come in person, and if they do not pay, they are jailed or given other forms of punishment if they are guilty.

The following year, in October, the lieutenant returns with more money and makes a new repartimiento.[108]

Similar procedures were undoubtedly followed in the Villa Alta district, and it is clear that town officials gained a certain amount of power over their villagers—and often some material perquisites as well—by cooperating with the alcalde mayor. A good example of a common practice comes from the Mixe town of Tonaguia in 1654. As was customary throughout the district, the lieutenant of the alcalde mayor issued money and raw cotton for textile production to the gobernador, alcalde, and three regidores of the pueblo. These officials were in turn responsible for organizing the repartimiento and were obligated to distribute eight reales (as advance payment) and eight pounds of cotton to all the village households, which would then weave the required cotton mantles. This particular group of officials, however, was skimming a profit right off the top, usurping one real and one pound of cotton per household before making the distribution.[109] Since textile repartimientos occurred every few months, such a scam could be quite profitable for cabildo officials who got away with it. Many villagers no doubt tolerated the practice in the expectation that they would do the same when it was their turn to serve. For some gobernadores, the incentives for remaining in the good graces of the alcaldes mayores could be quite powerful, even in times of acute oppression. When virtually the entire district (ninety pueblos) protested to the viceroy of the electoral abuses of Alcalde Mayor Quiroz in 1698, it was noted that "this petition does not speak for the gobernadores of San Francisco Cajonos, Santa María Yaviche, Choapan, Latani, San Juan Jalahui . . . , San Pedro Javee, Zoochila, and Camotlán, who are all followers of the said alcalde mayor."[110]

Repartimientos were organized in at least two ways. Apart from those that were administered separately to each Indian household were the *repartimientos de común*, in which the town officials were given the sole responsibility of paying back what was owed by the community as a whole at collection time. (The example just given from Tonaguia was of this type.) As Marcello Carmagnani points out, this system placed even more control in the hands of Indian authorities and tended to strengthen the role of the principales as a group.[111] Thus, as long as the repartimientos continued (i.e., until the end of the colonial period), there was a powerful incentive for individuals to seek high office in their villages. In most Rincón communities, with the exception of Yae, these offices were theoretically open to all, but one could ascend the ladder much faster if one were a principal. Serving as regidor, alcalde, or gobernador surely brought prestige and relief from the menial chores of the servicios bajos, but equally important, it also provided an opportunity for a man to partially recoup the repartimiento losses incurred during those years when he was out of office.[112]

Hypothetically, then, the greater the volume of repartimientos administered by the alcaldes mayores, the stronger the principal stratum became. One might also surmise that since the Rincón was the source of most of the disputes over cacique and principal status in the district, it is likely that repartimiento obligations were especially heavy there. Confirmation of this point must await further research, but, nonetheless, a likely motive for seeking principal status through the Spanish courts has been established. On the other side, granting such status was also advantageous to the trading interests of the Spanish magistrates. They depended heavily on the cooperation of village authorities, who rotated yearly. Especially where the villages were so small, it was good politics for the alcalde mayor to satisfy as many people as possible in their status aspirations. It could in no way hurt his own operations, and provided one of the few means he had of "keeping the Indians happy" at no inconvenience to himself. Denial of noble status to the litigants, on the other hand, would have augmented the already high degree of factionalism in the villages and hence endangered the official's trading interests. In sum, the alcaldes mayores needed the cooperation of Indian nobles to help them exploit the Rincón communities, while these same nobles, short on wealth and hereditary prerogatives, needed the legal confirmation of their status that only the alcaldes mayores could provide.

CONCLUSION

The evidence discussed in the preceding pages suggests two developmental phases of the native nobility in colonial Villa Alta. The first phase, ending about 1730, saw the steady elimination of the cacicazgos and the collapse (or at least the attenuation) of many of the cacique lineages. Cacicazgos appear to have been strongest and lasted longer in the Bixanos and Chinantec zones, though even here they were weak and impoverished compared with the large estates of the Valley of Oaxaca and the Mixteca Alta. In most pueblos of the district, cacique families went into decline well before 1730, in some places as early as the late 1500s. The second phase of the nobility's saga was a phenomenon of the eighteenth century and endured until the very end of the colonial rule. It was characterized by a desperate attempt on the part of the caciques and principales to maintain their prestige and political power in the face of growing opposition from the macehuales. The fight for political control was also lost, however, like the struggle for cacicazgos that preceded it, and the general picture that emerges is one in which power was exercised primarily by village officials rather than hereditary caciques, who had little wealth or influence. The imposition of the Spanish type of town government with annually elected officials provided avenues of status achievement, and many commoners were able to use the cargo system to achieve principal status. It would be wrong, however, to assert that Spanish colonialism tended to eliminate the hereditary nobility or that it tended to level status differences in Indian communities. The colonial regime did strip the native nobility of much of its political power, and the records indicate that in the Rincón, especially, the important cacique lineages at the time of the Conquest were soon crushed. But as we have seen, in the eighteenth century a new type of nobility, combining aspects of both descent and achievement and composed largely of principales, developed in their wake. These nobles were people of little wealth or power, but thanks to the support of the alcaldes mayores they were able to retain their position of high prestige along with the newcomers who used the cargo system to achieve the same ends.[113] The financial gains that the repartimiento system made available to cabildo members provided another incentive for participating in the civil cargo system, especially for the commoners. This led to increased socioeconomic differentiation within the pueblos, though in no case was it of sufficient magnitude to lead to class divisions.

The result of these developments was a distinctive type of community organization, ridden with factionalism and characterized by an exceedingly large number of nobles and a dwindling pool of commoners. In some respects, the different cargo duties prescribed for principales and macehuales in late colonial times are similar to patterns found in modern Zapotec villages. Today it is not unusual for literate men to enter the system midway at the level of *secretario* and later rise to the positions of *alcalde* and *presidente*. Others never go beyond the cargos of *policía* and *regidor*.[114] According to Laura Nader, in the modern cargo system of the Rincón community of Talea de Castro

a man starts as policia and presumably works up the ladder to presidente, alcalde, and possibly principal, but where he enters the ladder in Talea depends on who he is and where he fits into the social strata. And his position in the social strata will depend on the degree of formal education, ability to speak Spanish, and power position of his family in the town. This recognition of the facts of social stratification results in making certain positions exclusive: a monolingual Talean could not become presidente, but he could become an alcalde. A man who can type or who has completed six years of schooling, or has come to the United States as a bracero, will never start out as a policia. It is unlikely that sons of principales would enter the hierarchy as policia, et cetera. Such exclusive recruitment changes the image of the vertical ladder for Talea; it becomes, instead, either two ladders standing vertically side by side, one with fewer rungs than the other (for those that enter at midpoint, the secretario level), or two ladders laid sideways one above the other, for a Talean no longer may be progressing up the ladder when he passes from policia to regidor, but rather he is progressing sideways.[115]

The resemblance to the late colonial pattern is evident, but with two important differences: the criteria governing social status have, of course, changed somewhat and the social strata are today much less concrete and more informally organized. Now no named strata have any basis in law, and today's principales in Talea who decide the town's governmental policies numbered only thirteen in 1957.[116] It might be said that the cargo system today *reflects* the social strata in the community but no longer plays a pivotal role in *determining* their contours as it did in the eighteenth century. This is, of course, the result of 150 years of history and a consequence of the community's increasing integration into Mexican national society. Principales today no longer form a stratum in and of themselves, but constitute a sort of advisory council for political matters. Just when the shift from status group to advisory council occurred is difficult to say, but it probably took place in the midnineteenth century.

During the course of the eighteenth century, however, the villages of the Villa Alta district were divided into two antagonistic *status groups* of nobles and commoners, in sharp contrast to the Valley of Oaxaca, where a number of cacique lineages persisted as *class-like groups* still in control of patrimonial lands. The peculiar character of colonial exploitation in the Sierra Zapoteca first stripped the native nobility of what little wealth it had, then, after 1730, redefined the rules of the game and created a new category of late colonial nobility based on the conflicting principles of descent and achievement. The outcome was a relatively impoverished group of insecure status seekers whose position required continual validation by Spanish colonial authorities. Sadly, by resorting to colonial courts and employing the Spanish legal system to maintain invidious distinctions among themselves, the Indians simply played into the hands of the alcaldes mayores. Their dependence on the colonial regime increased and as a consequence the firm control and repression necessary for the continuation of the repartimientos de efectos was never endangered.

CHAPTER 6

RELIGION

ONE OF THE GREAT ironies of Spanish colonization in Latin America is that the aspect of indigenous culture that the conquerors tried hardest to eradicate—native religion—is the one that has often shown the greatest resilience in post-Conquest years. Indigenous religious beliefs and practices did not remain unchanged, of course, as they became syncretized in various ways with European Catholicism. But even today, after four and one-half centuries of proselytization and forced acculturation, Indian components of worship are still vigorous in many places. While most Mesoamerican Indians now profess to be nominal Catholics, they are frequently aware—as in the case of the Cajonos town of Yalalag—that their religion is not *entirely* Catholic.[1]

One of the reasons why the "spiritual conquest" of Mesoamerica met with only limited success is that in some areas, at least, early colonial Spaniards and Indians never fully understood each other's religions. Convinced that pagan beliefs and ceremonies were really propitiating the devil, many colonial clerics were too busy trying to stamp them out to take the time to reflect on their meaning. The Indians, on the other hand, though some did undoubtedly convert sincerely to Christianity, could not help but bring their own understandings about the supernatural to the Catholic rituals they were forced to perform. The result, in the long run as well as the short, has been a gap in understanding between the Indian faithful and orthodox Catholics—the clergy in particular—that has been slow to narrow.

PRE-HISPANIC BACKGROUND

Sources on pre-Hispanic religion in the Sierra Zapoteca are limited to a handful of brief comments and observations made by Spaniards who did not fully comprehend the subject. Overall, however, religion in the three Zapotec zones under study seems to have conformed fairly well to the broad outline of Zapotec religion sketched for the Valley of Oaxaca and other Zapotec regions by Joyce Marcus.[2] Most fundamentally, Zapotec religion was animatistic, attributing life to many features of the natural world that Westerners consider inanimate. While the Zapotecs did recognize a supreme being, more attention was devoted to a series of powerful supernatural forces created by the supreme being, including lightning, sun, earthquakes, fire, and clouds. There was no anthropomorphic pantheon comparable to the Christian God, the Holy Family, and multitude of saints, nor do the Zapotecs appear to have shared a concept of "god" in the European sense. The feature of Zapotec religion that was most widely misunderstood, however, was its strong emphasis on ancestor worship, especially royal ancestors. As Marcus argues,

> This practice was widely misunderstood by the sixteenth-century Spaniards, who usually mistook the images of venerated, deceased rulers for the "idols" of "gods." Since the venerated rulers varied from town to town, the Spaniards wound up with dozens of "gods" . . . , giving rise to the notion of an extensive anthropomorphized Zapotec pantheon. Such misconceptions pervade even the best accounts of Zapotec religion, including those of Fray Juan de Córdova, Francisco de Burgoa, Gonzalo de Balsalobre, and the *Relaciones geográficas* of 1579–1581.[3]

One of the surface similarities that Zapotec religion shared with Spanish Catholicism was a trained, hierarchical priesthood. Marcus distinguishes between high priests (*uija-tào*), ordinary priests (*copa pitào*), sacrificers (*ueza-eche*), and young men who were educated to enter the priesthood (*bigaña*). In addition, diviners (*colanij*) used the 260-day ritual calendar (*pije* or *piye*) to determine auspicious days for a wide variety of human activities.[4] This priestly hierarchy applies best to the Valley Zapotecs; it was probably less elaborate in the underdeveloped Sierra Zapoteca. By the mid-sixteenth century, the Spanish regularly used the term *vigana* to refer to priests in this region, though there is no doubt that some of them were widely known and of very high status. They may sometimes have been the same persons as the caciques, or at least exercised considerable political power. Dávila Padilla, for example, mentions a cacique don Alonso in the Bixanos community of Comaltepec who was

> the greatest idolator of all, in whose lineage had always been the priests of the idols that they call *Viganas*, which means he who guards the gods. This was also the name for the boys that served the altar and offered incense and copal or locust resin to the idols. Some of these *Viganas* were so distinctive and dedicated to this office that not only did they live apart and aloof, but were also sexually incapacitated, a sign of their reverence for the altar.[5]

One of the few references to a Sierra Zapotec high priest concerns a contemporary of don Alonso's in Choapan. Described as *Coquitela* (*coqui* means "male ruler"), the "*summo sacerdote de los Viganas*," he was supposedly regarded as the son of the sun. When he died in 1558 or 1559 he was buried by the viganas with a considerable quantity of gold and some live women servants.[6] The viganas themselves were all of noble birth, the second sons of caciques and principales. Kept apart while young as they learned their profession, they were numerous and revered and castrated to assure their purity and devotion.[7] Tabaa in the 1550s had eight viganas, and Fray Jordán de

Santa Catalina managed to round up a total of thirty in the entire Cajonos zone.[8] While the documentation is thin, unquestionably some high priests were very influential men. The second Spanish corregidor of Nexitzo Yagavila, arriving at his post in 1534, was astounded by his encounter with a high priest named Yagaeche, who was a homosexual and practiced human sacrifice and ritual cannibalism. The corregidor referred to him both as a cacique and a "pope," though there was also another cacique in Yagavila named Gavice.[9]

Virtually no direct information on the religious practices of the Chinantecs and Mixes in the pre-Hispanic period has surfaced. The Mixes, however, seem to have had concepts of the supernatural similar to those of the Zapotecs, judging from early-eighteenth-century sources to be discussed below. The one brief reference to Mixe ritual cannibalism fails to explain its context.[10] It is impossible to say, however, whether the Chinantecs and Mixes had priestly hierarchies comparable to that of the Sierra Zapotecs.

Many have commented on both the similarities and differences between Mesoamerican religions and Spanish Catholicism. For the Zapotecs, at least, the similarities would include a formalized, hierarchical, full-time priesthood; fasting and penance; confession; feasting; a complex pantheon of supernatural beings; possession and worship of wooden and stone images; and reliance on a calendar for naming and observing many aspects of the ritual cycle. These broad resemblances made possible a significant degree of syncretism between the two traditions during the course of Catholic missionization. At the same time, however, sharp differences influenced the course of change. The Indians' basically animatistic orientation; strong emphasis on ancestor worship; the ritual sacrifice of animals and humans; blood offering by piercing the tongue, ears, nostrils, and other body parts; ritual dancing and intoxication; ritual cannibalism; and use of hallucinogenic substances for divination alternately puzzled and shocked the Spaniards. Despite periodic colonial campaigns to eradicate them, the worship of local spirits, animal sacrifice, and ritual intoxication persist today, integrated, if only loosely, with other Catholic forms.

Both Spaniards and Indians, out of necessity and frustration, concentrated on the outward ritual forms of each other's religions and tended to impute to them their own meanings and understandings. This common colonial process bedevils any scholarly analysis, the present one included, that relies mainly on documentation produced by the conquerors, so the following account must be regarded as preliminary. After providing a view of the administrative and social roles of the friars and the secular clergy in the Villa Alta district, I will discuss the persistence of indigenous beliefs and practices—and Spanish attempts to eradicate them. The chapter concludes with some observations on cofradías and the cult of the saints in the eighteenth century, and a chronology of the process of colonial syncretism in the region.

THE DOMINICAN PRESENCE

As we saw in chapter 2 the Dominican order thoroughly dominated the spiritual conquest of the Sierra Zapoteca, beginning especially with the arrival of Fray Jordán de Santa Catalina and his colleagues in 1558. The Dominicans were to remain virtually unchallenged as spiritual and often temporal guardians of the internal life of the Indian pueblos until the start of the eighteenth century. Their crucial years of consolidation in the region were between 1558 and 1576, led by Santa Catalina and, beginning in 1561, his successor, Fray Pedro Guerrero. During these years the Indians realized for the first time that the friars were intent on nothing less than the complete eradication of their religious system. The military conquest was complete and the pueblos recognized that they had no choice but to nominally accept the new religion. Some native priests understandably bridled at the thought of submission, one in Cajonos Tabaa going so far as to hang himself rather than convert. He advised the rest of the pueblo to follow him, but when Guerrero and the town's corregidor burned the priest's body in front of all the inhabitants, the people promised to surrender their idols and become Catholics. The news of this event spread quickly throughout the region, and many Indians arrived in Villa Alta to turn over their images of clay, stone, and precious stones, causing a number of Spanish vecinos to embark on a disruptive search for booty.[11]

Burgoa's account indicates that Fray Pedro Guerrero was among the most zealous and energetic Dominicans ever to arrive in the Sierra, and a number of fundamental changes took place during his fifteen years as vicar in Villa Alta (1561–76). Guerrero was probably the first missionary to master the Mixe language, and soon thereafter he learned Zapotec as well. He also initiated contact with the Chinantec Guatinicamanes, at great personal risk. Though almost certainly exaggerating, Burgoa claims that Guerrero congregated and built churches in 160 pueblos in the Sierra. While this is very unlikely, congregating even a quarter of this number would have been a remarkable accomplishment, given the tiny number of Dominicans and other Spaniards in the region at that time.[12] Guerrero was also the first to appoint Indian *fiscales* in the pueblos, an act that must have had considerable repercussions for community life. The fiscales were the friars' chief assistants and were placed in charge of the liturgy and catechism. They were paid a nominal salary (at least at first) and given considerable authority, even over the principales. Fiscales appointed by Guerrero in 1559–60 in the Chinantec towns of Lachixila and Petlapa were empowered to make sure that everyone was properly married in the Christian manner, that men and women who were not did not live together, and that there were no religious sacrifices or public drunkenness. The officials were to teach the *doctrina,* assemble public gatherings for this purpose, and punish any villagers who did not obey.[13]

It is difficult to say how effective these appointments were at first, particularly in the Guatinicamanes. The friars soon found that the Chinantecs were the most difficult Indians to work with in the entire region. Their language was especially difficult to learn and their scattered settlement pattern also posed many problems, as this passage from Burgoa makes clear:

> [The Chinantecs are] an isolated and untamed people, almost impossible to discipline as they live in *rancherías* in hollows and thickets of trees. They communicate very little among themselves, and are so mountainous that the original *padres* found no way to bring them together. The mountain ridges are very inaccessible and the people take advantage of this ruggedness so as to be neither found nor seen.[14]

Burgoa's lament echoes a pessimism that was prevalent among the clergy throughout the Bishopric of Oaxaca in the 1570s. Despite the considerable efforts directed toward congregation and missionization, the priests were too few and the Indians too many to permit much progress in rugged areas like the Sierra Zapoteca. In January 1577, Bishop Albuquerque wrote a very dispirited letter to the crown in which he despaired of ever making adequate progress toward conversion of the Indians because of the lack of personnel, the mountainous terrain, the variety of languages, the prevalence of dispersed settlement, the widespread "idolatry," and the mistreatment of the Indians by the corregidores.[15] Just seven years earlier, the crown had acceded to the bishop's request that all the Indians in Oaxaca be ordered to learn Nahuatl, in compensation for the church's inability to supply enough clerics fluent in the local languages.[16] While such a decree appears naive to modern observers, the fact that Nahuatl became the standard written language in highland Mixe pueblos in the seventeenth century suggests that the order may have had some effect.

Exact figures are unavailable, but in the late sixteenth and early seventeenth centuries there was never more than a handful of clerics to missionize the Villa Alta district's twenty to thirty thousand Indians, and many Indians saw a priest only seven or eight times a year, if that. Reinvigorated in 1558 with four Dominicans, the Doctrina of Villa Alta was for a time the only parish center in the entire district (except for a secular priest or two at Tanetze in the Rincón). Three of the friars spent their time in the pueblos while Fray Fabián de Santo Domingo remained in the villa, where he ran a school for sons of Spanish vecinos and noble Indian families. By 1568 the staff had increased to six, and in the 1570s a separate doctrina was established in the important Mixe town of Totontepec. A separate Chinantec parish followed, perhaps toward 1585, and in the seventeenth century two additional seats were established in the Mixe towns of Juquila and Quetzaltepec (these were offshoots of the Nejapa doctrina—founded in 1560—but served some Mixe towns in the Villa Alta district as well). Choapan became the parish center of nine Bixanos communities in 1603, while San Francisco

Cajonos, the last of the Dominican doctrinas to be established, became cabecera of fifteen pueblos in 1623.[17]

The one zone the Dominicans never fully controlled was the Rincón. While some Nexitzo communities were administered by the friars from Villa Alta, the parish of Tanetze was in the hands of the secular church well before the close of the sixteenth century, and seculars were also installed at Yae when it became a cabecera after the congregaciones. The end of Dominican hegemony in the district as a whole came in the first decade of the eighteenth century when Bishop Maldonado, aided by the viceroy and the audiencia, secularized twenty-seven Dominican doctrinas throughout the bishopric, while considerably increasing the number of parishes. The six Dominican doctrinas functioning in the Sierra at that time—Villa Alta, San Francisco Cajonos, Choapan, Totontepec, Juquila Mixes, and Quetzaltepec—were expanded to eighteen secular parishes between 1705 and 1707. The bishop claimed that before the reorganization the Dominicans had only twelve friars in the district; by 1705 the seculars numbered twenty-one.[18] By the middle of the eighteenth century the number of parishes in the district had stabilized at twenty, and essentially the same divisions were still intact as late as 1864.[19]

CLERICS AS COLONIZERS

Like most other Spaniards in the region, the clergy owned little property and depended on the Indian population for their livelihood. The sole known agricultural enterprise operated by churchmen was a sugar mill near Cajonos Zoochila run by Augustinians from Antequera in 1590s.[20] The only Dominican enterprise that has come to light was a sheep and goat ranch near Nejapa in the 1560s where the friars produced milk, cheese, and wool for their own consumption.[21] The most common supplement to the regular fees paid by the Indians was trade, and it appears that the commercial practices of many Dominicans and secular clergy differed little (at least in kind) from those of the Spanish merchants and political officials. In the remote Chinantec Guatinicamanes, as early as 1575, one secular priest was forcing cloths, altar hangings, and retables for the church on a reluctant population. As usual, the prices charged were excessive and the goods were "sold" on credit.[22] Before the end of the century, clerics were regularly including cotton mantles in the fees they demanded, a practice that no doubt increased during the eighteenth century.[23] Others conducted their own repartimientos de efectos (when they could evade the vigilance of the alcaldes mayores); for example, a Dominican in Choapan in the midseventeenth century traded in wax and fish for at least twenty years.[24]

Costs to the Indians for rituals increased as the clergy became more entrenched and the celebration of masses and fiestas became routine. These expenditures were especially burdensome for the smaller communities, as

TABLE 19.   Annual Church Fees and Payments in San Juan Yalahui, 1707

Offerings for eight ritual occasions	77 pesos
Required gifts for curate	16 pesos, 22 cotton mantles
Food for curate during his visits	11 pesos, 4 reales
Fees for masses	23 pesos
Payments to vicar and other annual expenses	19 pesos, 3 unpaid servants
Total: over 150 pesos a year plus labor	

Source: AGI México 879, 6.

shown in table 19 for San Juan Yalahui, which had a population of about 205 (45 casados) in 1707 and had no resident priest. To these community expenses must be added sums paid by individual families for baptism (amount unknown), marriage (4 pesos, 1 real), and death rites (2 pesos, 4 reales). Given such realities, it is not surprising that a steady stream of complaints about various priestly excesses emanated from the pueblos of the district, beginning in 1581 and continuing unabated thereafter. The parishioners did not protest the curates' right to be there, but they did object to what they considered unjust demands for servants, food, labor, and goods; excessive fees; and cruel treatment.[25]

Conditions were especially oppressive under the secular clergy in the second half of the eighteenth century, leading to local uprisings against priests on at least four occasions. In Mixe Totontepec the curate provoked the entire community in 1748 by ordering (for unknown reasons) that no one leave the town and then whipping someone who did.[26] A violent confrontation occurred in Bixanos Latani in 1783 when an angry mob attacked the *casas parroquiales*. The people's complaints about their priest were quite specific: he (1) treated them badly; (2) demanded excessive fees and personal service; (3) called the Indians *brutos, animales,* and *perros* (brutes, anmals, and dogs); (4) inflicted unusually cruel whippings; (5) punched a cacique who came drunk to communion; and (6) did not pay people who tended his fields and looked after his sheep.[27] Other uprisings are mentioned for Cacalotepec in 1779 and Yahuive in 1812, the latter involving several pueblos.[28]

These rebellions were symptomatic of the considerable power wielded by the clergy. During the sixteenth and seventeenth centuries, rarely, if ever, were the Dominicans denied support by the alcaldes mayores and the viceroys in their plans for congregaciones and appointments of parish seats. Friars had the power to designate Indian fiscales, had access to community treasuries, and came to assume considerable secular authority in many pueblos. The alcaldes mayores did not object to the friars' meddling in Indian affairs so long as they were not disruptive and did not interfere with the repartimientos. In fact, priests sometimes served as surrogate lieutenants for the magistrates in remote areas. In the Choapan area in 1653, Indian officials of eleven towns complained of the excessive authority of their long-standing vicar, Fray Juan Noval: "He acts as lieutenant of the alcalde mayor in Choapan, attending the market and making offers as if he were a *regidor* in a town of Spaniards. He checks to see if the scales are correct and levies fines as if he were a judge."[29]

Such broad authority was frequently enforced by the infliction of physical punishment, whipping being the standard form throughout the colonial period. In late colonial times, penalties of six to sixteen lashes were administered to male offenders by the fiscales or church topiles for such infractions as (1) failing to attend mass, rosary recitations, or doctrina classes; (2) drunkenness; (3) wife beating; (4) disrespect of one's parents; and (5) disrespect of the curate.[30] The early pretenses made about priestly benevolence had largely vanished by the 1780s, exemplified by the matter-of-fact comment of one curate that he saw no alternative to whipping, for instilling fear in the Indians was the only way to get their respect.[31] Once the political conquest was completed in the 1550s, the priests' involvement in the internal affairs of many communities made them the most frequent Spanish participants in the controlled violence that was so much a part of colonial life. Whipping not infrequently got out of hand, and Indian men, even pueblo officials, sometimes died from the lashes they received. A pregnant woman lost her baby after being whipped in the Dominican monastery in Villa Alta. Torture in other forms was also employed by the friars in the sixteenth century.[32]

Not until the mideighteenth century were there signs that clerical authority in the region was successfully challenged, and even these involved relatively minor incidents. It had long been the custom for priests to invalidate village elections if they did not like the candidates selected, but in Yae in 1759 the curate's disapproval of the newly elected mayordomos of the Cofradía del Ilustrísimo Sacramento was ultimately ignored. The Zapotecs took their case to court in Mexico City and won a ruling that forbid the priest to interfere.[33] The church was challenged again in 1762 when newly appointed Alcalde Mayor Lorenzo Basco usurped the priests' centuries-old practice of appointing Indian fiscales in the villages.[34] While too much should not be made of this incident, we have already seen that the alcaldes mayores sought to tighten their grip on Indian communities as the commercial possibilities for trade in cochineal and cotton mantles increased in the late eighteenth century. Greater production demands were placed on Indian households, necessitating adjustments in everyday life. Probably fewer families had the time to attend required religious functions and perform all the services desired by the priests. Faced with such situations, it was inevitable that some clergy would clash with the alcaldes mayores and would come to accept a somewhat diminished role in pueblo and district affairs in the late colonial period.

THE CAMPAIGN AGAINST IDOLATRY

The tangible activities of the friars in the sixteenth century were impressive—the congregation of towns, building of churches, organization of parishes, initiation of catechism classes, and the regular administration of the sacraments. Yet as time went on, it became increasingly clear that their ultimate goal of implanting the Christian doctrine was a very elusive one. Religious instruction could be carried out only intermittently in the Sierra and was severely handicapped by lack of personnel and ignorance of Indian languages. The friars were dependent on native interpreters and Indian fiscales and were rarely in a position to notice covert resistance or distortions in the message they sought to deliver. Fewer than 10 percent of the district's 100-plus communities had resident priests, and the inhabitants were accustomed to long periods of relatively unsupervised religious life punctuated several times a year by clerical visits, usually for major fiestas. That indigenous "idolatry," as the Spanish called it, was still going on was never a secret to any reasonably alert missionary or bishop. Driven partially underground during the first strong wave of proselytization of 1558–76, indigenous religious systems continued to function in a truncated fashion. Yet it seems that not until the late seventeenth century did many Spanish civil and ecclesiastical officials become aware of the *extent* of the apostasy of the Indians. Perhaps the Dominicans had been aware of it all along, but other Spaniards were alarmed to discover that idolatry was not confined to an occasional sacrifice of a turkey in the bush or prayers dedicated to a household "idol," but that entire communities routinely held pagan ceremonies throughout the whole district, presided over by the elected cabildo officials and native shamans, or *maestros de idolatría*.

To understand the full historical significance of these religious phenomena, it is necessary to go beyond the common syncretic model, which would posit an essentially indigenous religious system coated with a "veneer" of Catholicism. Nancy Farriss, in her recent study of the Yucatec Mayas, has shown the utility of viewing both Christianity and Mesoamerican religions as complex systems with a variety of levels. In her view, religious change is best studied not as a shift from one religion to another or even from one level to another, but "as a set of horizontal, mutual exchanges across comparable levels."[35] Farriss distinguishes three broad strata: (1) the universal level, concerned with an all-encompassing concept of the divinity, whether single or multiple; (2) the parochial or corporate level, concerned with community patron deities or saints; and (3) the private or "magical" level, which "involves the manipulation of highly discrete and localized supernatural forces for the benefit of the individual and his family."[36] These three levels are roughly comparable to the sociocultural levels of the state, the community, and the family. The two higher ones comprise the public, collective sphere of religious activity and in the Mesoamerican case were the most vulnerable to Spanish missionizing. Indian private worship, usually associated with health and food production, involved domestic ritual and was addressed to somewhat humbler spirits. Farriss notes that Maya private ritual in Yucatan has survived more or less intact, in part because the colonial clergy regarded it more as "superstition" than "idolatry" and developed a fairly tolerant stance toward it. While important differences in native religion and Catholic missionizing distinguished the Sierra Zapoteca from Yucatan, Farriss's general model can fruitfully be applied to the case at hand to elucidate the critical points of transformation in the process of religious syncretism.

As we saw earlier, the pre-Conquest Zapotecs did recognize a supreme being, an infinite and incorporeal being for whom no images were ever made and who never came into direct contact with mortals. Lightning (*cocijo*) and clouds (*zaa*), from which the Zapotecs had descended, were the most powerful supernaturals with which the Zapotecs dealt.[37] Such entities, related as they are to rain, and hence to agriculture, can thus be connected to the immediate concerns of human existence, but as universal forces they were also central to a "transcendental theology addressing itself to the larger question of where we come from, why we are here, and where we are going when we leave."[38] The sources on idolatry in the colonial Sierra Zapoteca are often vague as to the purpose of specific rituals and the supernaturals being worshiped, but confessions and testimony collected from almost all the pueblos in the Villa Alta district in the first decade of the eighteenth century (to be discussed below) make no mention of a supreme deity, lightning, or clouds.[39] Traditionally among the Zapotecs, at least, communication with such powerful forces was done through the priesthood, but in most parts of the Sierra the high priests had disappeared or were greatly weakened by the 1570s. Lower priests may have continued for a time, but surely the secrecy in which they would have had to conduct their activities would have placed limits on their influence. The only known reference to a priestly hierarchy of any sort in the seventeenth century appears in a letter to the crown from the bishop of Oaxaca in 1679 that mentions a "*summo sacerdote o Pontifice*" with four assistants in San Francisco Cajonos.[40] It is entirely possible, however, that the bishop was misinformed and was describing a particularly influential Zapotec shaman.

It thus seems reasonable to posit that the universal component of native religion in the Sierra was much impoverished by 1576. Without a vigorous priestly élite to interpret such abstract concepts, the average peasant was at a loss. The friars, of course, were at the same time trying to impose their own supreme deity and Christian universalism, but with little success. The Zapotecs and other groups were more accustomed to addressing supernatural life forces than "gods" as viewed by Westerners. The Zapotec expression used by sixteenth-century Spaniards to indicate the Christian deity was *Pitào Dios* (*Betao Dios* in the Sierra). But what they failed to understand was that *pitào* did not refer to a specific deity, but rather to the "great breath" or "great spirit," a sacred life force within lightning or a supernatural being.[41] We may conclude that the spiritual conquest of the Sierra Zapotecs, as in other parts of Mesoamerica, greatly eroded the universal level of native religion without establishing any effective Catholic replacement. Farriss's observation for the Yucatec Mayas applies equally well to the present case:

> If the vast majority of colonial Maya found the concept of a distant, all-encompassing god who meted out rewards and punishments in the hereafter meaningless or irrelevant, it was surely as much the fault of the content of the message as of the manner of instruction. The concerns of the Maya peasant, Spanish conquest notwithstanding, were still confined to the welfare of his family and his village, his hunting grounds and beehives, and above all his milpa; and his negotiations were directed to the less awesome beings who were in charge of them. If anything, religious universalism suffered a decline after the conquest.[42]

While the native priesthood and universal religion were much attenuated in the Sierra after the 1570s, worship of indigenous supernaturals continued to thrive at the parochial and private levels. Though the priests were gone, shamans or diviners—the maestros de idolatría—continued to function much as before, basing their prognostications and curing on the ritual 260-day calendar and even coming to assume some of the former priestly roles. The maestros were enlisted by individuals, families, and town officials to perform rites and make predictions on all kinds of occasions that involved high degrees of uncertainty. The shamans controlled the ritual calendar (consisting of twenty "months" of thirteen days each), and through this medium and by divining with *habas* (dried beans) or kernels of corn they designated propitious days for many activities. Indians consulted them upon the birth of a child, for naming a newborn, when selecting a wife, for celebration of a marriage, for curing illness, on the death of a relative, for construction of a new house, for retrieval of lost objects, at planting and harvest time, before going hunting or fishing, and in times of famine and epidemics.[43] Depending on the problem, the shaman usually prescribed some sort of penitence, offering, or sacrifice to community supernaturals. Penitence took the form of fasting, ritual bathing, and sexual abstinence for a specified number of days. Offerings could be of food, blood from one's nose, ears or tongue, or feathers of the macaw bird, purchased especially for this purpose. Sacrifice, the ultimate offering, was of turkeys or cocks and, among the Cajonos pueblos, infant dogs and occasionally a deer. The important element was the offering of the blood of the animal after it had been beheaded, or in the case of the deer, the offering of the heart itself.[44]

Virtually every pueblo in every ethnic zone had at least one shaman; most had between three and ten, depending on the size of the community.

While women were sometimes mentioned, most of the shamans were men. Shamanism was a part-time calling to which some people were drawn, not a designated office, and a town might have many or few such specialists depending on the circumstances. While literacy was advantageous to an aspiring maestro, it was not essential; apparently people of any rank were eligible for the role—macehuales, principales, caciques, and town officers. Most maestros operated with the aid of a small "calendar book" that was handed down to them or purchased in another pueblo. Written in the Roman alphabet, these books contained the names of all the days in the ritual calendar.[45]

Most shamans also ingested hallucinogenic drugs to aid them in predicting the future. The most common was an herb called *cuanabetao* (in Nahuatl, *coaxoxouhqui*), which was ground up and mixed with water. Others included mushrooms, *amuiguia* (identified with the Nahuatl *patlepilzintle*), *noce* or *noee*, and even a kind of beetle.[46] By taking any of these substances, the shaman received visions and was able to impersonate a god or gods. In Cajonos Betaza, for example, a maestro who took cuanabetao might impersonate Guitzanatao, Gogue, Golana, Vixea (a female god), or Guxio.[47] In many pueblos, shamans stated that taking hallucinogens also helped them cure illness.

The objects of devotion of the shamans and the people in general during the seventeenth century remain obscure, but they seem to have been of two types: (1) spirits that inhabited the earth, trees, stones, and certain mountains and (2) spirits of deceased ancestors.[48] Stone images (perhaps of ancestors) were placed in inaccessible sacred spots and in caves on the outskirts of virtually every pueblo, and many families also had small ones in their homes. All of these supernaturals were worshiped for their life-giving qualities—for health, good harvests, and occasionally for rain.

None of these private beliefs and rituals will come as a surprise to anyone acquainted with Oaxaca ethnography, for most of them are part of a general religious complex found throughout the state in both historical and contemporary periods.[49] Bishop Gillow, in his visita to the Sierra Zapoteca in the 1880s, noted that "idolatry" was still strong in the region and that turkeys and dogs were still sacrificed regularly.[50] As late as the 1960s, ritual practices (including sacrifice) in connection with shrines and the ceremonial calendar still existed in Zapotec pueblos in many parts of Oaxaca.[51] Indeed, among the Mixes, a calendar book turned up as late as 1945 and *curanderos* (shamans) continued to take mushrooms for visions to contact supernatural beings and predict the future. Sacrifice remains very important today and in the highland Mixe pueblos is directed at Mount Zempoaltépetl and other mountains, the earth, thunder, lightning, air, and ancestors.[52] The persistence of indigenous private religion is thus well documented and generally parallels the situation in Yucatan, where Farriss notes that "the modern ethnographic literature contains descriptions of many domestic rituals, especially those surrounding childbirth, illness and death, which could have been copied almost verbatim from colonial documents." [53]

But what of native religion at the parochial level? Colonial proselytization may have failed with respect to both universal and private understandings, but at the level of community ritual Christianity was most competitive with indigenous doctrines. The friars introduced Christian forms of public worship as essentially community forms, each carried out collectively by the inhabitants of a pueblo under the guidance of a patron saint that had been assigned to them. Images of other saints, Christ, or the Virgin Mary that came into the possession of particular towns also came to acquire special significance. The Christian God may have been incomprehensible to most Indians, but the saints were more tangible and, most important, could be worshiped as community-specific beings. Farriss believes that Christian ritual had essentially won the battle at the community level in Yucatan following the idolatry trials of the 1560s conducted by Fray Diego de Landa. The Franciscans, shocked to find that many Maya rituals were continuing even in pueblos where Christianity seemed to thrive, launched a determined purge that eventually banished native rites to the milpas and the forest where they continued for the benefit of individuals and families, no longer for whole communities. [54] A comparable process can be discerned in the Sierra Zapoteca of Oaxaca, but with one important difference: the turning point came about 140 years later than in Yucatan.

The earliest surviving record of civil court trials for idolatry in the Villa Alta region dates from the midseventeenth century. The first case, tried in 1665 by Alcalde Mayor Diego de Villegas y Sandoval, was relatively minor: a man from Cajonos Yojovi confessed to sacrificing cocks so that his corn and beans would grow and was given a sentence of one hundred lashes and one year's service in the church of Villa Alta. [55] In 1666 several individuals from Lachirioag and Yatee, including the gobernador of the latter town, were tried for sacrifices held to ensure good harvests. The accused from Lachirioag were released because of insufficient evidence; the gobernador of Yatee was removed from office and given two hundred lashes, his companion one hundred lashes. [56] Such deviations from orthodox Christianity, together with another minor case in 1668 involving a man from Yatzachi El Alto, [57] were dealt with in summary fashion. Though the penalties were characteristically harsh, the cases were apparently regarded as routine occurrences by the alcalde mayor and other Spanish vecinos of Villa Alta. It was not long, however, before the church began to take an active role in the extirpation of idolatry in the Sierra Zapoteca and other parts of Oaxaca, led by Bishop Nicolás del Puerto and his successor Isidro Sariñana y Cuenca.

The focus of attention in the Sierra was the Cajonos Zapotec zone, especially San Francisco Cajonos, which quickly acquired a reputation as one of the most idolatrous pueblos in the Villa Alta district. Whether it deserved its fame is an open question. Bishop Del Puerto jailed an Indian "pope" and four other practitioners from San Francisco in 1679, noting that the former regularly heard confessions from the villagers.[58] The vast majority of the surviving court cases involving idolatry pertain to Cajonos Zapotec pueblos. The Cajonos Zapotecs may have been especially vulnerable since many of their towns—like San Francisco—were located on or near the road between Villa Alta and Antequera, and Spaniards were continually passing by. As we will see shortly, the rest of the Sierra's population was engaged in similar religious practices. At any rate, by the 1680s the alcalde mayor began to remit idolators that came his way to the bishop for punishment.[59] Magistrates in other jurisdictions of Oaxaca were apparently doing the same, for in 1689 Bishop Sariñana y Cuenca noted that idolatry was so common in the bishopric, and the prisoners so many, that a special ecclesiastical jail was needed in Antequera.[60]

In September 1700 an incident in San Francisco Cajonos brought to a head the church's growing concern about idolatry.[61] On September 14, two fiscales of the pueblo, one of them a cacique, alerted the two Dominicans in charge of the parish to a pagan ceremony scheduled to take place that night in a private home. The friars sent two other Spaniards as hidden observers, and at 11:00 P.M. they witnessed a local shaman leading a prayer session with his calendar book. Men, women, and children were in attendance, including the gobernador and two alcaldes. The ceremony was due to conclude with the sacrifice of a turkey and the offering of tamales and macaw feathers, but the proceedings came to a halt when the house was raided by the friars, the two Indian fiscales, and several other Spaniards. The next day the fiscales remained at the Dominican monastery while the friars notified their provincial in Antequera of what had happened. It quickly became apparent that most of the pueblo and its five sujetos were outraged at the betrayal of the fiscales and that there would soon be violence. It came at night on September 15 when an angry mob attacked the monastery, demanding that the two fiscales be relinquished. Fearful for their lives, the Dominicans complied, but only after one Indian was shot and killed by a Spaniard. On September 16, the hapless fiscales were roundly condemned by the pueblo. They were whipped and jailed, then taken to San Pedro Cajonos, where they were whipped again and secretly killed.

Alcalde Mayor Juan Antonio Mier del Tojo immediately ordered an investigation and discovered that virtually all the Cajonos pueblos were in sympathy with the killing of the two traitors. Betaza even sent messengers as far afield as Latani, Yahuive, and Comaltepec in Bixanos country to alert the people to what had happened and seek their support in resisting Spanish attempts to quash all indigenous religious ritual. In Villa Alta, thirty-four Cajonos Zapotecs were jailed, including the gobernador and all the alcaldes of San Francisco and its sujetos. Legal proceedings dragged on until January 7, 1702, when the alcalde mayor finally pronounced sentence: fifteen prisoners were condemned to death without right of appeal, seventeen others were given suspended death sentences with the right of appeal to the Real Sala del Crimen in Mexico City, and two received only lashes. The death sentence of the first fifteen was carried out on January 11, 1702, in a most grisly manner, calculated to have maximum symbolic effect and instill fear in the Indians. The prisoners were beheaded in the Villa Alta jail, and their heads were taken to San Francisco Cajonos, where they were displayed on stakes in the center of town. The bodies were quartered and the resulting sixty pieces of flesh were displayed prominently in trees lining the section of the road from Villa Alta to Antequera that passed through San Francisco, San Pedro, and San Miguel Cajonos. The fate of the other seventeen is unknown, though Bishop Gillow guessed that they were spared from execution.

The entire episode amounted to an epic tragedy. Over 180 years later, private native rituals were still being held in the Cajonos pueblos, but the fiscales were by then widely recognized as the "Venerable Martyrs of Cajonos," their defense of the religion commemorated in San Francisco by a few paintings and two crosses with miraculous curing powers.[62] Bishop Gillow proposed in 1889 that the martyrs be canonized by the church, reasoning that such an official act would help promote Catholicism and discourage idolatry.

The Cajonos incident occurred at a time when the office of bishop in Oaxaca was temporarily vacant. It was filled with the appointment of Fray Angel Maldonado on July 10, 1702, just six months after the execution of the Zapotec prisoners in Villa Alta. Bishop Maldonado launched a pastoral visita of the bishopric almost immediately after his arrival in Oaxaca, beginning, for obvious reasons, at San Francisco Cajonos.[63] He seems to have gone to the Sierra with two objectives in mind. One was to investigate at first hand the nature and extent of indigenous religious practices in one of Oaxaca's most idolatrous regions. The other objective was related to what the bishop saw as a partial solution to the problem—the secularization of the understaffed Dominican doctrinas in the Sierra Zapoteca and elsewhere. The bishop's strategy was successful, at least in the Villa Alta district.

The inquiry into idolatry in the Sierra begun by Bishop Maldonado in 1702 produced a large quantity of extraordinary documentation on native religious practices in Zapotec and Mixe villages.[64] Fear aroused by the executions of the Cajonos prisoners was still running high in the pueblos, and the bishop was able to gather detailed confessions from officials and shamans in fifty towns during his visita. Two years later, perhaps when he had decided in earnest to go after the Dominicans, Maldonado sent to Villa Alta Lic. Joseph de Aragón y Alcántara, curate of Ejutla, and appointed him comisario del Santo Oficio and juez visitador general. During November and December 1704 and January 1705, Aragón y Alcántara collected verbal and written confessions from the rest of the villages in the Villa Alta district, with the notable exception of the Chinantec communities. All details were duly recorded and the Indians absolved of their sins. During the process, ninety-nine of the calendar books used by Zapotec diviners were confiscated and ultimately sent to Spain along with the written proceedings. The bishop also received the enthusiastic cooperation of Diego de Rivera y Cotes, alcalde mayor in Villa Alta from 1703 to 1708.

Even though most of them were prepared according to a common formula, the confessions left no doubt that idolatry was still widespread in all the pueblos of the district. Rituals and sacrifices were not limited to private affairs in homes and milpas, but frequently involved entire community populations in public (though secret) ceremonies. The news that every village held several community sacrifices each year was especially galling to the bishop, for it meant that Catholic rituals had not replaced indigenous ones at all, but had simply been added to the repertoire.

Details of these communal events show surprisingly little variation from pueblo to pueblo, with little difference between the Zapotec and Mixe versions. Most villages held two to four ceremonies a year, though in Betaza the annual number was said to be between eight and thirteen.[65] The purpose of the rites was to draw the entire pueblo together to ask for prosperity, good health, and good harvests. Interestingly, the occasions chosen are of both pre- and post-Conquest derivation, and many sacrifices coincided with important Catholic fiestas or state-mandated civic occasions. Many towns held communal sacrifices on New Year's Day when the newly elected cabildo officials took office. Two pueblos scheduled native rites at Easter, and twelve held similar ceremonies during the fiesta for the Virgin of Rosario in October or on All Saints' Day in November. Most popular of all were pagan ceremonies held in conjunction with Catholic patron saint fiestas, at the time of planting in February or May and at harvest time.[66]

The task of organizing the rituals fell to the village alcaldes, and the number held in a given town depended on the energy and initiative of its elected officials. The events were financed by contributions of one or two reales, collected by the regidores from all households. Attendance at the rites was mandatory and there is no doubt about their importance for maintaining pueblo identity and a sense of cultural integrity, as the death of the martyrs of Cajonos so dramatically illustrated. The same symbolism was evident in Tabaa in 1703, shortly after Bishop Maldonado's visit. Some people, including a few shamans, were reluctant to attend the communal sacrifices for fear of being discovered, but the alcaldes and regidores insisted on holding them and sometimes whipped men who failed to attend.[67] Communal rites were always held in secluded sacred places outside populated areas, though in many pueblos it was customary to first light candles in the church. In some, all men, women, and children participated; in others, men attended the pagan rites while the women took candles to the church.[68]

Worshipers prepared themselves for the ceremonies several days in advance by fasting, abstaining from sexual relations, and taking ritual baths at dawn. Some also confessed with the maestros. The rituals themselves were conducted by two or three shamans and involved the sacrifice of a few turkeys, cocks, puppies, a deer, or some combination of the same. The blood was sprinkled on the stone idols being propitiated and also on an offering of macaw feathers, imported from Guatemala. All participants were required to bring small bags of *pisiete*, a wild tobacco mixed with a bit of lime, which they sprinkled on the feathers. Sacrificial blood was also sprinkled on small tortillas that the shaman blessed and then consumed after the ceremony (the resemblance here to the Catholic mass is striking). Prayers were said, and in at least one community (Betaza) a maestro took a feather from an image of the Virgin in the church and tied it on his head while praying to the Zapotec gods. The ceremony concluded with a ritual meal—sometimes a true feast—in which the sacrificed animals were eaten and pulque was consumed. The feasts might include the entire population, but sometimes only the maestros, cabildo officials, and principales were allowed to partake.[69]

The bishop and alcalde mayor, both recently arrived in Oaxaca, were alarmed that all of this had been taking place in such elaborate fashion for so long. Especially distressing to them was the testimony of two elderly men from Betaza who said that they and many others in the pueblo had forgotten the Christian doctrine, even though their priest visited them seven times a year.[70] On December 23, 1704, Alcalde Mayor Rivera y Cotes had all the confiscated idols and other religious paraphernalia from the Cajonos pueblos brought to the plaza in Villa Alta and burned. He and Bishop Maldonado jointly recommended to the viceroy that three measures be taken: (1) that all pueblos in the district be congregated in settlements of at least four hundred casados each, (2) that a Spanish teacher be placed in every town, and (3) that the alcalde mayor be permitted to place lieutenants in any town where he deemed necessary. They also argued that the Indians should be forced to plant more community milpas to augment their impoverished *bienes de comunidad*, or community treasury. The viceroy approved the plan in 1706, much to the consternation of the Indians, who had offered the alcalde mayor considerable sums of money (one town as much as five thousand pesos) if he would abandon his plans for congregation. Yet it appears that very little came of these measures. There is no evidence that any congregaciones were ever carried out, and the program was most likely abandoned. Spanish teachers were indeed installed in some pueblos, though they seem to have had little impact other than to increase the already high degree of dissension.[71]

We have seen that these traumatic years of the early eighteenth century did not put an end to indigenous religious worship, nor did they extinguish the sacrificial complex, which continues today. Various references to persistent idolatry continued to surface during the eighteenth century.[72] Nonetheless, the years 1700–6 were an important watershed, for henceforth idolatry came to play a lesser role in community life. The pure shock value of

the Cajonos incident and Bishop Maldonado's visita cannot be entirely dis-
counted. A revealing incident occurred in Betaza after the bishop's visit. As
in many other pueblos, the cabildo frequently had shamans take hallucinogens in times of uncertainty to foresee future developments that would
affect the welfare of the people. In this instance, the officials were concerned
about their ability to carry on with the traditional communal ceremonies in
the face of increased Spanish surveillance. An alcalde gave this account of
how the shaman described his vision: "[the gods] told him that the people
were now in the hands of God the Father, that the Christian doctrine and the
Spaniards would come and take over ancestors, which were our idols, and
that the first to go would be *Gogue yaachila*, and that they would take it and
burn it in the plaza of Villa Alta."[73]

This was a self-fulfilling prophecy in many ways, for in succeeding decades many pueblos of the Sierra Zapoteca came to abandon their communal
pagan ceremonies. Where the rituals continued, they were less important,
and the practice of ancestor worship seems to have declined as well. No
mention of either exists after 1735,[74] and we may conveniently take this date
as marking the ascendance of Catholic over pagan ritual at the community
level. From this time forward, indigenous religious elements would be of
central importance only at the private level. The most important trend during the remainder of the eighteenth century was not the persistence of parallel pagan beliefs—though this occurred, to an extent—but the final flowering of the community cult of the saints and the emergence of *cofradías*
(religious brotherhoods) as an important element in village life. This was
not a replacement of indigenous religion with Christianity, but rather the
full development of a new syncretic form of community worship that had
been in the making for some time. It is tempting to speculate that indigenous ancestors and community saints had finally become fused into a single
set of tutelary community gods, though we have no direct evidence. In any
case, to use Farriss's terms, this change was the culmination of "a gradual
shift in emphasis from the old, risky, and increasingly dysfunctional (because necessarily secret) idolatry, which itself was becoming infused with
Christian elements, to the less obviously syncretic worship of saint-deities in
the churches."[75] While the case of the Sierra Zapoteca is not unique, the fact
that this shift took so long and came so much later than in central Mexico
and Yucatan testifies to the regional, discontinuous nature of the process of
religious syncretism in Mesoamerica.

THE CULT OF THE SAINTS

By the second half of the eighteenth century idolatry had faded into the
background and public ritual in the Sierra focused almost exclusively on
outwardly Christian form. Complaints from curates and bishops about Indian customs in this period rarely mentioned idolatry, concentrating instead

on what they regarded as excessive expenditures and licentious behavior connected with Catholic celebrations.[76] From the clerical point of view, the main problem was no longer how to bring Catholicism to the Indians, but rather how to control aspects of syncretized Catholic worship that they felt had gotten out of hand. It is clear that fiestas had become quite popular with the Indians, and, as elsewhere in Mesoamerica, community patron saints were especially important objects of devotion. But fiestas for the saints had become much more than religious occasions; they were also celebrations of community identity, power, and prestige vis-à-vis other communities. This trend became manifest as early as 1691 in the Rincón when Yagavila, a cabecera with a resident priest, complained to the bishop and the viceroy that the fiestas for Holy Week, Corpus Christi, Purificación, and Ramos were being celebrated in other towns in the parish rather than in Yagavila. This was seen as a slight to the hegemony of the head town of the parish.[77] As time went on and affection for the saints (perhaps syncretized with indigenous community ancestors) increased, Catholic fiestas gradually came to express a collective community identity in much the same way as the pagan ceremonies had before 1735.

Up until the mideighteenth century, most pueblos in the district celebrated seven or eight fiestas a year (not including smaller barrio feast days), with priests always in attendance for at least part of the proceedings. The three most important were Holy Week, Corpus Christi, and the festivities for patron saints; other popular fiestas were for Purificación, Espíritu Santo, Rosario, and Natividad. This was in the main standard church policy in the district and perhaps in the bishopric as a whole. The secularization of the Dominican doctrinas around 1706 may have served as a catalyst for more elaborate and more frequent fiestas, as many secular priests were well known to be more concerned with their finances than with preaching. Unscrupulous curates occasionally upped the number of fiestas to the point that the Indians lost their enthusiasm and came to view them as a burden. This happened in 1763 in the Chinantec cabecera Teotalcingo and its seven sujetos, where the people were being forced against their will to celebrate nineteen fiestas a year. The cost to the parishioners was considerable; the village of Petlapa, with only sixty-five casados, calculated that each year it paid the curate 104 pesos plus 107 cotton mantles in fiesta-related fees alone.[78] Priestly excesses on such a grand scale were not typical, however, and after 1749 were expressly prohibited by viceregal policy. Henceforth, curates in the Villa Alta district were instructed by the bishop that the only required fiestas were for patron saints and those sponsored by formally erected cofradías. The rest were voluntary.[79] This policy did not completely curb exploitation by overly zealous priests, but the Teotalcingo case shows that even the isolated Chinantecs were sufficiently informed to lodge a protest when this policy was contravened.

The role of cofradías in fiesta sponsorship is only sparsely documented for the Sierra Zapoteca, but the available information indicates that the brother-hoods in this region were primarily a late colonial phenomenon. As William Taylor and I have shown, most cofradías in Oaxaca generally were founded in the eighteenth century after the secularization of the Dominican parishes. Organized to support the cults of particular saints and pay for their ex-penses, Oaxaca cofradías were small, rarely self-supporting, and narrowly religious in origin and function. Their properties, if they had any, and their records were managed by the parish priests.[80] Cofradías in the Villa Alta district seem to have been founded, or at least became important, between 1743 and 1778. In 1743 Alcalde Mayor Juan Francisco de Puertas made routine visits to all the pueblos of his jurisdiction and offered the general observation that most communities had no *bienes de comunidad* because they used their only resource—corn grown on communal land—entirely for vil-lage fiestas.[81] If cofradías existed at that time, they must have played only a minor role in fiesta financing, for the magistrate did not mention them.[82] Records of the visita of Bishop Ortigoza in 1778–84, on the other hand, leave no doubt about the central role of cofradías in village fiestas by that time.[83] The bishop found large numbers of cofradías and *hermandades* (the difference between them, if any, is not clear) throughout the entire district. Some towns had only one or two, but most had several. At the top of the scale was the parish of Choapan, with five cofradías and twenty-six herman-dades; the Mixe parish of Quetzaltepec had fourteen hermandades.

Few, if any, of these sodalities had been formally erected in the church. Much to the bishop's dismay, he found that most of their expenditures were for fireworks, food, drink, and dances at fiestas; many of them were in the business of loaning money to villagers at interest rates of 25 percent or more (in Mixe Tlahuitoltepec, the curate noted that "most of the principales are firmly in the power of the mayordomos") and that many others were insol-vent and deeply in debt. Some cofradías had debts of several hundred pesos, while others were solvent. Two in the Cajonos pueblo of Yae and two her-mandades in Yovego each had assets of slightly over two hundred pesos. The many brotherhoods in Choapan had an average net worth of 130 pesos each. Most of these funds came from the sodalities' money lending and from their own cornfields, which the parish priest of Villa Alta said were often better tended than the members' private ones. If we assume the minimum cost of a village fiesta in the 1770s to be fifteen pesos,[84] it is clear that many cofradías possessed both the funds and the enthusiasm to celebrate the saints in style. Not to be outdone, those that lacked the requisite funds took up collections from their members or relied on personal contributions from their officers, the mayordomos.

To Bishop Ortigoza's way of thinking, the sumptuous fiestas sponsored by these brotherhoods were little more than drunken parties that the impover-ished Indians could ill afford. (Most of the curates shared this view, but since they derived part of their income from such occasions they were not

about to take the lead in suspending them.) He abolished many of the cofradías on the spot (probably those that were in debt), and ordered the curates
not to allow the rest to spend any funds on fireworks, food, or liquor. Still
others he attempted to consolidate, as in the case of the thirty-one sodalities
in Choapan. The parish priest was given two years to confiscate all their
funds and use them to found one general cofradía that would serve the entire
parish. While the bishop was manifestly upset with the direction the Indian
cofradías had taken, he also recognized how important they were in stimu-
lating the people's interest and in financing the church: "I must confess that
the cofradías have brought a thousand disorders, excesses, and some expenses for the Indians. But all of this is a necessary evil that the zeal and
vigilance of the bishops and priests, aided by the Royal Jurisdiction, can
remedy in part."[85]

Closely related to cofradías were the *barrios,* which like the brotherhoods
appear to be of post-Conquest origin. Ethnographers have noted the absence
of Mixe or Zapotec terms for barrios, which are invariably named for
Catholic saints, as they were in colonial times. With the exception of Yalalag
and a few other Cajonos communities, modern barrios in the Sierra are not
residential units. Where they exist, their function is primarily religious:
each barrio has a patron saint and a mayordomo in charge of organizing and
financing the saint's fiesta, often taking up a collection from the members.
Barrios may also own land and use the products to pay for fiestas. In Nexitzo
Talea, the religious function of the barrios has receded somewhat, and
Nader stresses their role as "savings and loan associations" that lend money
to their members, using the interest earned for their patron saint fiestas.[86]

While Nader suggests that the barrios of Talea are of recent origin and
grew up to replace financing of fiestas by individuals, the historical evidence
indicates otherwise. Named barrios were quite common in the colonial period, some towns having just two and others as many as six. The descriptions of their functions are virtually indistinguishable from accounts of the
cofradías. Each barrio had its mayordomo who organized the patron's annual fiesta. Like the cofradías, barrios also owned property and lent money.
In the late eighteenth and early nineteenth centuries, barrios and cofradías
seem to have been virtually synonymous, though one document refers to a
barrio of San Juan in San Mateo Cajonos that contained more than one cofradía. Barrios were clearly older in the Sierra, the first mention of them
coming from Betaza in 1703, several decades before the appearance of cofradías. Perhaps barrios were introduced by the Dominicans as a means of
organizing worship of the saints, then were reshaped into cofradías by the
secular clergy in the second half of the eighteenth century.[87]

Shortly after Bishop Ortigoza's visita of 1778–84, an important shift began in methods of fiesta financing that affected barrios and cofradías alike.
Until the close of the 1780s, they were able to pay for their fiestas with proceeds from property, interest earnings, contributions from members, and

occasional donations from the community milpas of their pueblos.[88] In some towns, such as Yatee, this system apparently survived into the early years of the nineteenth century.[89] Others, however, encountered problems that seem to have begun with the arrival of Villa Alta's first subdelegado, Pablo de Ortega (1790–96). In 1808, a mayordomo of Lachirioag complained of having to finance a village fiesta out of his own pocket. Before 1790, he stated, mayordomos took up collections for each fiesta and could also count on the fruits of the community milpa. However, Subdelegado Ortega had outlawed these methods of fiesta financing and since then mayordomos had had to spend their own money. This particular individual was in trouble with the town's principales because he could not afford to provide them with the customary meal for the fiesta of Trinidad.[90] Mayordomos of Solaga and Roayaga found themselves in similar positions in 1832. By that time the practice of individual sponsorship by mayordomos had become more entrenched, though many people regarded it as unjust. In Roayaga, a group of fifty people actually seceded from the barrio Dulce Nombre de Jesús in a dispute over individual sponsorship. They founded a new barrio, Trinidad, and in 1832 were attempting to institute a system in which all members contributed equally, despite pressures from town officials who preferred that mayordomos assume the responsibility.[91] Similar changes were probably occurring in other pueblos in the district at the close of the colonial period, and the principal cause seems to have been pressure from the subdelegados, who replaced the old alcaldes mayores with the introduction of the new intendancy system. Much like Bishop Ortigoza a few years before, these magistrates attempted to limit the amount of surplus the Indians spent on their fiestas, reasoning that forcing individuals to pay the bills themselves would lead to more moderation. Whether or not this can be called a policy at some level is far from clear, but as Taylor and I have shown, the shift from group to individual sponsorship was occurring throughout Oaxaca at this time.[92]

Conspicuously lacking in all these social mechanisms for celebrating the saints is any formal connection between community civil and religious offices. As we saw in chapter 5, most towns had well-developed hierarchies of civil cargos, but religious offices were not included. Cofradía and barrio offices existed parallel to the political ones, and it was not until the very end of the colonial period that increasing reliance on rotating sponsorship of fiestas by all community households may have brought the civil and religious posts together in a single system.[93]

CONCLUSION

Though many aspects of religious worship in the colonial Sierra Zapoteca remain to be clarified, a rough sketch of the major syncretic developments and their timing has been presented. An early period of persistence of native religion more or less intact came to a close by 1576, Fray Pedro Guerrero's last year as Dominican vicar in Villa Alta. By this time, the Indian priesthood had all but vanished (at least at the upper levels), leaving the shamans to carry on as the principal indigenous religious specialists in most villages. Catholicism had begun to make itself felt, but the Dominicans of this period had their greatest impact not in the religious sphere, but in the areas of settlement and sociopolitical organization. Indigenous religious universalism was effectively stifled for all but perhaps an enlightened few, not to be replaced with any viable Christian variety.

The second era, from 1576 to 1700, can be called the period of idolatry, as both Catholic and pagan rituals coexisted—and to some extent competed—at the parochial level. Whether consciously or not, the Dominicans presided over a process of intermingling religious elements in both directions. Once the last major round of congregaciones was completed in the early years of the seventeenth century, the pressures of conversion appear to have been lighter. The result was the beginning of a syncretic "Catholic" cult of the saints, tempered by community pagan rituals that had absorbed some Christian elements and were often held on the same days as the church ceremonies. Identification with the saints was increasing, but community identity still revolved fundamentally around the worship of local spirits and ancestors, as the uprising at San Francisco Cajonos made clear.

The Cajonos incident of 1700 marked the end of an era and ushered in the third period of syncretism, which lasted until about 1790. The death of the two martyrs ultimately hastened the departure of the Dominicans from the district and their replacement with secular clergy who were less tolerant of the lingering forms of indigenous worship. The campaign against idolatry in the late seventeenth and early eighteenth centuries and continued pressures thereafter greatly diminished—and in many pueblos, probably extinguished—the role of communal pagan rituals and the village shamans. Faced with staunch opposition from the clergy, the Indian "underground" religion atrophied. As idolatry faded, the saints became more important in community life and an increasingly syncretized form of Catholicism became dominant with the founding of the cofradías in the second half of the eighteenth century. A telling comment on the course that syncretism had taken was made inadvertently by Bishop Ortigoza during a visit to the Mixe pueblo of Quetzaltepec in 1782. In this town, as in others in the Chinantec zone, native dances that had once been held in conjunction with pagan ceremonies were now a part of fiestas for the saints. The same brightly colored macaw feathers were still being used, but now they had found a place in public, "Catholic" rituals to complement their role in indigenous blood offerings.[94] This is but one symbol of the triumph of a modified Catholicism at the parochial level. While this shift put an end to the most obvious forms of indigenous worship, propitiation of local spirits continued with the help of the shamans at the private level.

The beginning of a fourth syncretic period can be discerned about 1790, when the Bourbon-inspired intendancy system began to take hold in the Villa Alta district. This era continued well into the nineteenth century, which lies beyond the scope of this book. I would hypothesize, however, that it was characterized by civil administrative attempts to suppress fiesta expenditures, and later on by the banning of most forms of communal and cofradía property. As the colonial period came to a close, sponsorship of village fiestas increasingly rested on the shoulders of individual mayordomos. Assuming that this trend intensified during the nineteenth century, pressure would have mounted for all households in these small communities to take their turn at sponsorship. The result, it would appear, was the emergence of the civil-religious hierarchy in its classic form in which cofradía offices became integrated with civil ones to form a unified ladder of prestige and community service.[95]

In conclusion, it is worth noting that the general trajectory of religious syncretism in the Sierra Zapoteca differs in important respects from those recently advanced for other regions of Mesoamerica. The nature and timing of the stages is very different from the account of colonial Tlaxcala given by Hugo Nutini and Betty Bell.[96] They define a three-stage syncretic process that reached completion in the midseventeenth century when Catholic religious ideology was successfully internalized. For Aztec central Mexico, William Madsen, following Jiménez Moreno, believes that syncretism had eliminated most vestiges of paganism by about 1555.[97] In the Sierra Zapoteca, on the other hand, Catholic and indigenous religion, both of them modified by the other, persisted as dual, compartmentalized traditions as late as the early eighteenth century. It is noteworthy that the Sierra produced no equivalents of the Virgin of Guadalupe in the Valley of Mexico or Tlaxcala's Virgin of Ocotlán, both of which served as powerful symbols of a new, syncretized Catholic ideology.

In its outward form, the syncretic process in the Sierra more closely resembled the experience of the Yucatec Maya as described by Nancy Farriss.[98] In both regions, Catholic forms eventually took over public ritual in the towns, leaving a diminished but important residue of local spirits and ritual at the private level. This has led to a twentieth-century system in which pagan and Christian cults function on different levels and worship two sets of deities. Indigenous spirits are never confused with the saints, and the two forms of worship are regarded as two complementary ways of dealing with the supernatural.[99]

Yet we have seen that the timing of syncretism in Yucatan and the Sierra Zapoteca was substantially different. According to Farriss, the Maya gave up their pagan community rituals before 1600, while in the Sierra Zapoteca they continued as an important focus of community identity over a century longer. Such marked regional differences challenge us to seek better explanations of the processes involved. Contrasting Yucatan with central Mexico,

William Madsen notes that the relative isolation and decentralization of the Mayas, the hostile interpersonal relations they had with early Spaniards, and the snail's pace of the conquest in the peninsula all help explain the persistence of aspects of Maya religion.[100] These same factors also help explain the differences between central Mexico and the Sierra Zapoteca, but we are still left with accounting for the big gap in chronology between the Sierra and Yucatan. The small numbers of friars and sheer difficulty of access of many Sierra communities were two important factors, and a third was the linguistic barrier. All but the most dedicated friars lacked incentives for learning local varieties of Zapotec, Mixe, or Chinantec, long after Nahuatl and Yucatec Maya had become lingua francas in their respective regions. It is also quite possible that the nature of the indigenous religions themselves and the missionary tactics of the different mendicant orders and the secular clergy influenced the course of syncretism. Certainly the Dominicans' failure to understand Zapotec ancestor worship was a major factor in Oaxaca. In any case, the Sierra Zapoteca stands out as a region in which indigenous beliefs and practices persisted in some form long after they had disappeared or combined with Catholic forms in other parts of Mesoamerica.

CHAPTER 7

CONCLUSION

THE PRECEDING CHAPTERS have dealt with a region of colonial Mexico that had a large Indian population but a tiny and impoverished group of Spanish colonists, virtually no haciendas, little mining activity of consequence during most of its colonial history, and one of the most inaccessible geographical settings in southern Mesoamerica. Nor were the pre-Hispanic Indian societies of the district as developed as those that have commanded most of the attention of anthropologists and historians. Quite clearly, the Sierra Zapoteca of Villa Alta was a peripheral area of New Spain. But like other peripheral parts of the colonial world, it provided large quantities of raw materials and cheap labor without which the core regions never would have developed.

A long line of urban merchants and alcaldes mayores succeeded in converting the Sierra's isolation and rusticity into a commercial bonanza in which large profits from textiles and cochineal were monopolized by a very few for over a century and a half. This basic contradiction—profits for the few among poverty and exploitation for the many—was of course central to the entire colonial enterprise in New Spain, but it was especially sharp in the Villa Alta district. Economic monopolies encompassing only a few individuals at a time played a major role in reshaping the internal structure of the Indian communities and also set the terms for their articulation with the outside world. Spaniards in the district had no interest in acquiring land, and once the dislocations of the sixteenth century had begun to fade, most colonial adventurers in the Sierra—for that is what they were—recognized that it was to their advantage to keep the corporate, landholding Indian communities intact. In this, the native inhabitants of the district were only too happy to cooperate. The battle they faced in the seventeenth and eighteenth centuries had less to do with retaining their territorial and political integrity than with preserving their traditional forms of community organization, which inevitably came into conflict with the conscious and unconscious designs of colonial civil and ecclesiastic officials. This led to a paradox: marked continuities in the some areas of Indian social life, particularly in family life and subsistence activities, and important changes in others, especially in social stratification, political organization, and communal forms of religious worship.

176

It is difficult to sum up the trajectory of change over a 300-year period for a district as ethnically diverse and ecologically variegated as Villa Alta. Furthermore, the information is most complete for the Zapotec groups and frequently lacking for the Mixes and Chinantecs. With this proviso, the data available do show certain trends. The sixteenth century was especially traumatic for the peoples of the Sierra, who were not accustomed to the domination of powerful lords from within and without as were the inhabitants of many other parts of Oaxaca. The Spaniards' prolonged and bloody attempts at conquest in the first half of the century wreaked havoc on the native nobility and alienated the rest of the indigenous population. A modicum of stabilization arrived at midcentury, due largely to the proselytizing efforts of the Dominicans, but it was continually threatened by continuing population decline, the trauma of the congregaciones, and further serious erosion in the authority of the native nobility.

The seventeenth century, by contrast, was a time of adjustment, accommodation, and colonial consolidation. The repartimientos de efectos of the alcaldes mayores became well entrenched during the period, even though they would not reach their peak volume until much later. In the Indian communities, the caciques generally lost out to the growing influence of the gobernadores and the cabildos (except perhaps among the Mixes). Spaniard and Indian learned to adjust to each other in the interest of mutual survival, but their societies and cultures remained separate and polarized. The processes of acculturation and syncretism had begun but had yet to bear fruit in overtly new institutions. The seventeenth century can be called a period of estrangement, a condition most evident in the lack of a market system in the district before 1700 and the marked compartmentalization of Catholic and indigenous religious rituals in Indian communities.

The eighteenth century, particularly the decades of the 1730s and 1740s, ushered in a new era when a number of long-term processes culminated in a significant restructuring of society in the Sierra Zapoteca. Indian society experienced a number of changes, at once demographic, economic, social, political, and religious. At the same time, a type of social and cultural integration took place between Indians and Spaniards, most evident in the economic, political, and religious spheres. Acculturation reached a new stage in the eighteenth century, and while Indian and Spaniard were in most respects still worlds apart, they came to depend on each other in new and different ways, establishing for the first time a kind of symbiosis.

The demographic recovery of the Indian population laid the foundation for the new late colonial society. Though still well below pre-Conquest levels, the population was on the rebound by the early eighteenth century. During the latter half of the colonial period the greatest gains were in the highland area. Despite the presence of more people, the number of settlements did not change appreciably and new ways had to be devised—or old ones revived—to accommodate the larger numbers in village social structures.

One response to population growth was the appearance of a regional Indian market system in the first decade of the eighteenth century. While Spanish officials were involved to some extent in the founding of new marketplaces, only the *plazas* in Villa Alta, Choapan, and Zoochila were regularly attended by Spaniards; the remainder were almost exclusively Indian. The market system was also a reaction to increasing economic specialization in the region, stimulated by the increasingly heavy demands of the cochineal and textile repartimientos of the alcaldes mayores. Population growth made possible ever larger and more demanding repartimientos, which in turn diverted some labor from subsistence activities and pumped more cash into the economy. Indians who previously had had little use for a system of local markets now began to depend on it to meet many of their daily needs.

Another fundamental change in the eighteenth century occurred in the area of religious worship, with the triumph of pagan-Catholic syncretism at the parochial or community level. While the clergy lost some of its power to the Spanish magistrates in the late eighteenth century, forces already set in motion much earlier finally came into their own. The campaign against idolatry, particularly in the aftermath of the Cajonos rebellion, greatly reduced the incidence of communal pagan rituals and other community forms of indigenous worship, at least in the Zapotec portions of the district. They were replaced with the Catholic saints, and a new localized and syncretized form of religion at the community level flowered in the latter half of the eighteenth century with the establishment of numerous cofradías throughout the district.

The later colonial period also brought with it a fundamental shift in the social and political organization of Indian communities. This was most evident in the Zapotec villages, above all in the Rincón. After 1730 a "new nobility" arose, in good measure on the coattails of the Spanish magistrates in Villa Alta. The villagers had a problem: the traditional hereditary nobility with pre-Hispanic roots was now either moribund or gone entirely, and the only available replacements were individuals and their descendants who had distinguished themselves in the higher municipal offices. The Spanish colonial regime had thrown the indigenous stratification system into disarray, first by destroying the cacique lineages in the sixteenth and seventeenth centuries, then by continuing to recognize a privileged noble group based on the mutually inconsistent principles of heredity and achievement. Another problem was the small size of the villages themselves. Even with the population growth in the highlands, there were still not enough adult males to adequately staff all the municipal offices and also permit exemptions for those of noble status. The result was a high degree of internal conflict in many communities that only the alcaldes mayores in Villa Alta were in a position to mediate.

At the same time, the magistrates themselves had a problem: as the volume of their repartimientos increased, the alcaldes mayores became ever more dependent on the Indian officials who helped administer them in their respective communities. It would have been bad for business to deny confirmation of noble status to the long line of plaintiffs who arrived in Villa Alta. The outcome was an ever-expanding status group of Indian principales who in a number of villages came to outnumber the macehuales. In the end, the magistrates' attempts to placate the Indians in their status aspirations and avoid conflict simply served to perpetuate that conflict.

It was thus through the trading activities and legal decisions of the alcaldes mayores that Spaniards and Indians (at least the Zapotecs) came to depend on each other in symbiotic fashion in the eighteenth century. The priests, of course, were not without their influence but were much less needed; by the late colonial period many aspects of village spiritual life could and did function quite well in their absence. The clergy, especially the Dominicans, had been dominant in the first half of the colonial period, but the second half clearly belonged to the alcaldes mayores. It was no accident that the restructuring of indigenous status groups and the increase in power and commercial monopolies of the magistrates coincided with Oaxaca's boom years between 1740 and 1790. Expanding internal demand for low-cost textiles and the growing international market for cochineal had a major impact on the activities of the magistrates and, through them, on the social, political, and economic structures of the Indian communities of the district.

Late colonial peasant society in the Sierra Zapoteca thus exemplified two contradictory tendencies recently identified by Eric Van Young:

> one of increasing internal social differentiation, strongly encouraged if not wholly initiated by the Spanish conquest, and probably gaining momentum in the late colonial period; and a second of the continuing survival and vigor of the corporate, landholding Indian peasant villages during the same time. The apparent contradiction consists in the fact, well established by anthropologists studying both contemporary and historical peasant communities, that the cosmological assumptions and social arrangements characteristic of such communities normally push toward *minimizing* internal social distances in favor of egalitarianism and intragroup solidarity.[1]

While I agree that this contradiction was prevalent throughout much of late colonial Mexico, I would suggest that it took different forms in different regions. In his study of the Guadalajara region in the eighteenth century, Van Young shows how the expansion of a regional, commercial agricultural economy coupled with Indian population growth led to increasing conflict over land between Spaniards and Indians and heightened social and economic differentiation in Indian communities. "The increased economic chafing in individual pueblo communities produced intragroup tensions and a potential for open conflict that ill accorded with the cosmological assumption underlying group identity, or with the functional prerequisites of the village as a corporate landholding entity."[2] Van Young goes on to argue that in the Guadalajara region, Indian villages resolved these tensions by engaging in legal and extralegal conflict over land with neighboring non-Indian landowners, especially the owners of large haciendas.

Van Young's analysis may perhaps be generalized to other areas of colonial Mexico where haciendas competed with Indian villages for land, but it surely does not apply to the Sierra Zapoteca, which had virtually no haciendas or non-Indian landowners. The integrity of Sierra villages as units was never really threatened in late colonial times. Instead, the chief cause of village social differentiation and conflict was the machinations of the alcaldes mayores, especially in the Rincón. In this case the lawsuits that stemmed from this conflict were internal to the communities, and they were resolved by recourse to Spanish authority in Villa Alta. The monopolistic repartimiento system had the effect of limiting the Indians' ability to resolve these tensions, for the officials who exploited them and those empowered to hear legal appeals were one and the same.

The distinctiveness of the Villa Alta district in the late colonial period can be further appreciated by comparing it with the more developed Valley of Oaxaca. One of the most obvious differences was the persistence in the Valley of a number of important cacique lineages from pre-Hispanic times well into the colonial period. Beginning with the Conquest itself, which in the Valley was quick and peaceful, the Spaniards were eager to gain the allegiance of the caciques, who held positions of considerable power in their pre-Hispanic town-states. The nobles responded by rapidly adopting the Spanish life-style, and all those who could afford it moved to the city of Antequera. They were also quick to grasp the importance of written law and had the good sense to obtain legal confirmation of their landholdings before the Spaniards became interested in acquiring land themselves.[3] Valley caciques were integrated rapidly into the colonial economy through silk raising and trade in cattle, sheep, and cochineal. To a significant extent, they used this new European-style wealth and their position as cultural brokers to maintain their status and power in their home villages. Long after the native nobility of regions like Michoacán and the Valley of Mexico, not to mention the Sierra Zapoteca, had gone into decline, the cacique stratum in the Valley of Oaxaca still enjoyed considerable status, wealth, and power. In some cases—notably in Cuilapan and Etla—this pattern continued into the late eighteenth century. This was possible because the caciques acquired an independent economic base in the sixteenth century and held on to their patrimonial lands. Two centuries later some of them could still lay claim to some of the largest landed estates in the Valley.[4] As a consequence, distinct strata of caciques, principales, and macehuales persisted in the Valley well into the nineteenth century.

Up in the Sierra Zapoteca, as we have seen, the picture was quite different. The Spanish conquerors there encountered strong Indian resistance. Pacification of the region was extremely brutal and dragged on for thirty-five years. The Spanish soon realized that the Sierra nobility possessed neither wealth nor much power, and saw little to be gained from recruiting caciques as brokers. Instead, many nobles were summarily hanged or thrown to the dogs and Spanish control did not take hold until the 1550s. In contrast to those of the Valley, few Sierra caciques were able to develop independent economic bases of their own. They did not attempt to gain legal confirmation of their holdings until the second half of the sixteenth century or even later, and ultimately found themselves in competition with the cabildos of their own communities. Further, their lack of appreciation of the Spanish concept of individual private property also put them at a disadvantage. The result was that few Sierra cacique lineages survived the sixteenth century, and the few that did languished for some time before vanishing altogether shortly after 1730. The title of cacique continued, but it was held by newcomers who were never able to convincingly document their claims of descent from pre-Hispanic ruling families. And these newcomers were no wealthier than their predecessors.

I suggest that the striking differences in stratification in Indian society in the Valley and the Sierra had their roots not only in the contrasting nature of the pre-Hispanic societies in the two regions but also in the different modes of integration into the colony's essentially capitalist market system. In the Valley, a number of cacique lineages persisted as a *class*, based on wealth, because they had held on to their land and established an independent economic base. In the Sierra, late colonial families regarded as caciques were largely merged with the *principal* stratum, which greatly expanded in size in the eighteenth century. Socioeconomic differentiation was on the upswing in the Villa Alta district in late colonial times. More cash came into circulation and there was some trading of cochineal and cotton textiles in the Indian marketplaces. Even more important were the opportunities for economic gain open to those who served the higher cabildo posts in their capacity as facilitators of the magistrates' repartimientos de efectos. Nonetheless, it is quite clear that the economic differences between nobles and commoners were neither as sharp nor as significant as they were in the Valley. In the Sierra, the late colonial nobility constituted a relatively impoverished, yet significant *status group*, the membership of which was in a constant state of flux.[5]

We have seen that the Sierra status group of principales persisted in the eighteenth century because the alcaldes mayores needed it to keep their repartimientos running smoothly. Only by working to create and maintain such a buffer group could they continue to utilize the high degree of force and repression their business required. In the Valley, on the other hand, the native nobility had long ceased to act as a buffer group. By late colonial times, their services as cultural brokers were much less in demand because of the Valley's vigorous market system, which served Indian and Spaniard alike and created a web of interdependence between them.[6] Accordingly, the use of physical coercion to achieve economic ends was no longer as necessary or as desirable as it had been in earlier days. In the Sierra, in contrast, economic relations between Indian and Spaniard were governed by the monopolistic system of the repartimiento until the very end of the colonial period, and the use of force was ever present. The most significant form of trade thus bypassed the fledgling Sierra market system altogether, but it was precisely this repartimiento activity that linked the district to colony and world markets and that required a cushion of Indian nobles to operate smoothly.

In his study of colonial Huamanga, Peru, Steve J. Stern distinguishes among three different forms employed by Spaniards to gain access to Indian labor or its products. The first, the "indigenous form," "mobilized native labor on the basis of traditional Andean norms and relationships."[7] But the other two most concern us here:

> A second mode of extraction, the "state form," used the formal legal institutions of the state to mobilize a labor force (the mitas), or gain access to revenues (tributes). This form of exploitation facilitated more direct control of productive processes and labor relationships by colonials, despite dependence upon the state for access to labor. A third path, the "private form," involved extraofficial relations arranged directly between colonials and the Indians they exploited. These more direct relations included long-term servitude such as yanaconaje; wage labor agreements; more ambiguous arrangements, such as asiento contracts, that mixed elements of long-term bondage and free sale of labor-power; and extralegal coercions to serve the personal (extraofficial) interests of state functionaries and their allies. Though not necessarily illegal, nor completely divorced from formal and informal uses of state power, these kinds of extractions reflected the emergence of forces in "civil society." They circumvented the official labor-tribute patrimony of the state, as well as the limits imposed by kuraka mediators who operated within the traditional norms of Andean labor. These arrangements enabled entrepreneurs to assert their most direct control over production and labor.[8]

In their broad outlines, these three types of labor control apply equally well to colonial Mexico. Regarding the Villa Alta district, the preceding chapters have dealt with both the second and third types at some length. Of these, the repartimientos de efectos were by far the most important and had the farthest-reaching consequences for Spanish and Indian society alike. They would appear to fall into Stern's third category, in that their impetus and capitalization lay ultimately with the urban merchants in Oaxaca and Mexico City. The alcaldes mayores, despite their power, were in this sense only brokers. Yet it must be recognized that such a large volume of goods would never have been produced or exchanged without the application of force that only the apparatus of the state could provide. This is why the magistrates were so indispensable to the functioning of the system. Even though their repartimientos were technically illegal, the practice was so well known and so widely tolerated that it had become, in effect, part of the expected duties of office.

For these reasons and others the repartimiento de efectos cannot be regarded as a strictly capitalist institution. It was not based on a mode of production involving "free wage labor," but rather fed off the Indian subsistence economy by imposing a tributary or colonial form of production backed up by political force. Yet the repartimientos constituted the crucial links between the production process, which was noncapitalist, and the colonywide and world markets, which were capitalist. William Roseberry reminds us that "during capitalism's mercantilist phase, the primary mechanism for expansion and consolidation was not through capitalist relations of production but through capitalist relations of exchange. Within the sphere of circulation, the 'system' as a whole was capitalist; within the sphere of production, the 'system' encompassed, in a none too systematic manner, a wide variety of formations."[9] Thus a merchant could be engaged in capitalist accumulation, even though the producers were not in a capitalist mode of production. It is, therefore, evident that the cochineal repartimientos of the seventeenth and eighteenth centuries involved the Sierra Zapoteca in a mercantile capitalist world economy, but a world economy that contained multiple modes of production linked only at the level of exchange.[10]

Comparing once again the Villa Alta district and the Valley of Oaxaca (a comparison that could probably be extended to other areas, notably the Mixtèca Alta), we find in the late colonial period two contrasting modes of articulation or integration with the larger capitalist world system. In the Sierra the crucial link between the production process and the capitalist system of exchange was the alcalde mayor himself, with his monopolistic and coercive tactics. The real financiers may have been the urban merchants, but they had to work through the magistrates because the regional market system in the district was primitive and inadequate to their needs. In the Valley, on the other hand, the important links between Indian peasant production and the capitalist system were more often than not the merchants themselves. In this region the repartimientos of the alcaldes mayores were smaller in volume, less monopolistic, and of less economic import than those in the Sierra. The Valley had a vigorous regional market system dating back to pre-Hispanic times, and merchants based in Antequera and elsewhere were able to exploit it to deal more directly with Indian producers. As I have tried to show, these contrasting modes of articulation—via monopoly and force in the Sierra and via a regional market in the Valley—had far-reaching consequences for Indian society. The continued class-like manifestation of the cacique stratum in the Valley was due to a greater direct involvement in the market economy by the Indians themselves. In the Sierra, on the other hand, the "restratification" of status groups in many communities in the

eighteenth century occurred because of the brokerage functions and monopolies of the Spanish magistrates. Their activities effectively prevented class
differences from arising in Indian communities, but actively maintained instead a fluid noble status group. Thus on the eve of independence, the people
of the Sierra remained enmeshed in a system of coercive colonial relationships reminiscent in many ways of sixteenth-century society in the more developed regions of New Spain.

ALCALDES MAYORES AND SUBDELEGADOS OF VILLA ALTA, OAXACA

COMPILED FROM DOCUMENTS in the Archivo del Juzgado de Villa Alta; the Archivo General de la Nación, Mexico City; and the Archivo General de Indias, Seville.

ALCALDES MAYORES

1529–31	Luis de Berrio
1531	Pedro Asensio
1531–37	Graviel de Aguilera, Corregidor
1537–41	?
1542–44	Francisco de Sevilla, Alcalde Mayor de los Zapotecas, Chontales, y Mixes
1545	Juan Núñez Sedeño, Alcalde Mayor y Juez de Residencia
1546–48	?
1549	Cristóbal de Chávez
1550	Luis de León Romano, Juez de Comisión en la Provincia de Oaxaca
1551	Cristóbal de Chávez (see 1549)
1552	?
1553–55	Alonso de Buiza (or Buyca)
1556–60	Juan de Salinas
1560–62	Juan Enríquez de Noboa
1563	Juan de Salazar, Alcalde Mayor de Villa Alta y Nejapa
1564	?
1565–66	Gerónimo Flores, Alcalde Mayor de Villa Alta y Nejapa
1567–69	Fernando Dávalos
1570	Francisco de Valdivieso, Alcalde Mayor de Villa Alta y Nejapa
1571	Bartolomé Tofiño
1572–74	?
1575–76	Juan de Canseco
1576	Cristóbal de Arellano
1577–79	?
1580–81	Hernando Altamirano
1582–83	?
1584	Ruy Díaz de Mendoza
1585	Juan Enríquez de Noboa (see 1560–62)
1586–87	Juan de Medina
1588	Cristóbal Holgado (or Salgado)
1588	Gabriel Mejía
1589	Antonio Gracida, Alcalde Mayor y Comisario del Santo Oficio de la Inquisición
1589–91	Bartolomé Mejía

1591–92	Bartolomé de Zárate
1593	Nicolás de Espíndola
1594–1600	?
1601	Lic. Francisco Manjárez
1602	?
1603	Hernando de Molina Roxas
1604–5	?
1606	Jorge Mejía y Peralta
1608	Juan Velázquez de la Cueva
1609–17	?
1618	Francisco de Trexo
1619	?
1620–21	Pedro de Tovar
1622–24	?
1625–26	Manuel Ruiz de Contreras
1627–29	?
1630	Pedro de Almazán
1631	?
1632	Diego Orejón
1633	?
1634	Tomás Morán de la Cerda
1634	Capitán Juan de Vargas
1635	Antonio de la Plaza Equiluz
1631–38	Pedro de Guzmán y Rivera
1639	?
1640–42	Gerónimo de Bañuelos y Carrillo
1643	?
1644–47	Almirante Juan López de Oláez, Caballero del Orden de Santiago (COS)
1647–51	Gobernador Martín de Robles Villafaña Ballero (COS)
1651	Diego de Gamarra
1652–53	Andrés de Aramburu
1653–55	Capitán Diego de Villegas y Sandoval (COS)
1656	?
1657	General Pedro Sáenz Izquierdo (COS)
1658	?
1659–61	General Pedro Fernández de Villaroel y de la Cueva (nephew of the Viceroy Duque de Albuquerque)
1662	Felipe de Leyva de la Cerda
1664	Joseph Martínez de Alarcón
1665	General Pedro Fernández de Villaroel y de la Cueva (see 1659–61)
1666–67	?
1668	Cristóbal del Castillo Mondragón (COS)
1669	?
1670	Juan Niño de Tabora, Maestre de Campo
1670–72	Fernando Velasco y Castilla, Conde de Santiago y Calimaya, y Adelantado de las Islas Filipinas
1673	?
1674–75	Luis Carrillo de Medina y Guzmán, Capitán de la Guardia del Virrey
1676	?
1677–83	Cristóbal del Castillo Mondragón (COS) (see 1668)
1679	Luis Carrillo de Medina y Guzmán (see 1674–75)
1684–86	Capitán don Alonso Muñoz de Castilblanque

1687–91	Juan Manuel Bernardo de Quiroz (COS)
1692–96	Capitán Miguel Ramón de Nogales (COS)
1697–1702	Capitán Juan Antonio Mier del Tojo
1703–8	Diego de Rivera y Cotes, Maestre de Campo
1709–12	Capitán Antonio de Miranda y Corona
1712	Gaspar Agüero de los Reyes y San Pelayo (appointed but did not arrive)
1713–15	?
1716–18	Juan de Santander Rada
1717	Sebastián de Aziburu Arechaga (appointed but did not arrive)
1717–21	Gaspar Agüero de los Reyes y San Pelayo (see 1712)
1719	Joseph Francisco de Madrigal
1722–23	?
1724–29	Martín de Hechartena
1730	Antonio Blanco de Sandoval, Teniente Coronel de Caballería
1731–34	?
1735–36	Joaquín de Padilla y Estrada
1737	Juan Martín de Iriarte
1731–38	Pedro Angel de Irigoyen
1739–42	Juan Francisco de la Puerta, Teniente Coronel de Caballería
1743	Manuel Valentín Bustamante y Bustillo (never arrived?)
1744	Joseph de Azevedo
1745–49	Pedro Angel de Irigoyen (see 1731–38)
1749–51	Phelipe de Rivas Ramírez de Arellano (COS)
1753–56	Francisco Xavier de Barroeta
1757	Agustín de Olloquiegui
1758–61	?
1762	Alonso de Basco y Vargas (COS), Teniente de Navío de la Real Armada
1763–65	?
1766	Francisco Xavier de Barroeta (see 1753–56)
1767–69	Joseph de Molina y Sandoval (COS), Brigadier de los Reales Ejércitos
1770	Alonso de Basco y Vargas (see 1762)
1771–76	Sancho Pisón (or Pissón) y Moyua, Primer Teniente del Regimiento de Reales Guardias Españolas de Infantería
1777	?
1778–79	Sancho Pisón y Moyua (reappointed)
1780–84	Francisco Marty, Capitán de Granaderos del Regimiento de Infantería de Voluntarios Extranjeros
1784–89	Pablo de Ortega, Jurado Capitán de las Milicias de Caballería de la Costa de Xicayán

SUBDELEGADOS

1790	Pablo de Ortega (Interim)
1790–96	Bernardino María Bonavía y Zapata, Sargento Mayor de los Reales Ejercitos
1797–1801	Bernardo Ruiz de Conejares
1801–2	José Carlos de Gordon Urquijo (Josef de Gordon)
1803–6	Juan Antonio de Llaguno
1807–10	?
1811	Julián Nieto Posadillo
1811–21	?

APPENDIX B

GLOSSARY OF SPANISH TERMS

Agencia. Dependent hamlet in a *municipio*

Alcabala. Sales tax

Alcalde. Judge and *cabildo* member

Alcalde mayor. Spanish official in charge of a district

Alcaldía mayor. Political district headed by an *alcalde mayor*

Alguacil. Constable

Alguacil mayor. Chief constable

Arriero. Muleteer

Arroba. Unit of measure; about 25 pounds

Aviador. Financial backer of an *alcalde mayor*

Barrio. Neighborhood in a community

Bienes de comunidad. Community revenues on deposit in royal treasury

Caballería. Unit of agricultural land; about 105 acres

Cabecera. Head town

Cabildo. Municipal council

Cacicazgo. Estate of a *cacique*

Cacique. Hereditary Indian chieftan or local ruler

Carga. Unit of measure; generally one-half a *fanega*, or about three-quarters of a bushel

Cargo. Burden or office

Casta. Group of mixed racial ancestry

Cédula. Royal order

Cofradía. Sodality; a lay brotherhood responsible for financing religious services and maintaining the church

Congregación. Congregation or concentration of scattered settlements into one community

Corregidor. Spanish officer in charge of a local Indian district

Corregimiento. Jurisdiction or office of a *corregidor*

Curato. Parish administered by secular clergy

Derrama. Unofficial local tax levy

Despoblado. Abandoned town site

Doctrina. Religious doctrine; parochial jurisdiction or its head town

Ejido. Municipal common lands

Encomendero. Possessor of an *encomienda*

Encomienda. Grant of an Indian town or towns, carrying the right to assess tribute

Entrada. Spanish military foray or invasion

Escribano. Secretary or scribe

Español. Spaniard or Creole

Estancia. Subordinate Indian community; ranch

Expediente. File of papers bearing on a case

Fanega. Unit of dry measure; 1.5 bushels

Fiscal. Low-ranking Indian official

Gobaz. Zapotec term for low-ranking Indian official

Gobernador. Appointed head of an Indian municipality

Grana. Cochineal

Hacendado. Owner of an hacienda

Hacienda. Landed estate used for both ranching and agriculture

Intendente. Spanish provincial political official; head of an *intendencia*

Juez de primera instancia. Judge of first instance

Juez de residencia. Judge presiding at a residencia

Legajo. Bundle (of documents)

Lienzo. Colonial Indian painting on cloth

Macehual. Indian commoner

Maestro de idolatría. Indian shaman or curer

Manta. Cotton cloth or mantle

Matlazáhuatl. A disease, probably typhus or yellow fever

Mayeque. Dependent serfs

Mayor. Indian chief constable

Mayordomo. Majordomo; custodian, frequently for a *cofradía*

Municipio. Municipality

Naboría. Indian of intermediate status between slave and free who was forced to work for a particular Spaniard or Spanish town

Nopal. Type of cactus used for producing cochineal

Padrino. Godfather or godparent

Parentela. Family or kin group

Partido. District

Petate. Palm-mat

Principal. Member of Indian upper class or status group

Procurador. City or town attorney

Pueblo. Town or village; usually refers to small and medium-size Indian communities

Ranchería. Small settlement or hamlet

Rancho. Ranch

Real. Monetary unit; one-eighth of a peso

Regidor. Councilman in a *cabildo*

Repartimiento. Labor draft

Repartimiento de efectos or mercancías. Forced distribution of money for production purposes or sale of goods to Indians by a Spanish official

República de indios. Indian community

Residencia. Inquiry taken concerning the conduct of a Spanish official who had completed his term of office or had been removed from it

Sacristán. Sexton

Serrano. Resident of the mountains or *sierra*

Subdelegado. Late colonial Spanish official replacing the *corregidor* and *alcalde mayor*

Sujeto. Subject town

Tameme. Indian carrier

Tasación. Tribute valuation

Teniente. Deputy or assistant

Terrazguero. A Spanish colonial term for *mayeque*, Indians of roughly the status of serfs

Tianguis. Indian market

Tierra caliente. A warm, low-altitude region or "hot country"

Topil. Low-ranking Indian official

Trapiche. Sugar mill

Vara. Unit of measure of roughly 33 inches; staff or office of a *cabildo* member
Vecino. Permanently residing Spanish household head in Spanish colonial towns
Vigana. Zapotec term for priest or young man in training for the priesthood
Visita. Tour of inspection; community or church ministered by nonresident clergy
Vista de ojos. Boundary inspection

NOTES

THE FOLLOWING abbreviations are used in the notes:

AGI   Archivo General de Indias, Seville
AGN   Archivo General de la Nación, Mexico City
AJPA   Archivo Parroquial de Villa Alta, Oaxaca
AJVA   Archivo del Juzgado de Villa Alta, Oaxaca
AMT   Archivo Municipal de Talea de Castro, Oaxaca
BN   Biblioteca Nacional, Madrid
CCG   Colección Castañeda Guzmán, Oaxaca
CDII   *Colección de documentos inéditos relativos al descubrimiento, conquista y organización de las antiguas posesiones españolas de América y Oceanía* . . . , 42 vols., Madrid, 1864–84.
ENE   *Epistolario de Nueva España, 1505–1818.* Francisco del Paso y Troncoso, ed., 16 vols., Mexico City, 1939–42.
PNE   *Papeles de Nueva España.* Francisco del Paso y Troncoso, ed., 9 vols., Madrid, 1905–36.

In references to archival sources, the major volume (usually *legajo*, but sometimes *tomo*) appears first; the *expediente*, when given, is in large italic figures; and the folios, when given, always follow a colon. Thus, AGN Mercedes 3, *789:* 309v, stands for Archivo General de la Nación, Mexico City, Ramo de Mercedes, tomo 3, expediente 789, folio 309 versa. For citations that do not fit this format, key abbreviations or even full Spanish terms are supplied. Legajos in the Archivo del Juzgado de Villa Alta (AJVA) are identified by the type of cases they contained (Civil, Criminal, or both) and their earliest and latest dates. These are followed by the expediente number in italics, as in AJVA Civil y Criminal 1682–1882, *57.* Note that the location and organization of the AJVA holdings has changed since I completed my research (see Bibliography).

PREFACE

1. Some of the recent works that emphasize diversity and regionalism in Mesoamerica include MacLeod and Wasserstrom; Farriss, *Maya Society;* Harvey and Prem; Taylor, *Landlord and Peasant* and *Drinking;* and Chance, "Colonial Ethnohistory of Oaxaca."
2. See García Martínez for a recent study of the colonial Sierra Norte de Puebla.
3. Hunt, p. 227.
4. Two noted examples are Gibson, *Aztecs,* and López Sarrelangue. A recent exception is Farriss's *Maya Society,* which stresses the discontinuities of the "second conquest" in late colonial Yucatan (chapter 12).
5. Van Young, pp. 56–57. See also Taylor, *Drinking;* and Carmagnani, "Una forma mercantile," "Los recursos," and "Local Governments."
6. Taylor, *Landlord and Peasant.*
7. Wallerstein.

CHAPTER 1

1. For example, Whitecotton, a summary of research on all time periods up to the present, is limited almost exclusively to the Valley. The same holds true for most of the Zapotec portions of Flannery and Marcus.

2. For a summary, see Chance, "Colonial Ethnohistory of Oaxaca."

3. There are some notable exceptions, such as Zeitlin; Hamnett, *Politics and Trade;* Carmagnani, "Una forma mercantile," "Los recursos," and "Local Governments"; Brockington; Romero Frizzi, *Economía y vida;* Pastor, *Campesinos y reformas;* and Hunt. Howard Cline's work on the Chinantecs (*Papeles de la Chinantla*, 3 : 44–57) has a useful bibliography.

4. Gerhard, *Guide,* p. 367.

5. Nader, *Talea and Juquila,* pp. 201–2.

6. Beals, p. 6.

7. De la Fuente, "Los zapotecos de Choapan," pp. 144–45; Weitlaner and Cline, pp. 523, 532.

8. Nader, "The Zapotec," p. 331; Whitecotton, p. 15.

9. Weitlaner and Cline, p. 525.

10. Nader, "The Zapotec," p. 331.

11. For more information on the languages of the Sierra Zapoteca, see Reeck.

12. De la Fuente, *Relaciones,* pp. 33–34, 39, 53; "La cultura zapoteca," p. 235; "Los zapotecos de Choapan," p. 153; *Yalalag,* p. 16.

13. Nader, *Talea and Juquila,* p. 204.

14. Weitlaner and Cline, p. 525.

15. AGI Justicia 205, 5.

16. Kuroda, p. 12.

17. Cline, "Native Pictorial Documents," p. 120.

18. De la Fuente, "Algunos problemas," p. 246; Roger Reeck, personal communication.

19. Beals, p. 7.

20. Schmieder, p. 46.

21. Nader, "The Zapotec," p. 333.

22. Gerhard, *Guide,* pp. 196, 369.

23. AGN Tierras 812, *2;* Tierras 2682, *21;* AGI Justicia 205, 5.

24. Burgoa, *Palestra,* p. 96.

25. Borah and Cook, *Aboriginal Population,* p. 83.

26. Marcus, "Aztec Military Campaigns," pp. 314–18.

27. Barlow, p. 123.

28. PNE, 4:47.

29. AGI Justicia 191, *2.*

30. AGN Tierras 812, *2;* AGI Justicia 205, *5;* Dávila Padilla, pp. 635, 637; Burgoa, *Geográfica descripción,* 2:151.

31. AGN Tierras 812, *2.*

32. Pérez García, 1:64.

33. Beals, p. 18.

34. Gerhard, *Guide,* p. 371; Gay, 1:240.

35. Burgoa, *Geográfica descripción,* 2:147.

CHAPTER 2

1. Cortés, p. 147; Gay, 1:345.

2. Díaz del Castillo, pp. 360–63; Gay, 1:364–400.

3. Cortés, pp. 227–28; Díaz del Castillo, pp. 409–10.

4. Gay, 1:424.

5. Díaz del Castillo, pp. 479–80, also mentions Alonso de Herrera, a captain who was in the Zapotecas at the same time as Figueroa. The two had a falling out and Herrera soon left the region.

6. Díaz del Castillo, pp. 479–80.

7. AGI Justicia 135, *1;* AGI México 96.

8. AGI Justicia 205, *5;* AGI Justicia 135, *1.* Lemoine, p. 194, notes that Villa Alta was officially designated as a villa by Marcos de Aguilar on January 23, 1527.

9. AGI Justicia 205, *5;* AGI Patronato 76, *2,* ramo 12.

10. AGI Justicia 230.

11. CDII, 13, 130; Cuevas, p. 40.

12. AGI Justicia 230:179v–210v.

13. AGI Justicia 230; ENE, 3:92.

14. Herrera, 9:209.

15. Varner and Varner, pp. 83, 84.

16. Cited in Kubler, 1:50.

17. AGI Justicia 191, *2;* AGI Justicia 135, *1.*

18. Dávila Padilla, p. 549.

19. AGN Mercedes 4:113–15.

20. AGI Justicia 230:6r.

21. AGI Patronato 20, *5,* ramo 21; López de Velasco, p. 230; García Pimentel, p. 69; Lemoine, p. 195. Cook and Borah, *Central Mexico, 1531–1610,* p. 89, give an estimate of 85 persons for 1568 based on thirty *vecinos* and a multiplier of 2.8. However, a factor of 5 would be more appropriate for the Spanish population, yielding a revised estimate of 150.

22. Gay, 1:380, 416, 435.

23. De la Fuente, "Documentos"; AGN Civil 390, *4;* AGN Tierras 335, *5;* AMT "Memoria y probanza de la fundación del pueblo de Talea, hoy Villa de Castro." These documents also mention a Fray Tequinaca, who remains unidentified.

24. Burgoa, *Geográfica descripción,* 2:132; Burgoa, *Palestra,* p. 97.

25. Kubler, 2:534; Burgoa, *Geográfica descripción,* 2:132.

26. Burgoa, *Geográfica descripción,* 2:134; Burgoa, *Palestra,* p. 99; Kubler, 2:534.

27. Burgoa, *Geográfica descripción,* 2:132, 133, 156, 158, 164; Gay, 1:557, 558, 607; Dávila Padilla, pp. 633–34.

28. AJVA Civil y Criminal 1682–1830; AGN General de Parte 1, *24: 5;* Burgoa, *Geográfica descripción,* 2:188.

29. Bevan, pp. 14–15.

30. AGN Tierras 2075, *1.*

31. AGN Mercedes 3, *788:*308v–309. The route to Antequera from the Rincón was through Tepanzacualco, Calpulalpan, and Ixtlán. Mixes followed a trail through the Hacienda San Bartolo that bordered on Ayutla (AJVA Civil 1759–97, *36*).

32. ENE, 3:50–52; AGN Mercedes 2, *452:*186v–187v; AGN Mercedes 3, *789:*309v.

33. CDII, 13:182; ENE, 16:33; ENE, 2:90; ENE, 3:55. Gay, 1:461, mistakes Zapotec San Miguel Tiltepec for Mixe Santa María Tiltepec. This uprising may be one of the events portrayed on the Lienzo de San Miguel Tiltepec; see Glass, p. 210 and Pérez García, 1:59–61.

34. ENE, 3:53, 60.

35. AGN Civil 1271:202r–v.

36. Burgoa, *Geográfica descripción,* 2:147.

37. AGI Justicia 230.

38. AGN Mercedes 3, *314:*122r–v.

39. PNE, 1.

40. AGI Justicia 205, *5.*

41. PNE, 1.

42. PNE, 1; Chance, *Race and Class,* p. 48.

43. AGN Mercedes 3, *785, 787*:307–308v.
44. Gerhard, *Guide*, p. 369.
45. Ibid.
46. AGI México 91.
47. AGN Mercedes 3, *785*:307–8; AGN Civil 1271:196v.
48. ENE, 3:50.
49. AGI Justicia 230.
50. ENE, 4:145.
51. ENE, 3:51.
52. ENE, 3:48–77.
53. AGN Mercedes 4:113–15.
54. See Appendix A for a list of known alcaldes mayores and subdelegados of Villa Alta.
55. AGN Mercedes 3, *802*.
56. AGN Civil 1271:196–197v; AGN Mercedes 3, *790*.
57. AGN Mercedes 2, *341, 452*; AGN Mercedes 3, *802*. The first of these documents is reproduced in Gay, 1:532–34.
58. AGN Mercedes 3, *314, 802*; AGN Civil 1271:196r.
59. AGN Mercedes 4:227r–v; AGN Mercedes 5:98r–v; AGN Mercedes 6:463–64; Burgoa, *Geográfica descripción*, 1:143; Gay, 1:558.
60. Two of the documents are dated 1521, one of them 1522, and two 1525. Their locations and the towns to which they refer are: Solaga, AGN Tierras 1301, *2* (published in De la Fuente, "Documentos," pp. 175–97); Lahoya (now Otatitlán de Morelos), De la Fuente, "Documentos," pp. 191–97; Yatzachi, AGN Civil 390, *4;* Juquila, AGN Tierras 335, *5;* Talea, AMT, "Memoria y probanza de la fundación del pueblo de Talea, hoy Villa de Castro." All these accounts appear to be based on *lienzos* painted in the second half of the sixteenth century. The Solaga and Juquila documents, both dated 1521, may be related to the Lienzos of San Juan Tabaa and San Miguel Tiltepec, which are also dated 1521. The falsification of dates on all these documents was probably done intentionally to enhance their "authenticity."
61. AGN Mercedes 5:98r–v, 110v; AGN Mercedes 8:245v.
62. AGN Mercedes 4, *30;* AGN Mercedes 84, 25v–26.
63. Gerhard, *Guide*, p. 197.
64. Gay, 1:559.
65. AGN Mercedes 6:461v–462v; AGN Mercedes 7:192r–v.
66. AGN Mercedes 28:269v–271; AGN Tierras 79, *4.* For more detail on the jurisdiction of Nejapa see Gerhard, *Guide*, pp. 195–99.
67. AGN General de Parte 5, *350.* See also AGN Mercedes 4:362r–v for 1556 and AGN General de Parte 3, *122* for 1587.
68. Gerhard, *Guide*, p. 369.
69. AGN Reales Cédulas Duplicadas 5, *57, 619, 730.*
70. AGN Mercedes 8:243v–244; AGN Mercedes 4:353v; AGN Indios 4, *877;* AGN Indios 5, *969, 971;* Zavala and Castelo, 6:285, 307–8, 310.
71. Zavala and Castelo, 3:188; ibid., 5:102–3; ibid., 6:315.
72. AGN Indios 4, *877.*
73. Kubler, 1:63.
74. Dávila Padilla, p. 549.
75. AGN Mercedes 11:26v; Zavala and Castelo, 2:413.
76. Zavala and Castelo, 2:310.
77. Dávila Padilla, p. 549; Kubler, 1:131, 171, 175.
78. Unless otherwise noted, the source for this section is the bundle of *Papeles de Analco* in APVA.
79. Tlaxcalans and others from central Mexico formed the nucleus of the Barrio of Jalatlaco in Antequera (Chance, "The Urban Indian").

80. The Lienzo de Analco, now at the National Museum of Anthropology in Mexico City, is a possible source of information on the conquest of Zapotec and Mixe villages in the vicinity of Villa Alta. It consists of a detailed map of a large region with numerous depictions of battles between Spaniards and Indians. However, as Glass, p. 86, observes, "the almost complete absence of any glosses, dates, place names, or glyphs of any description complicates its interpretation." Blom, pp. 131, 134–35, in his brief study of the lienzo, noted its stylistic affinities with the famous Lienzo de Tlaxcala and concluded that three interpretations are possible. It may represent the conquest of Cholula and Tenochtitlan, the conquests led by Pedro de Alvarado in Oaxaca in 1522 or 1524, or the wars fought with Sierra Zapotecs and Mixes before the founding of Villa Alta.

81. Nestepec disappeared in the 1580s or 1590s.

82. The names Analco and Papalotipac were used interchangeably into the early 1590s.

83. AGN General de Parte 1, *35*.

84. AJVA Civil 1584–1793, *20*.

85. AJVA Civil y Criminal 1682–1882.

86. AGN Indios 3, *917*.

87. Gerhard, *Guide*, p. 369.

88. Lachichina and Tepanzacualco: AGN Inquisición 437, *17*; AGN Mercedes 41:81v–82v; Zavala and Castelo, 7:35; Lachixila: AGN Reales Cédulas Duplicadas 19, *624*; Ocotepec and Ayacastla: AJVA Civil 1682–1882, *13*; Yovego: AJVA Civil y Criminal 1701–50, *22*; Cajonos and Yatzona: AJVA Civil 1697–1796, *43*; AJVA Civil 1708–1825, *39*.

89. AGN Reales Cédulas Duplicadas 5, *694*.

90. Díez de la Calle, p. 179.

91. CCG "Libro de elecciones de la hermita de Santo Domingo de Villa Alta;" AJVA Civil 1759–97, *60*.

92. AGI México 357.

93. AGI México 77, *600*.

94. AGN Reales Cédulas Duplicadas 29, *401*.

95. AGI México 600.

96. See AGI México 634, 689, 1222.

97. AGI México 1222.

98. AGN Reales Cédulas 90:116–21.

99. AJVA Civil 1793–1840, *71*.

100. The data are not sufficient to support an analysis of marriage patterns by race. Of the 332 marriages that took place between 1729 and 1810, both partners were racially identified in only twenty-eight cases. The one peninsular Spaniard married a creole woman; seven of the creole grooms took creole brides, three married mestizas, one a castiza, and two Indians; three of the six mestizos married mestizas, one a castiza, one a creole, and one an Indian; five Indian grooms married Indian women, another a mestiza; the two mulattoes both married Indians (APVA "Libros de Casamientos," 1729–1810).

101. AJVA Civil 1682–1882, *34*.

102. AGN Civil 26, *4*; AJVA Civil 1753–82, *66*.

103. AJVA Civil y Criminal 1682–1882, *40*.

104. Construction and repair of roofs was not a minor task in the humid climate of Villa Alta. Periodic fires—such as the one in 1634—also took a considerable toll (AGN Mercedes 41:81v–82v).

105. AJVA Civil y Criminal 1682–1882, *33, 40*; AGN Reales Cédulas Duplicadas 18, *104*; AGN Indios 7, *279*; AGN Indios 13, *435*.

106. AGN Indios 5, *969*; AGN Indios 7, *279*; AJVA Civil 1639–1843, *38*; AJVA Civil 1682–1882, *3*.

107. AJVA Civil 1793–1840, *72*.

108. AJVA Civil 1759–97, *59*.

109. AGN Reales Cédulas Duplicadas 24, *3;* APVA "Papeles de Analco"; AJVA Civil 1779–1802, *3.*

110. AJVA Civil 1753–1782, *34.*

111. AJVA Civil 1697–1796, *45.*

112. AGN Civil 1607, *1:*47v.

113. AJVA Civil 1779–1802, *5.*

114. One other such descendant, a principal, was living in Antequera in 1747 (AJVA Civil 1579–1825, *36*).

115. APVA "Papeles de Analco"; AJVA Civil 1753–82, *50;* Chance, "Urban Indian."

116. APVA "Libros de Bautizos de Analco," 1777–1800.

CHAPTER 3

1. Borah and Cook, *Central Mexico in 1548, Aboriginal Population;* Cook and Borah, *Central Mexico, 1531–1610, Mixteca Alta,* "An Essay on Method," and "Royal Revenues."

2. Borah and Cook, *Central Mexico in 1548;* Cook and Borah, *Central Mexico, 1531–1610, Mixteca Alta,* "Royal Revenues"; Gerhard, *Mexico en 1742.*

3. Borah and Cook, *Central Mexico in 1548.*

4. Ibid., pp. 18, 74.

5. Cook and Borah, "An Essay on Method," p. 75.

6. The variance for the mean ratio is 2.270, the standard deviation 1.507, and the standard error 0.233.

7. Also in parentheses in table 9 are estimates for two pairs of towns that were counted together in 1548: Huayatepec and Lahoya, and Lazagaya and Tagui. For each case the combined figure has been divided and a count assigned to each town proportionate to its size in 1568. Estimates for Villa Alta and Analco, also in parentheses, are arbitrarily the same as in 1568.

8. Cook and Borah, *Central Mexico, 1531–1610,* pp. 85–88.

9. Note that Region V (Zapotecas) employed by Cook and Borah for 1568 and again for 1622 (*Central Mexico, 1531–1610* and "Royal Revenues") includes much more than the Alcaldía Mayor of Villa Alta. Their total population estimates for Region V are therefore not comparable to those developed here, which apply only to the Villa Alta district.

10. Cook and Borah, "Royal Revenues," pp. 1–128.

11. Cook and Borah, *Mixteca Alta,* p. 47.

12. The variance for the mean ratio is 0.516, the standard deviation 0.714, the standard error 0.103. Once again, Lazagaya and Tagui have been separated. These 1622 estimates should be regarded as provisional. Cook and Borah's Region V—including the Districts of Villa Alta, Nejapa, Teococuilco, and some adjacent areas—proved to be a problem case. Different methods of calculating the total population of Region V produced widely varying estimates, from 42,646 to 25,837. "In connection with this discrepancy, it should be noted that for the 23 towns the population in 1641 [1622] is actually greater than in 1595. There may have been a real increase in population, the extension of Spanish control may have come later than has been generally assumed, or there may be a factor of selection in the data whereby the more important towns are represented at the expense of those which disappeared. The Zapotecas may have constituted a special case which deserves further examination" (Cook and Borah, "Royal Revenues," p. 65).

13. Cook and Borah, *Mixteca Alta,* especially figure 2, p. 41.

14. The estimate for Villa Alta is again arbitrary. Those for Betaza, Lachitaa, Yaa, Yatee, Yatzachi el Alto, Yohueche, and Yojovi are all averages of the 1703 figures and other counts done in these towns in 1701–4 (AJVA Civil 1584–1793, *14*). The estimate for Zoogocho is based on a 1704 casado count in AGI México 881, *19.* The estimates for Temaxcalapan, Yalahui, and Yatzona are averages of the 1703 figures and other counts done in 1707 (AGI México 879). The estimate for Tlahuitoltepec is an interpolation (see Cook and Borah, "An Essay on Method," pp. 74–75) derived by averaging a figure available for 1668 (AJVA Criminal 1607–95, *16*) with that for 1742.

15. The variance for the mean ratio is 0.960, the standard deviation 0.980, the standard error 0.115.

16. Villaseñor y Sánchez, pp. 148–202.

17. Cook and Borah, *Mixteca Alta*, p. 46.

18. Additional counts from 1743 (AJVA Civil 1635–1803, *39*) are available for Lachirioag, Xagacia, and Yalalag. They have been averaged with the 1742 figures.

19. See table 5.

20. The figure given for Metepec is an interpolation of the estimates for 1742 and 1789. The figures for the Trapiche de Yuguiba is from the 1777 church census (AGI México 2589, *58*).

21. The twenty-five pueblos for which censuses are available are Betaza, Lachitaa, Yaa, Yalalag, Yatee, Cacalotepec, Juquila, Lachichina, Lahoya, Lalopa, Talea, Tanetze, Yae, Yagallo, Yatoni, Yaviche, Yotao, Amatepec, Jareta, Jayacaxtepec, Moctum, Ocotepec, Tonaguia, Totontepec, and Tepitongo.

22. Cook and Borah, *Mixteca Alta*, p. 41.

23. *Division territorial . . . 1900, Division territorial . . . 1910, Censo general . . . 1921, Quinto censo . . . 1930, Sexto censo . . . 1940, Séptimo censo . . . 1950, VIII Censo . . . 1960, IX Censo . . . 1970.*

24. Miranda.

25. Miranda's 1794 count is the figure reported in the totals of the Revillagigedo census. This figure is considerably higher than corresponding ones in this analysis. Explanation of these differences must await further study. I suspect, however, that the Revillagigedo census totals contain many errors.

26. Cook and Borah, *Central Mexico, 1531–1610;* Borah and Cook, *Aboriginal Population.*

27. Cook and Borah, *Central Mexico, 1531–1610,* p. 47.

28. Borah and Cook, *Aboriginal Population.*

29. Cook and Borah, *Central Mexico, 1531–1610,* pp. 85–88.

30. The variance is 0.124, the standard deviation 0.352, and the standard error 0.088.

31. Cook and Borah, *Central Mexico, 1531–1610,* p. 53.

32. Nader, *Talea and Juquila,* p. 205.

33. Schmieder, p. 48.

34. De la Fuente, "Notas sobre lugares."

35. Ibid., p. 280.

36. Schmieder, p. 47.

37. Berg, p. 23.

38. Nader, *Talea and Juquila,* p. 202.

39. Schmieder, p. 54.

40. Nader, "The Zapotec," p. 340.

41. Schmieder, p. 50.

42. Beals, p. 7.

43. Nader, "The Zapotec," p. 340.

44. Beals, p. 6.

45. Schmieder, p. 72.

46. Ibid., p. 62.

47. Nader, *Talea and Juquila,* p. 202.

48. Schmieder, p. 70; Beals, p. 12.

49. Gerhard, "Congregaciones de indios," p. 375.

50. Díaz del Castillo, p. 410.

51. De la Fuente, "Algunos problemas," p. 248 fn.

52. De la Fuente, "Notas sobre lugares," pp. 282–88.

53. AGN Tierras 846, *1.*

54. De la Fuente, "Notas sobre lugares," pp. 282–88.

55. APVA "Papeles de Analco."

56. Pérez García, 1:64.

57. PNE, 1:393, 497.

58. Burgoa, *Geográfica descripción*, 2:215.

59. Farriss, "Nucleation versus Dispersal," pp. 196-99.

60. Gerhard, "Congregaciones de indios."

61. AJVA Civil y Criminal 1682-1882, *5*; AJVA Civil 1697-1796, *36*, *43*; AGN Tierras 846, *1*.

62. Gerhard, *Guide*, p. 372.

63. De la Fuente, *Yalalag*, p. 18.

64. AGN Mercedes 7:69r.

65. AJVA Civil 1708-1825, *3*; AGN Indios 24, *276*.

66. AGN Indios 11, *24*.

67. Pérez García, 1:58.

68. APVA "Papeles de Analco."

69. Pérez García, 1:59.

70. AGN Indios 24, *495*.

71. AGN Tierras 185, *9*.

72. PNE, 1:279.

73. AGN Indios 24, *91*.

74. AGN Tierras 171, *4*.

75. AGI México 881, *19*.

76. AJVA Civil 1779-1802, *72*. While there is no direct information, the district was probably not immune to the widespread famine of 1785-86. The famine may have triggered this epidemic.

77. AGN Indios 62, *39*.

78. Murguía y Galardi, fol. 28; AJVA Civil 1833-35, *4*; Martínez Gracida.

79. Pérez García, 1:64.

80. Nader, *Talea and Juquila*, p. 208.

81. Gerhard, *Guide*, p. 371; AGI Justicia 191, *2*.

82. PNE, 1:225, 254, 327.

83. AGI Justicia 230. Nexitzo Ixcuintepec is not to be confused with the Mixe town of the same name in the jurisdiction of Nejapa.

84. Gerhard, *Guide*, p. 371; AGN Indios 6, *segunda parte, 514*.

85. AGN Indios 6, segunda parte, *514, 713, 774, 805*.

86. AGN Indios 6, segunda parte, *923*.

87. AGN Tierras 2775, *8:2v*.

88. The factor 3.1 has been used to convert tributaries to total population. See Cook and Borah, *Mixteca Alta*, p. 41.

89. AGN Tierras 2775, *8*.

90. Ibid.

91. AGN Indios 24, *248*.

92. AGN Indios 6, segunda parte, *923*.

93. AGN Tierras 852, *1*.

94. AGN Indios 64, *205*; AJVA Civil y Criminal 1674-1810, *71*.

95. AGN Tierras 791, *2*; AGN Mercedes 76:34v-35v.

96. AGN Indios 34, *172*; AGN Indios 36, *257, 276, 321*; AGN Indios 37, *114*.

97. AJVA Civil 1631-1787, *15*; AGN Indios 16, *47*.

98. Miranda, p. 144.

99. AGN Tierras 167, primera parte, *2:21v*.

100. De la Fuente, "Documentos," p. 190, and "Algunos problemas," p. 244.

101. AJVA Civil y Criminal 1682-1882, *46*.

102. AGI México 879.

103. Nader, *Talea and Juquila*, p. 212.

104. Ibid., p. 208.
105. AGI Justicia 191, 2.
106. AJVA Civil 1579–1825, 3.
107. AJVA Civil 1697–1796, 31.
108. Olivera and Romero, p. 235, believe that Choapan is of post-Conquest origin.
109. PNE, 1:219, 735, 738; Gerhard, Guide, p. 371.
110. Gibson, Aztecs, pp. 435–41.
111. AGN Civil 246, 8.
112. Weitlaner and Cline, p. 534.
113. AGN Indios 6, segunda parte, 923.
114. Gerhard, Guide, p. 371; AGN General de Parte 1:43.
115. AGN Tierras 812, 2.
116. AGN Tierras 2682, 21.
117. AGN Indios 50, 211; AGN Tierras 442, 7.
118. AGN Mercedes 76:183–85.
119. Archivo del Estado de Oaxaca, expediente on Yaxoni and Reagui.
120. AJVA Civil y Criminal 1701–50, 22; AGN Indios 19, 317; AGN Indios 24, 257.
121. Beals, p. 38.
122. Beals, pp. 12, 14.
123. Schmieder, p. 70.
124. Gerhard, Guide, p. 370.
125. AJVA Civil 1682–1882, 41.
126. AJVA Civil 1682–1882, 63; AGN Indios 6, primera parte, 1015.
127. AGN Tierras 165, 2.
128. Cook and Borah, "Royal Revenues."
129. AJVA Civil 1761–78.
130. AJVA Civil 1682–1882, 13.
131. PNE, 1:49, 325, 326, 390, 438, 728, 732.
132. Beals, p. 11; AGN General de Parte 1, 1039.
133. AGN General de Parte 1, 1039, 1212; AGN Inquisición 129, 2.
134. AGN Indios 6, segunda parte, 923.
135. AGN Tierras 2785, 7; AGI Patronato 230B, 9.
136. AGN Tierras 2785, 7.
137. AJVA Civil y Criminal 1682–1882, 57; AGN Indios 13, 225.
138. Beals, p. 18.
139. Laviada, p. 127.
140. AJVA Civil y Criminal 1631–1787, 46; Villaseñor y Sánchez, p. 200.
141. Gerhard, Guide, p. 370; Burgoa, Geográfica descripción, 2:188–203.
142. Laviada, p. 164.
143. Gerhard, Guide, p. 371; AJVA Civil 1708–1825, 59.
144. AGN Indios 6, segunda parte, 690.
145. AJVA Civil 1635–1803, 49.
146. AGI México 91.
147. AGN Indios 16, cuaderno 1, 18.
148. AJVA Civil 1682–1882, 27.
149. AGI México 2588.
150. AJVA Civil 1693–1860, 5.
151. AGI Justicia 186, 6.
152. Gerhard, Guide, pp. 86–88, 368–70.
153. AGN Indios 6, segunda parte, 895.
154. AGN Tierras 558, 1.
155. AGN Tierras 2075, 1.

156. Dávila Padilla, p. 641.

157. Gerhard, *Guide*, p. 372.

158. Ibid., p. 195.

159. Ibid.

160. The discussion here refers to territorial, not ethnic, population. Not all Mixe towns to-day are 100 percent "Mixe." As in the four other ethnic zones, migration and mestization must be taken into account. For example, according to the national census, of the 13,826 residents in the municipio of Cotzocón in 1970, only 3,762 spoke Mixe as their primary language; 1,090 spoke Mazatec, 532 Chinantec, 500 Mixtec, and 217 Zapotec. The rest were Spanish speakers.

161. Chance, "Kinship and Urban Residence"; "The Urban Indian," pp. 621–27; "City and Country," p. 111.

162. Schmieder, p. 70.

163. Villa Rojas, p. 17.

CHAPTER 4

1. Taylor, "Landed Society," p. 397.

2. Spores, *Mixtec Kings*, p. 107; Taylor, "Landed Society," p. 399.

3. Hamnett, *Politics and Trade*, p. 3.

4. See Taylor, *Landlord and Peasant*, for a well-documented study of colonial land tenure in the Valley of Oaxaca.

5. AGN Tierras 2764, *30*.

6. AGN Mercedes 45:239v–240; AGN Indios 40, *137*.

7. AGN Mercedes 45:239v–240; AGN Mercedes 59:72r–v; AJVA Civil y Criminal 1682–1882, *43*; AJVA Civil 1734–97, *25*.

8. De la Fuente, *Yalalag*, p. 14.

9. PNE, 1:137, 158, 165, 173, 275.

10. AGN Mercedes 3, *501*.

11. AGN Inquisición 129, *2*; AGN General de Parte 3, *132*.

12. AJVA Civil 1672–1799, *2*.

13. AGN Indios 3, *482, 598*; AGN Indios 4, *33, 34, 421, 552*; Zavala and Castelo, 6:470–72.

14. Zavala and Castelo, 7:35.

15. AGN Indios 12, primera parte, *194*.

16. AGN Reales Cédulas Duplicadas 15, *70, 85, 124*; AGN Tierras 2934, *55*.

17. Zavala and Castelo, 8:78–79.

18. AGN Reales Cédulas Duplicadas 31, *56*; AJVA Civil 1584–1793, *12*.

19. AJVA Civil y Criminal 1701–50, *25, 26*.

20. AJVA Civil 1579–1825, *2*.

21. AJVA Civil 1753–82, *30*.

22. AGN Indios 69, *289*.

23. Zavala and Castelo, 8:279–80; AGN General de Parte 39, *110, 259*; BN 2449, *49*.

24. AJVA Civil y Criminal 1674–1810, *13*; Nader, *Talea and Juquila*, p. 209; Hamnett, *Politics and Trade*, p. 159.

25. AGN Civil 1607, *1*.

26. AJVA Civil 1779–1802, *34*; AGN Civil 1607, *1, 3*.

27. AJVA Civil y Criminal 1674–1810, *13*.

28. AJVA Civil 1779–1802, *35*.

29. AJVA Civil 1779–1802, *37, 51*.

30. Nader, *Talea and Juquila*, p. 209.

31. Esteva, p. 431.

32. AGN Indios 6, primera parte, *372*.

33. AGN Indios 6, primera parte, *325*.

34. AJVA Civil 1635–1803, *24*.

35. AJVA Civil 1697–1796, *49*; AJVA Civil 1635–1803, *13, 15, 18, 24*.

36. AJVA Civil 1635–1803, *24*.

37. AGN Civil 1607, *2*.

38. AJVA Civil y Criminal 1682–1882, *37*.

39. AJVA Civil 1753–82, *52*.

40. AGN Indios 32, *222*.

41. AGN Subdelegados 35:211–14.

42. AGN Clero Secular y Regular 188, *12*.

43. AJVA Civil 1697–1796, *2, 44*.

44. AJVA Civil 1779–1802, *26*; AGN Indios 92, *311*; AJVA Civil 1753–82, *67*.

45. AGN Indios 62, *39*.

46. AJVA Civil 1779–1802, *50*.

47. The two best sources on the cochineal trade in Oaxaca are Hamnett, *Politics and Trade*, and Dahlgren de Jordán, *La grana*. See also Chance, *Race and Class*, pp. 68, 111, 145–47.

48. Dahlgren de Jordán, p. 29.

49. AJVA Civil y Criminal 1682–1882, *54*.

50. Letter from the Bishop of Oaxaca to the Crown in 1663, AGI México 357.

51. AJVA Civil y Criminal 1682–1882, *22*.

52. AGN Tierras 2962, *106*.

53. AJVA Civil 1753–82, *52*.

54. Hamnett, *Politics and Trade*, p. 80.

55. Ibid., p. 5.

56. AGI México 600, *3*; AJVA Civil 1639–1843, *49*; Carmagnani, "Una forma mercantile," p. 140. For a recent overview of this practice in New Spain, see Pastor, "El repartimiento de mercancías."

57. The economic boom in Oaxaca was due to a number of factors, including the Bourbon economic reforms and the establishment of the intendancy system. Among the results were a substantial increase in the cochineal trade and a revival of the textile industry in Antequera. While the boom lasted into the second decade of the nineteenth century, the *repartimiento de efectos* declined somewhat with the establishment of the intendancy system between 1786 and 1790. For further details see Hamnett, *Politics and Trade*, pp. 149, 153; Chance, *Race and Class*, pp. 145–46; and Gibson, *Spain in America*, pp. 169, 171.

58. AGI México 1229.

59. See chapter 2; for comparison with other districts see Hamnett, *Politics and Trade*, pp. 16–17.

60. Summarized by Hamnett, *Politics and Trade*, p. 45. Hamnett's fine study provides considerably more detail on the financial, administrative, and political aspects of the *repartimientos* than can be discussed here.

61. Ibid., especially pp. 4–8.

62. Ibid., p. 7.

63. AGI México 600, *4*.

64. AJVA Civil 1639–1843, *49*; AGN Civil 192, *9*.

65. AGN Subdelegados 35:211–14.

66. Lee, pp. 457, 462.

67. Hamnett, *Politics and Trade*, p. 148.

68. Dahlgren de Jordán, p. 10.

69. Hamnett, *Politics and Trade*, p. 30. Further details on the cochineal trade in Oaxaca, including some production statistics, can be found in Hamnett; Dahlgren de Jordán; and Chance, *Race and Class*, pp. 145–47.

70. AGI Patronato 182, *50*; AJVA Civil 1693–1860, *15*; Chance, *Race and Class*, pp. 145–47.

71. AGI México 600, *4*.

72. Dahlgren de Jordán, Appendix 2.
73. AJVA Civil 1753–82, *36*.
74. AGN Subdelegados 35:211–14.
75. AJVA Civil 1753–82, *36*.
76. Hamnett, *Politics and Trade*, pp. 9, 32.
77. AGN Subdelegados 35:211–14.
78. Hamnett, *Politics and Trade*, p. 35.
79. AGN Industria y Comercio 20, *6;* Bustamante, 3:31.
80. Hamnett, *Politics and Trade*, p. 31.
81. AGN Inquisición 881, *3*.
82. Bustamante, 3:31.
83. Hamnett, *Politics and Trade*, pp. 13–14.
84. AGN Subdelegados 35:211–14; AGN Tierras 558, *1*.
85. Hamnett, *Politics and Trade*, p. 80.
86. AGN Tierras 558, *1;* AGN Tierras 559, *1;* AGN Civil 246, *8*.
87. AGN Subdelegados 35:211–14.
88. AGN Inquisición 881, *3*.
89. AGN Indios 30, *221*.
90. Hamnett, *Politics and Trade*, p. 76.
91. Ibid., pp. 75–76, 81.
92. AGN Tierras 558, *1;* AGN Inquisición 689, *34*.
93. Paraphrased by Hamnett, *Politics and Trade*, p. 79.
94. The first such rebellion on record was in Choapan in 1551 (AGN Mercedes 3, *786*). Other uprisings occurred during the seventeenth and eighteenth centuries in Choapan, Yaveo, and Latani (1684–85); Lachirioag (1660s); Huitepec (ca. 1712); Yojovi (1740s); Lachixila; San Francisco Cajonos; Yalalag; and Yagavila (AJVA Civil 1697–1796, *45;* Archivo del Estado de Oaxaca, Ramo de Juzgados 1684, *10;* AGN Indios 28, *205, 206*).
95. AJVA Civil 1682–1882, *61*.
96. AGI México 600; AGN Indios 19, *338–42*.
97. AGI México 600, *3;* AGI México 77.
98. AGN General de Parte 4, *431;* AGN Inquisición 881, *3;* AGI México 600, *3;* Hamnett, *Politics and Trade*, p. 80.
99. Hamnett, *Politics and Trade*, p. 76.
100. Ibid., pp. 75–81; AGN Subdelegados 35:211–14, 217r–v.
101. Hamnett, *Politics and Trade*, p. 150; Stein.
102. In the eighteenth century five pueblos in the district lacked the legally guaranteed minimum of 600 *varas* of *fundo legal:* Roavela, Jalahui, Xagalazi, Yagallo, and Tepantlali. Latani was also short on land. Most of these towns were forced to rent lands from neighboring communities (AJVA Civil 1759–97, *70;* AGN Tierras 354, *3;* AGN Tierras 442, 7).
103. PNE, 1:99, 137, 158, 193, 275, 279; AGI Justicia 205, *5;* BN 2449, *45, 49*.
104. Hamnett, *Politics and Trade*, p. 79.
105. AGN Mercedes 16:190r–v; AGN Mercedes 18:251v; AGN Mercedes 22:33v.
106. AGN Mercedes 39:31v–33; AGN Indios 14, *73;* AGN Indios 30, *298;* AGN Indios 31, *250*.
107. Nader, "The Zapotec," p. 341.
108. AGI Justicia 205, *5*.
109. AJVA 1579–1825, *3*.
110. PNE, 1:99, 137; BN 2449, *45*.
111. AJVA Criminal 1682–1816, *7;* AJVA Civil y Criminal 1697–1797, *20*.
112. Burgoa, *Geográfica descripción*, 2:232.
113. This explanation for the Valley of Tlacolula was suggested to me by John Paddock, whom I thank.

114. De la Fuente, *Yalalag*, pp. 131–40; AJVA Criminal 1682–1816, 7.

115. AJVA Civil y Criminal 1631–1787, *64*.

116. AJVA Criminal 1682–1816, *65*.

117. AGN Indios 32, *356*.

118. AJVA Civil 1579–1824, *3*.

119. De la Fuente, "Los Zapotecos de Choapan," p. 177.

120. AJVA Civil 1753–82, *19*; De la Fuente, "Los Zapotecos de Choapan," p. 177.

121. AJVA Civil y Criminal 1698–1865, *8*.

122. Bevan, pp. 14–15.

123. AJVA Civil 1693–1860, *5*; BN 2449, *5*; PNE, 1:137.

124. AGN Indios 31, *250*; AGN Indios 32, *188*.

125. AGN Indios 32, *311*.

126. AJVA Criminal 1695–1702, 7.

127. AGN Indios 25, *486*.

128. AGN Indios 66, *26*.

129. Dahlgren de Jordán, p. 12.

130. Ibid., pp. 12–13.

131. Ajofrín, 2:121–22.

132. AJVA Civil 1697–1796, *5*.

133. PNE, 4:142–43, quoted in Dahlgren de Jordán, pp. 18–19.

134. Burgoa, *Geográfica descripción* 2:289, quoted in Dahlgren de Jordán, p. 19.

135. AJVA Civil y Criminal 1697–1797, *1*; AJVA Civil y Criminal 1701–50, *46*.

136. Dahlgren de Jordán, p. 29.

137. AGI México 877.

138. Hamnett, "Dye Production," p. 76.

139. Hamnett, *Politics and Trade*, p. 63.

140. AGN Civil 26, *4*; AJVA Civil 1753–82, *15, 67*.

141. AGN Indios 12, primera parte, *188*; AGN Inquisición 689, *34*; AJVA Civil 1753–82, *19*; BN 2449, *45*.

142. AJVA Criminal 1748–71, *18*; AGN Indios 58, *79*; AGN Tierras 2771, *4*.

143. AGN Indios 64, *124*; AGN Tierras 2771, *4*.

144. AJVA Civil y Criminal 1697–1797, *1*; AJVA Civil y Criminal 1701–50, *16*.

145. AJVA Civil y Criminal 1631–1787, *52, 53*; AJVA Civil 1807–17, *92, 93*; AJVA Civil y Criminal 1674–1810, *31*; AGN Tierras 2771, *4, 5*; Berg, Jr., p. 22.

146. AGN Indios 64, *138 bis*; AGN Tierras 2771, *4, 5*; AJVA Civil 1635–1803, *36*.

147. AGN Tierras 2771, *4*; AJVA Civil y Criminal 1701–50, *16*; AVJA Civil 1753–82, *15*.

148. AJVA Criminal 1695–1702, *32*.

149. AJVA Civil 1584–1793, *22*.

150. AGN Tierras 2771, *8*; AJVA Civil 1639–1843, *40*; AGN Indios 32, *365*; AJVA Civil 1584–1793, *22*.

151. AJVA Civil 1635–1803, 28; AGN Tierras 2771, *8, 10*.

152. AGN Indios 62, *54, 72, 74*; AGN Indios 64, *45, 138 bis*; AJVA Civil y Criminal 1698–1865, *8*.

153. AGN Civil 26, *4*; AGN Indios 50, *54*; AGN Indios 64, *205*; AGN Indios 66, *178*; AGN Tierras 2771, *5*; AGI México 2588.

154. For the Valley of Oaxaca see Taylor, *Landlord and Peasant*, chapters 2 and 3.

155. The peak cochineal period in the 1770s and 1780s was probably an exception in many pueblos; see this chapter, above.

156. Carmagnani, "Una forma mercantile," p. 143.

157. Hamnett, *Politics and Trade*, pp. 49, 50.

CHAPTER 5

1. The use of colonial Nahuatl documentation has increased considerably in recent years in central Mexican studies. See, for example, Anderson, Berdan, and Lockhart.

2. Taylor, *Drinking;* Spores, *Mixtec Kings, The Mixtecs.*

3. Among the many examples that could be cited is Pedro Carrasco's use of a sixteenth-century census to study marriage and the family (Carrasco, "Family Structure"). Quantitative sources of various kinds were also indispensable in my previous study of Indians in the Spanish city of Antequera (See Chance, "The Urban Indian").

4. The only substantial native pictorial sources from the Villa Alta region are the Lienzos of Tabaa, Tiltepec, and Analco. See chapter 2, notes 33, 60, and 80. All of these deal primarily with the Conquest period, however, and have not yet been adequately interpreted. The AJVA does contain a number of colonial documents written in Zapotec and Nahuatl (see Chance, *Indice*). Unfortunately, the study of written Zapotec is in its infancy and lags far behind the analysis of written Nahuatl.

5. The only other local juzgado archive in Oaxaca that has thus far yielded comparable riches, though of a different sort, is in Teposcolula in the Mixteca Alta. For an inventory of its colonial holdings see Romero and Spores.

6. Taylor, *Drinking,* p. 24; Carmagnani, "Local Governments," presents an opposing point of view, hypothesizing a persistence and expansion of indigenous regional ethnic ties during the eighteenth century in Oaxaca as a whole. The data from Villa Alta do not support such an interpretation, however, nor, in my opinion, do data from other parts of Oaxaca.

7. De la Fuente, *Relaciones,* p. 34.

8. APVA "Libros de matrimonios" for Yetzecovi (1799–1809); Yalahui (1801–13); Lachirioag (1730–31, 1768–74); Temaxcalapan (1745–56); Tagui (1753–1800); Roayaga (1657–64); Yatzona (1721–75); "Libros de bautizos" for Yetzecovi (1730–83); Roayaga (1758–81); Lachirioag (1768–81); Yatzona (1722–32).

9. AGN Civil 374, *3.* This observation assumes greater significance when we consider that it is not uncommon for some community officials to lack a knowledge of Spanish today. This was the case in Yae itself when I visited the town in 1978.

10. AJVA Civil 1753–82, *19, 26;* AGI México 2588.

11. AGI Justicia 205, *5;* AJVA Criminal 1695–1702, *33;* AJVA Civil 1579–1825, *26.*

12. AJVA Criminal 1607–45, *4;* AJVA Civil y Criminal 1682–1882, *51, 63;* AJVA Criminal 1695–1702, *14;* AJVA Criminal 1682–1816, *8;* AGN Tierras 165, *2;* AGN Tierras 528, *3.*

13. AJVA Criminal 1682–1816, *27.*

14. AJVA Civil 1753–82, *22.*

15. Written Zapotec from the Sierra can profitably be compared with samples from the Valley of Oaxaca and other regions. Joseph W. Whitecotton (personal communication) has made a beginning in this area and finds that the differences are not great.

16. The documents are from Talea, Lahoya, Juquila, Solaga, and Yatzachi El Alto. See chapter 2, note 60 for citations.

17. A similar pattern is reported by García Martínez (p. 200) for the Sierra Norte de Puebla.

18. The date of this pilgrimage is uncertain, but Burgoa, *Palestra,* p. 98, confirms that it did take place, perhaps between 1545 and 1548. According to him, the request was made jointly by the Spanish cabildo of Villa Alta and the conquered Zapotec pueblos.

19. AGN General de Parte 1, *135, 174, 468, 737.*

20. AGN General de Parte 1, *376.*

21. AGN Indios 5, *1098.*

22. AGN Indios 7, *270* (Lalopa, 1618); AGN Indios 9, *72–74, 81* (Choapan, Xoconia, Yaa, Ayacastla, 1618); AGN Indios 12, primera parte, *186, 250* (Choapan, 1635); AGN Indios 14, *21* (Villa Alta, 1642); AGN Indios 27, *26* (Villa Alta, 1680); AGN Indios 30, *298, 323, 339, 387* (Puxmetacan, Toavela, Choapan, Tanetze, 1689–90); AGN Indios 42, *167* (Yae, 1719).

23. AJVA Civil 1697–1796, *1*; AJVA Criminal 1695–1702, *11*; AJVA Civil y Criminal 1701–50, *22*; AJVA Civil 1584–1793, *21*.

24. AJVA Civil y Criminal 1682–1882, *2*.

25. AGN Indios 14, *87*.

26. AGN Tierras 2682, *21*.

27. AGN Mercedes 3, *783*.

28. AGN Indios 5, *837–41*.

29. AGN Indios 1, *14*.

30. AGN Indios 3, *693*.

31. AGN Indios 13, *173*.

32. AGN Indios 19, *634*; AGN Indios 24, *478*.

33. AJVA Criminal 1682–1816, *18*; AGN Tierras 167, primera parte, *2*.

34. AJVA Civil 1635–1803, *38*.

35. AGN Tierras 2935, *177*.

36. Taylor, *Landlord and Peasant*, pp. 39–44; Pastor, *Sociedad y economía*, chapter 2. Spores, *Mixtec Kings*, p. 152.

37. The considerably more complex pattern of land tenure in the colonial Valley of Oaxaca included six types of Indian lands. Five were essentially communal arrangements and one was private. None appears to have involved corporate kin groups. See Taylor, *Landlord and Peasant*, p. 68.

38. AGN Indios 5, *839*.

39. AGN Indios 24, *478*.

40. AJVA Civil y Criminal 1701–50, *22*.

41. AGN Tierras 167, primera parte, *2*.

42. AGN Tierras 443, *3*.

43. AGN Tierras 2682, *21*.

44. AGN Tierras 163, *14*.

45. Corporate, landowning kindreds are relatively rare in the ethnographic literature but are known to exist (see Davenport). A cognatic (ambilineal) lineage or clan model, in which group members trace descent and inheritance from a founding ancestor through any combination of male or female links would fit with many characterizations of the Aztec *calpulli*, though these are also based on very slim evidence (see Kirchhoff; Wolf, pp. 135–36). Cognatic lineages have also been attributed to the pre-Hispanic Valley Zapotecs and the Cuicatecs, though again the evidence is problematic at best (see Whitecotton, pp. 153–57; Hunt, pp. 222, 231).

46. Romney, pp. 215–17.

47. AJVA Civil 1548–1793, *29*; AJVA Civil 1759–97, *55*, segunda parte; AJVA Civil 1697–1796, *26*.

48. Chance, "Social Stratification."

49. AGN Civil 374, *3*.

50. AJVA Civil 1753–82, *18*.

51. AJVA Civil 1807–17, *17*; AJVA Civil 1759–97, *55*, segunda parte.

52. That the lack of private property is in itself insufficient to explain this development is shown by the Cañada Cuicatec case. The Cuicatecs also lacked private property (Hunt, pp. 185, 203, 206), but they attained a higher degree of stratification than in the Sierra Zapoteca because of their extensive utilization of intensive irrigation. As a consequence, wealth and power were more highly centralized among the Cuicatecs, where each community had only one lordly family.

53. AGN Indios 3, *345*.

54. AGN Indios 12, segunda parte, *24*; AGN Indios 13, *70*.

55. AGN Indios 24, *34*.

56. AGN Indios 11, *85*.

57. Burgoa, *Geográfica descripción*, 2:184.

58. AGN Mercedes 3, *44*.

59. See chapter 2, note 60 for sources.

60. AGN Mercedes 7:68r–69r. The towns in question are Cacalotepec, Tagui, Yaneri (Yabago), Yagila (Yaxila), Yalalag, Yaa, Yohueche, and Lalana.

61. AGN Indios 1, *3, 127;* AGN General de Parte 1, *4, 20, 1184;* AGN General de Parte 2, *222.* The towns in question are Ixcuintepec (Tanetze), Lalopa, Temaxcalapan, Yagavila, Yagila, Yaci (Jocotepec), Tagui and Yalahui, Cacalotepec, Comaltepec, and Lobani.

62. AGN General de Parte 1, *1183;* AGN Indios 1, *307.*

63. AGN Indios 6, segunda parte, *1080.*

64. AJVA Civil 1631–1787, *16.*

65. AGN Indios 13, *225.*

66. AJVA Criminal 1682–1816, *21;* AGN Tierras 846, *1.*

67. AJVA Civil y Criminal 1682–1882, *63;* AJVA Civil 1635–1803, *2.*

68. AGN Indios 14, *93.*

69. AGN Indios 10, cuaderno 2, *192.*

70. AJVA Civil 1759–97, *70.*

71. AJVA Civil 1779–1802, *33.*

72. AJVA Criminal 1735–1821, *94;* AJVA Civil 1734–97, *19.*

73. AJVA Civil 1807–17, *4, 20.*

74. AGN Indios 6, primera parte, *1015.*

75. AJVA Civil y Criminal 1682–1882, *27.*

76. AJVA Civil 1779–1802, *21.*

77. AJVA Civil 1753–82, *73.*

78. AJVA Civil 1807–17, *65.*

79. AGN Indios 13, *80.*

80. AGN Indios 32, *346.*

81. AJVA Criminal 1748–71, *30;* AGN Indios 62, *55.*

82. AGN General de Parte 2, *1300.*

83. AGN Indios 6, primera parte, *125;* AGN Indios 17, *98;* AGN Indios 19, *102, 634–37.*

84. AJVA Civil y Criminal 1701–50, *9;* AGN Inquisición 746:57–62.

85. AGN Indios 30, *322.*

86. AGN Indios 19, *39.*

87. AGN Indios 28, *205–6.*

88. AJVA Civil 1639–1843, *38;* AGN Indios 21, *222.*

89. AJVA Civil y Criminal 1631–1787, *53.*

90. AGN Indios 56, *113.*

91. Note that these were *civil,* not civil-religious hierarchies. Chapter 6 will show that while religious sodalities (*cofradías*) were present in the pueblos of the Villa Alta district, they were not well integrated into the ranked hierarchy of offices. The fusion of civil and religious cargos into a single system, where it occurred, was mainly a late-eighteeenth-century and nineteenth-century development. See Chance and Taylor.

92. AJVA Civil 1759–97, *55,* tercera parte.

93. AJVA Civil 1759–97, *31.*

94. AJVA Civil 1779–1802, *23;* AJVA Criminal 1682–1816, *96;* AJVA Civil 1635–1803, *38;* AJVA Civil 1639–1843, *3;* AJVA Civil 1779–1802, *73.*

95. Archivo del Juzgado de Tlacolula, Oaxaca, bundles marked Civil y Criminal for 1797–1832 and 1776–95.

96. See Cancian for the best documented ethnographic study.

97. AJVA Civil y Criminal 1701–50, *28.* The only other extensive genealogy that has been located in the entire Villa Alta district comes from the Cajonos Zapotec town of Yatzachi El Alto. It was presented to the alcalde mayor in 1794 by a man who claimed descent from a cacique of the midsixteenth century and shows nine generations (AGN Civil 390, *4*).

98. AJVA Civil y Criminal 1674–1810, *13.*

99. AJVA Civil 1759–97, *55,* primera parte.

100. AJVA Civil 1753–82, *33*.

101. AJVA Civil 1753–82, *18*.

102. AJVA Civil 1635–1803, *56, 57*.

103. AJVA Civil 1635–1803, *57*.

104. AJVA Civil 1734–97, *27*.

105. AJVA Civil 1759–97, *8*.

106. AJVA Criminal 1682–1816, *96*.

107. AGN Clero Secular y Regular 188, *12*.

108. Dahlgren de Jordán, pp. 62–63.

109. AJVA Criminal 1607–45, *4*.

110. AGN Indios 30, *322*.

111. Carmagnani, "Una forma mercantile," p. 141.

112. I do not wish to imply that competition for top offices was lacking in communities in other districts of Oaxaca and New Spain generally. My point is that the especially heavy repartimientos in the Villa Alta district made this region distinctive and that, within it, the Rincón stood out as the area with the greatest amount of "status seeking." The extent to which this phenomenon occurred elsewhere in colonial Mexico, and the role played by the Spanish magistrates in maintaining it, awaits further research.

113. These generalizations apply only tentatively to the Mixes, Chinantecs, and Cajonos Zapotecs, for which the late colonial data on stratification and cargos are quite thin. It is likely, however, that the pattern described for the Nexitzo and some Bixanos towns was not foreign to the other zones. The difference was probably one of degree rather than kind.

114. Nader, "The Zapotec," p. 349.

115. Nader, *Talea and Juquila*, p. 264.

116. Ibid., p. 253. I have chosen Talea for comparison because it shows the most parallels with the colonial data. This does not mean that Talea is necessarily "typical" of modern Rincón communities. Nader has shown that in Juquila, for example, the role of the principales is somewhat different. Unfortunately, the fine-grained comparison she makes between the two pueblos is not possible for the colonial period, given the sources available.

CHAPTER 6

1. De la Fuente, *Yalalag*, p. 274.

2. Marcus, "Archaeology and Religion," "Zapotec Religion."

3. Marcus, "Zapotec Religion," p. 345.

4. Ibid., p. 350.

5. Dávila Padilla, p. 635.

6. Ibid., p. 637; Burgoa, *Geográfica descripción*, 2:151.

7. Burgoa, *Geográfica descripción*, 2:168.

8. Dávila Padilla, p. 638.

9. AGI Justicia 191, *2*.

10. Ibid.

11. Burgoa, *Geográfica descripción*, 2:154–55.

12. Ibid., pp. 141–64. See chapter 3 for details on some of these congregaciones.

13. AGI México 358.

14. Burgoa, *Palestra*, p. 238.

15. AGI México 357.

16. AGN Reales Cédulas Duplicadas 47, *287*.

17. Burgoa, *Geográfica descripción*, 2:141–42, 148, 180, 206, 218, 222, 229, 232, 234; García Pimentel, p. 72; Gerhard, *Guide*, p. 372.

18. AGI México 880, 881, *13, 19*; Gay, 1:370.

19. Villaseñor y Sánchez, pp. 190–201; Orozco y Berra, pp. 177–83.

20. AGN Indios 4, *358*.

21. AGN Mercedes 5:175r.
22. AGN General de Parte 1, *205*.
23. AGI México 357 (1595); AGI México 879, *6* (1707).
24. AGN Indios 17, *130*.
25. AGN General de Parte 2, *1219* (Cajonos pueblos, 1581); AGI México 357 (twelve pueblos, 1595); AGN Inquisición 1, *13* (San Miguel Tiltepec, 1598); Zavala and Castelo, 7:369–71 (Totontepec, 1640); AGN Indios 30, *443* (Yae, 1691); AGI México 2588, *36, 38* (Cajonos pueblos and Yae, 1778); AGN Indios 69, *325* (Yaveo, 1794).
26. AJVA Criminal 1748–71, *18*.
27. AGN Civil 246, *8*.
28. AGI México 2588; AGN Indios 88:293–316.
29. AGN Indios 17, *130*.
30. AGI México 2588, *19*.
31. AGI México 2588, *22*.
32. AGI México 358; AGN Indios 17, *130*.
33. AGN Indios 58, *119*.
34. AGN Tierras 2931, *3*.
35. Farriss, *Maya Society*, p. 295. Chapter 10 of her work describes the model in detail and applies it to the Maya case.
36. Ibid., p. 296.
37. Marcus, "Zapotec Religion," pp. 345–47.
38. Farriss, *Maya Society*, p. 296.
39. AGI México 882.
40. AGI México 357.
41. Marcus, "Zapotec Religion," pp. 345, 349.
42. Farriss, *Maya Society*, p. 305.
43. Alcina Franch, "Calendarios zapotecos," p. 124, and "Calendario y religión," p. 214.
44. AGI México 882; AJVA Civil y Criminal 1701–50, *32*.
45. AGI México 882; Alcina Franch, "Calendarios zapotecos," "Calendario y religión"; Zilbermann. All ninety-nine surviving calendar books are from Zapotec pueblos; it is uncertain whether Mixes and Chinantecs used them as well.
46. AGI México 882; Alcina Franch, "Calendario y religión," pp. 216–17; AJVA Civil y Criminal 1701–50, *32*.
47. Ibid.
48. AGI México 882; AJVA Civil y Criminal 1701–50, *32, 36*.
49. The role of the shaman in the Sierra Zapoteca seems nearly identical to that described for the southern Zapotec region in the seventeenth century by Balsalobre. See Alcina Franch, "Calendario y religión."
50. Gillow, pp. 203–9.
51. Nader, "The Zapotec," p. 351.
52. Villa Rojas, pp. 21, 37, 55–57; Kuroda, pp. 71–84.
53. Farriss, *Maya Society*, p. 288.
54. Ibid., pp. 289–90.
55. AJVA Criminal 1607–95, *22*.
56. AJVA Criminal 1607–95, *7, 30*. An extract from the Yatee case, expediente 7, has been published by De la Fuente, "Documentos," pp. 182–83.
57. AJVA Criminal 1607–95, *32*.
58. AGI México 357.
59. AJVA Criminal 1682–1816, *3;* Gillow, p. 128.
60. AGI México 357.
61. The following account is based on the documents and summary published by Gillow, pp. 103–224.

62. The martyrs of Cajonos are also the subject of several large, mural-size paintings that adorn the walls of the church of San Juan de Dios in the city of Oaxaca today.

63. Gay, 2:368, 370.

64. AGI México 881, 882. These sources were cited in the previous discussion of universal and private religious practices in the district. Two other scholars have made extensive use of this material: Zilbermann and especially Alcina Franch, "Calendarios zapotecos," "Calendario y religión," and "Los dioses."

65. AJVA Civil y Criminal 1701–50, *32*.

66. Alcina Franch, "Calendario y religión," p. 218.

67. AJVA Civil y Criminal 1701–50, *36*.

68. AGI México 882.

69. AGI México 882; AJVA Civil y Criminal 1701–50, *32, 36*.

70. AJVA Civil y Criminal 1701–50, *32*.

71. AGI México 811, *11*; AGI México 882.

72. AJVA Civil y Criminal 1701–50, *4* (Yatee, 1706); AJVA Civil y Criminal 1682–1831, *42* (Yatzachi, 1710); AJVA Civil 1682–1882, *45* (Lalopa, 1714); AJVA Civil 1635–1803, *4* (Yalalag, 1735); AJVA Civil y Criminal 1697–1797, *13, 15* (Yalalag, 1735, extract published by De la Fuente, "Documentos," pp. 176–78); AGI México 2588 (Betaza, 1784); AGI México 2587 (Yae, 1784).

73. AJVA Civil y Criminal 1701–50, *32*.

74. The 1735 reference is to Yalalag, AJVA Civil y Criminal 1697–1797, *13, 15*. Communal ceremonies did not disappear everywhere at once and may have lasted longer in Mixe pueblos. Carrasco, "Ceremonias públicas," reports on one such ceremony that took place in Tamazulapan in 1951.

75. Farriss, *Maya Society*, p. 313.

76. Many observations are made in the records of the visita of Bishop Alonso de Ortigoza in the late 1770s and early 1780s (AGI México 2587, 2588).

77. AGN Indios 30, *448*.

78. AGN Tierras 282, *4*.

79. AGI México 2588, *29*.

80. Chance and Taylor, pp. 10–12.

81. AJVA Civil 1635–1803, *39*.

82. Records from the Mixe pueblo of Quetzaltepec and the Cajonos pueblo of Lachirioag in the seventeenth century make clear that responsibility for fiesta financing rested with the cabildo officials who used their towns' bienes de comunidad and took up collections from village households (AGN Tierras 165, *2*; AGN Indios 30, *370*).

83. AGI México 2587, 2588.

84. Gibson, *Aztecs*, p. 118.

85. AGI México 2587.

86. De la Fuente, *Yalalag*, p. 28; De la Fuente, *Relaciones*, pp. 26–27; Beals, p. 31; Nader, *Talea and Juquila*, pp. 236–37.

87. AJVA Civil y Criminal 1701–50, *32* (Betaza, 1703); AGI México 2588, *41* (Yaa, 1779); AJVA Civil 1779–1802, *14* (Yatoni, 1786); AJVA Civil y Criminal 1682–1831, *31* (Totontepec, 1789); AGN Tributos 25, *19* (Choapan, 1790); AJVA Civil 1793–1840, *33* (San Mateo Cajonos, 1807); AJVA Civil 1821–33, *5, 11* (Solaga and Roayaga, 1832); AJVA Civil 1821–33, *52* (Roayaga, 1832).

88. AJVA Civil y Criminal 1701–50, *32*; AJVA Civil 1779–1802, *71*.

89. AGN Tierras 1349, *1*.

90. AJVA Civil 1793–1840, *43*.

91. AJVA Civil 1821–33, *5, 11, 52*.

92. Chance and Taylor, pp. 17–20.

93. This matter is discussed at length in Chance and Taylor.

94. AGI México 2588, *49*.

95. This hypothesis has yet to be tested in full for the Sierra Zapoteca specifically, but evidence from several parts of colonial Mexico presented in Chance and Taylor makes it the most likely course of development. A modern civil-religious hierarchy in Mixe Tlahuitoltepec is described by Kuroda, chapter 4.

96. Nutini and Bell, pp. 288—304.

97. Madsen, pp. 378—79.

98. Farriss, *Maya Society*, chapter 10.

99. De la Fuente, *Yalalag*, p. 265; Beals, p. 88; Madsen, p. 388.

100. Madsen, p. 384.

CHAPTER 7

1. Van Young, pp. 56—57.

2. Ibid., p. 58.

3. Taylor, *Landlord and Peasant*, chapter 2.

4. Ibid.

5. My usage of the terms *class* and *status group* follows that of Max Weber. Class is wholly economically determined while status has to do with social honor and prestige.

6. This topic is discussed at greater length in Chance, "City and Country."

7. Stern, p. 189.

8. Ibid., pp. 189—90.

9. Roseberry, p. 66.

10. Foster-Carter, p. 74.

BIBLIOGRAPHY

MOST OF THE SOURCES employed in this study are unpublished, as one would expect for a region so little studied as the Sierra Zapoteca. Researching a little-known, peripheral region of colonial Mexico has both its rewards and its frustrations. While the present study led to the discovery of some new and unexpected material on colonial Indians and Spaniards, the unevenness of the documentation and the large gaps that exist for many topics proved to be a constant problem. I utilized four main archives: the Archivo del Juzgado de Villa Alta (AJVA) in Villa Alta, Oaxaca; the Archivo Parroquial de Villa Alta (APVA); the Archivo General de la Nación (AGN) in Mexico City; and the Archivo General de Indias (AGI) in Seville. An inventory of the colonial holdings of the AJVA can be found in my *Indice del Archivo del Juzgado de Villa Alta, Oaxaca: época colonial,* though the large quantity of nineteenth- and twentieth-century material remains to be catalogued. The Villa Alta Juzgado archive is one of the very few in Oaxaca known to contain large colonial holdings (it is second only to the Juzgado archive of Teposcolula in the Mixteca Alta), and without it this study would not have been possible. As of this writing, the colonial materials have been removed from the Villa Alta Juzgado and placed in the office of the Tribunal Superior de Justicia in the city of Oaxaca. While the organization of documents in *legajos* (bundles) described in my inventory no longer applies, it is hoped that none of the material was lost in the move.

Ostensibly, the Villa Alta municipal archive contains little or no documentation generated before the twentieth century. I did hear rumors that a quantity of old papers was stored in a private home somewhere in the village but was never able to confirm them. If such documents do indeed exist, they should be mainly from the nineteenth century, since Villa Alta had no *cabildo* between 1640 and the 1820s. Finally, it goes without saying that municipal and parish archives in the many villages in the area studied may contain valuable material. This remains uncharted territory.

Obviously, the greatest deficiencies in the historical record pertain to the pre-Conquest period. Apparently no pre-Hispanic manuscripts survived from the Sierra Zapoteca. Nor did many Spanish chroniclers pay much attention to the region, apart from Francisco de Burgoa, who wrote in the late seventeenth century. Of the surviving *relaciones geográficas* of 1579–81, so important for ethnohistorical reconstruction in many areas, none pertain to villages in the Villa Alta district. Nor is there any local equivalent of the Spanish-Zapotec dictionary and grammar for Valley Zapotec compiled by Fray Juan de Córdova in the midsixteenth century. The AJVA does contain a number of colonial documents written in Zapotec (using Roman script) and a few in Nahuatl, but all of these date to the seventeenth and eighteenth centuries. Given these limitations, I predict that further advances in our knowledge of the pre-Hispanic cultures of the region will come primarily from archaeology.

For the sixteenth century, most of the information on the Villa Alta district is located in the AGN and AGI; very little of it has been published. The Ramo Tierras of the AGN has many lawsuits over land that provide much valuable information. Other ramos I utilized extensively include Indios, Mercedes, General de Parte, and Reales Cédulas Duplicadas. Spores and Saldaña have published useful indexes of the Oaxaca material in the Ramos Mercedes, Indios, and Tributos of the AGN.

211

The AGI contains much valuable early material, most of it in the Audiencia de México section. Of special significance are three legajos that contain the papers of the *visita* of Bishop Angel Maldonado in the first decade of the eighteenth century. In addition to the "confessions" of shamans from throughout the district, they include ninety-nine Zapotec calendar books that were used for divination. The Justicia section contains a lengthy *residencia* taken on Villa Alta's first alcalde mayor, Luis de Berrio, in 1531 and the record of a 1539 trial of one of the early *corregidores* in the district.

The AJVA contains much of interest from the midseventeenth century onwards, particularly the late colonial civil suits over noble status that emanated from the Zapotec pueblos. Documentation is most plentiful for the Cajonos and Nexitzo Zapotec pueblos and often hard to come by for Bixanos Zapotec, Chinantec, and Mixe pueblos. Numerous criminal cases pertaining to assaults, homicides, and thefts were not utilized in this book.

The APVA is small and contains mainly registers of vital statistics for Villa Alta and a few surrounding Indian communities, beginning in the eighteenth century. One significant exception is a bundle of papers pertaining to the lands of Analco that dates back to the sixteenth century.

Ajofrín, Fray Francisco de. *Diario del viaje que por orden de la Sagrada Congregación de Propaganda Fide hizo a la América septentrional en el siglo XVIII*. 2 vols. Madrid: Real Academia de Historia, 1958–59.

Alcina Franch, José. "Calendario y religión entre los zapotecos serranos durante el siglo XVII," in *Mesamérica: Homenaje al Doctor Paul Kirchhoff*, coordinated by Barbro Dahlgren, pp. 212–24. Mexico City: Instituto National de Antropología e Historia, 1979.

———. "Calendarios zapotecos prehispánicos según documentos de los siglos XVI y XVII," *Estudios de Cultura Nahuatl* 6 (1966): 119–33.

———. "Los dioses del panteón zapoteco," *Anales de Antropología* 9 (1972): 9–43.

Anderson, Arthur J. O., Frances Berdan, and James Lockhart, trans. and eds. *Beyond the Codices: The Nahua View of Colonial Mexico*. Berkeley and Los Angeles: University of California Press, 1976.

Barlow, Robert H. *The Extent of the Empire of the Culhua Mexica*. Ibero-Americana, no. 28. Berkeley and Los Angeles: University of California Press, 1949.

Beals, Ralph L. *The Ethnology of the Western Mixe*. University of California Publications in American Archaeology and Ethnology 42 (1945): 1–176. Berkeley.

Berg, Richard Lewis, Jr. *El impacto de la economía moderna sobre la economía tradicional de Zoogocho, Oaxaca y su area circundante*. Trans. Victoria Miret and Ana Zagury. Mexico City: Instituto Nacional Indigenista, 1974.

Bevan, Bernard. *The Chinantec and Their Habitat*. Instituto Panamericano de Geografía e Historia, Pub. 24. Mexico City, 1938.

Blom, Franz. "El Lienzo de Analco, Oaxaca," *Cuadernos Americanos* 4 (1945): 125–36.

Borah, Woodrow, and Sherburne F. Cook. *The Aboriginal Population of Central Mexico on the Eve of the Spanish Conquest*. Ibero-Americana, no. 45. Berkeley and Los Angeles: University of California Press, 1963.

———. *The Population of Central Mexico in 1548: An Analysis of the "Suma de visitas de pueblos."* Ibero-Americana, no 43. Berkeley and Los Angeles: University of California Press, 1960.

Brockington, Lolita Gutiérrez. *The Leverage of Labor: Managing the Cortés Haciendas in Tehuantepec, 1588–1688*. Durham and London: Duke University Press, 1989.

Burgoa, Fray Francisco de. *Geográfica descripción*. 2 vols., 2d ed. Mexico City: Talleres Gráficos de la Nación, 1934.

———. *Palestra historial*. Mexico City: Talleres Gráficos de la Nación, 1934.

Bustamante, Carlos María de. *Cuadro histórico de la revolución mexicana*. 5 vols. Mexico City: Talleres Linotipográficos "Soría," 1926.

Cancian, Frank. *Economics and Prestige in a Maya Community*. Stanford: Stanford University Press, 1965.

Carmagnani, Marcello. "Local Governments and Ethnic Government in Oaxaca," in *Essays in the Political, Economic and Social History of Colonial Latin America*, ed. Karen Spalding, pp. 107–23. Newark, Del.: University of Delaware, 1982.

———. "Los recursos y los estrategias de los recursos en la reproducción de la sociedad india de Oaxaca," *Nova Americana* (Torino) 4 (1981): 263–80.

———. "Una forma mercantile coatta: Il "repartimiento" nella regione messicana de Oaxaca nell'ultimo terzo del secolo XVIII," *Wirtschaftskräfte und Wirtschaftswege*, vol. 4: *Übersee und allgemeine wirtschaftsgeshichte*, pp. 139–45. Stuttgart: Klett Cotta, 1978.

Carrasco, Pedro. "Ceremonias públicas paganas entre los mixes de Tamazulapan," in *Summa anthropológica en homenaje a Roberto J. Weitlaner*, pp. 309–12. Mexico City: Instituto Nacional de Antropología e Historia, 1966.

———. "Family Structure of Sixteenth-Century Tepoztlan," in *Process and Pattern in Culture: Essays in Honor of Julian H. Steward*, ed. Robert A. Manners, pp. 185–210. Chicago: Aldine, 1964.

Censo general de habitantes, 30 noviembre de 1921, Estado de Oaxaca. Mexico City: Talleres Gráficos de la Nación, 1927.

VIII Censo general de población, 1960, Estado de Oaxaca. Vol. 1. Mexico City: Dirección General de Estadística, 1963.

IX Censo general de población, 1970. Vol. 11. Mexico City: Dirección General de Estadística, 1973.

Chance, John K. "City and Country in Colonial Oaxaca: An Economic View," *Journal of the Steward Anthropological Society* 10 (1979): 105–14.

———. "Colonial Ethnohistory of Oaxaca," *Supplement to the Handbook of Middle American Indians*, vol. 4, ed. Victoria R. Bricker and Ronald Spores, pp. 165–89. Austin: University of Texas Press, 1986.

———. *Indice del Archivo del Juzgado de Villa Alta, Oaxaca: Epoca colonial*. Vanderbilt University Publications in Anthropology, no. 21. Nashville, 1978.

———. "Kinship and Urban Residence: Household and Family Organization in a Suburb of Oaxaca, Mexico," *Journal of the Steward Anthropological Society* 2 (1971): 122–47.

———. *Race and Class in Colonial Oaxaca*. Stanford: Stanford University Press, 1978.

———. "Social Stratification and the Civil Cargo System among the Rincón Zapotecs of Oaxaca: The Late Colonial Period," in *Iberian Colonies, New World Societies: Essays in Memory of Charles Gibson*, ed. Richard L. Garner and William B. Taylor, pp. 143–59. 2d ed. Private printing, 1985.

———. "The Urban Indian in Colonial Oaxaca," *American Ethnologist* 3 (1976): 603–32.

Chance, John K., and William B. Taylor. "Cofradías and Cargos: An Historical Perspective on the Mesoamerican Civil-Religious Hierarchy," *American Ethnologist* 12 (1985): 1–26.

Cline, Howard F. "Native Pictorial Documents of Eastern Oaxaca, Mexico," in *Summa Anthropológica en homenaje a Roberto J. Weitlaner*, pp. 101–30. Mexico City: Instituto Nacional de Antropología e Historia, 1966.

———, ed. *Papeles de la Chinantla*, vol. 3. Mexico City: Museo Nacional de Antropología. 1961. (Original ed., 1910, by Mariano Espínosa.)

Colección de documentos inéditos relativos al descubrimiento, conquista y organización de las antiguas posesiones españolas de América y Oceanía, sacados de los archivos del reino, y muy especialmente del de Indias. 42 vols. Madrid: Imprenta de Frías y Compañía, 1864–84.

Cook, Sherburne, F., and Woodrow Borah. "An Essay On Method," in their *Essays in Population History* 1: 73–118. Berkeley and Los Angeles: University of California Press, 1971.

———. *The Indian Population of Central Mexico, 1531–1610*. Ibero-Americana, no. 44. Berkeley and Los Angeles: University of California Press, 1960.

———. *The Population of the Mixteca Alta, 1520–1960*. Ibero-Americana, no. 50. Berkeley and Los Angeles: University of California Press, 1968.

———. "Royal Revenues and the Indian Population of New Spain, ca. 1620–1646," in their

Essays in Population History 3 : 1 – 128. Berkeley and Los Angeles: University of California Press, 1979.

Cortés, Hernán. *Cartas y documentos,* ed. Mario Hernández Sánchez-Barba. Mexico City: Porrúa, 1963.

Cuevas, Mariano, ed. *Documentos inéditos del siglo XVI para la historia de México.* Mexico City: Talleres del Museo Nacional, 1914.

Dahlgren de Jordán, Barbro, compiler. *La grana cochinilla.* Mexico City: J. Porrua, 1963.

Davenport, William. "Nonunilinear Descent and Descent Groups," *American Anthropologist* 61 (1959): 557 – 72.

Dávila Padilla, Agustín. *Historia de la fundación y discurso de la provincia de Santiago de México, de la Orden de Predicadores.* 3d ed. Mexico City: Editorial Academia Literaría, 1955.

De La Fuente, Julio. "Algunos problemas etnológicos de Oaxaca," *Anales del Instituto Nacional de Antropología e Historia* 4 (1952): 241 – 52.

――――. "La cultura zapoteca," *Revista Mexicana de Estudios Antropológicos* 16 (1960): 233 – 46.

――――. "Documentos para la etnografía e historia zapoteca," *Anales del Instituto Nacional de Antropología e Historia* 3 (1949): 175 – 97.

――――. "Notas sobre lugares de Oaxaca, con especial referencia a la toponimia zapoteca," *Anales del Instituto Nacional de Antropología e Historia* 2 (1947): 279 – 92.

――――. *Relaciones interétnicas.* Mexico City: Instituto Nacional Indigenísta, 1965.

――――. *Yalalag: Una villa zapoteca serrana.* Mexico City: Museo Nacional de Antropología, 1949.

――――. "Los zapotecos de Choapan, Oaxaca," *Anales del Instituto Nacional de Antropología e Historia* 2 (1947): 143 – 205.

Díaz del Castillo, Bernal. *Historia verdadera de la conquista de la Nueva España.* Mexico City: Porrúa, 1966.

Díez de la Calle, Juan. *Memorial y noticias sacras y reales de las Indias Occidentales.* 2d ed. Mexico City: Bibliófilos Mexicános, 1932.

División territorial de los Estados Unidos Mexicanos correspondiente al censo de 1910, Estado de Oaxaca. Mexico City: Dirección de Estadística, 1918.

División territorial de la República Mexicana formada con los datos del censo verificado el 28 de octubre de 1900, Estado de Oaxaca. Mexico City: Dirección General de Estadística, 1906.

Esteva, Cayetano. *Nociones elementales de geografía histórica del Estado de Oaxaca.* Oaxaca: San Hernán Hnos., 1913.

Farriss, Nancy M. *Maya Society under Colonial Rule: The Collective Enterprise of Survival.* Princeton: Princeton University Press, 1984.

――――. "Nucleation versus Dispersal: The Dynamics of Population Movement in Colonial Yucatan," *Hispanic American Historical Review* 58 (1978): 187 – 216.

Flannery, Kent V., and Joyce Marcus, eds. *The Cloud People: Divergent Evolution of the Zapotec and Mixtec Civilizations.* New York: Academic Press, 1983.

Foster-Carter, Aidan. "The Modes of Production Controversy," *New Left Review* 107 (1978): 47 – 77.

García Martinez, Bernardo. *Los pueblos de la sierra: El poder y el espacio entre los indios del norte de Puebla hasta 1700.* Mexico City: El Colegio de México, 1987.

García Pimentel, Luis, ed. *Relación de los obispados de Tlaxcala, Michoacán, Oaxaca y otros lugares en el siglo XVI.* Mexico City: Casa del Editor, 1904.

Gay, José Antonio. *Historia de Oaxaca.* 2 vols. Mexico City: Talleres "Verano," 1950.

Gerhard, Peter. "Colonial New Spain, 1519 – 1786: Historical Notes on the Evolution of Minor Political Jurisdictions," in *Handbook of Middle American Indians,* vol. 12, ed. Robert Wauchope and Howard F. Cline, pp. 63 – 137. Austin: University of Texas Press, 1972.

――――. "Congregaciones de indios en la Nueva España antes de 1570." *Historia Mexicana* 26 (1977): 347 – 95.

――――. *A Guide to the Historical Geography of New Spain.* Cambridge: University Press, 1972.

———. *México en 1742*. Mexico City: José Porrúa e Hijos, 1962.

Gibson, Charles. *The Aztecs under Spanish Rule*. Stanford: Stanford University Press, 1964.

———. *Spain in America*. New York: Harper & Row, 1966.

Gillow, Eulogio G. *Apuntes históricos*. Mexico City: Imprenta del Sagrado Corazón de Jesús, 1889.

Glass, John B., with Donald Robertson. "A Census of Native Middle American Pictorial Manuscripts," in *Handbook of Middle American Indians*, vol. 14, ed. Robert Wauchope and Howard F. Cline, pp. 81–252. Austin: University of Texas Press, 1975.

Hamnett, Brian R. "Dye Production, Food Supply, and the Laboring Population of Oaxaca, 1750–1820," *Hispanic American Historical Review* 51 (1971): 51–78.

———. *Politics and Trade in Southern Mexico, 1750–1821*. London: Cambridge University Press, 1971.

Harvey, H. R., and Hanns J. Prem, eds. *Explorations in Ethnohistory: Indians of Central Mexico in the Sixteenth Century*. Albuquerque: University of New Mexico Press, 1984.

Herrera y Tordesillas, Antonio de. *Historia general de los hechos de los castellanos en las islas y tierrafirme del mar océano*. 17 vols. Madrid: Tipografía de Archivos, 1934–57.

Hunt, Eva. "Irrigation and the Socio-Political Organization of Cuicatec Cacicazgos," in *The Prehistory of the Tehuacan Valley*, vol. 4, ed. Fredrick Johnson, pp. 162–259. Austin: University of Texas Press, 1972.

Icaza, Francisco A. de. *Conquistadores y pobladores de Nueva España*. 2 vols. Madrid: Imprenta de "El Adelantado de Segovia," 1923.

Kirchhoff, Paul. "The Principles of Clanship in Human Society," in *Readings in Anthropology*, ed. Morton H. Fried, 2:259–70. 2d ed. New York: Crowell, 1968.

Kubler, George. *Mexican Architecture of the Sixteenth Century*. 2 vols. New Haven: Yale University Press, 1948.

Kuroda, Etsuko. *Under Mt. Zempoatépetl: Highland Mixe Society and Ritual*. Osaka, Japan: National Museum of Ethnology, 1984.

Laviada, Iñigo. *Los caciques de la sierra*. Mexico City: Editorial Jus, 1978.

Lee, Raymond L. "Cochineal Production and Trade in New Spain to 1600," *The Americas* 4 (1948): 449–73.

Lemoine V., Ernesto. "Algunos datos histórico-geográficos acerca de Villa Alta y su comarca," in *Summa Antropológica en homenaje a Roberto J. Weitlaner*, pp. 193–202. Mexico City: Instituto Nacional de Antropología e Historia, 1966.

López de Velasco, Juan. *Geografía y descripción universal de las Indias*. Madrid: Fortanet, 1894.

López Sarrelangue, Delfina Esmeralda. *La nobleza indígena de Pátzcuaro en la época virreinal*. Mexico City: Universidad Nacional Autónoma de México, 1965.

MacLeod, Murdo J., and Robert Wasserstrom, eds. *Spaniards and Indians in Southwestern Mesoamerica: Essays on the History of Ethnic Relations*. Lincoln: University of Nebraska Press, 1983.

Madsen, William. "Religious Syncretism," in *Handbook of Middle American Indians*, vol. 6, ed. Robert Wauchope and Manning Nash, pp. 369–91. Austin: University of Texas Press, 1967.

Marcus, Joyce. "Archaeology and Religion: A Comparison of the Zapotec and Maya," in *Ancient Mesoamerica: Selected Readings*, ed. John A. Graham, pp. 297–314. 2d ed. Palo Alto: Peek Publications, 1981.

———. "Aztec Military Campaigns against the Zapotecs: The Documentary Evidence," in *The Cloud People: Divergent Evolution of the Zapotec and Mixtec Civilizations*, ed. Kent V. Flannery and Joyce Marcus, pp. 314–18. New York: Academic Press, 1983.

———. "Zapotec Religion," in *The Cloud People: Divergent Evolution of the Zapotec and Mixtec Civilizations*, ed. Kent V. Flannery and Joyce Marcus, pp. 345–51. New York: Academic Press, 1983.

Martínez Gracida, Manuel. *Colección de cuadros sinópticos de los pueblos, haciendas y ranchos del Estado de Oaxaca*. Oaxaca: Imprenta del Estado, 1883.

Miranda, José. "Evolución cuantitativa y desplazamientos de la población indígena de Oaxaca en la época colonial," in *Estudios de historia novohispana* 2 : 129–47. Mexico City: Universidad Nacional Autónoma de México, 1967.

Murguía y Galardi, José María. "Extracto general que abraza la estadística toda en su primera y segunda parte del estado de Guaxaca y ha reunido de orden del Supremo Gobierno y yntendente de provincia en clase de los cesantes José María Murguía y Galardi." 1827. Unpublished manuscript, Benson Latin American Collection, University of Texas-Austin.

Nader, Laura. *Talea and Juquila: A Comparison of Zapotec Social Organization.* University of California Publications in American Archaeology and Ethnology 48 (3): 195–296. Berkeley: University of California Press, 1964.

————. "The Zapotec of Oaxaca," in *Handbook of Middle American Indians*, vol. 7, ed. Robert Wauchope and Evon Z. Vogt, pp. 329 59. Austin: University of Texas Press, 1969.

Nutini, Hugo G., and Betty Bell. *Ritual Kinship: The Structure and Historical Development of the Compadrazgo System in Rural Tlaxcala.* Princeton: Princeton University Press, 1980.

Olivera, Mercedes, and María de los Angeles Romero. "La estructura política de Oaxaca en el siglo XVI," *Revista Mexicana de Sociología* 35 (1973): 227–87.

Orozco y Berra, Manuel. *Geografía de las lenguas y carta etnográfica de México.* Mexico City: J. M. Andrade y F. Escalante, 1864.

Paddock, John, ed. *Ancient Oaxaca.* Stanford: Stanford University Press, 1966.

Paso y Troncoso, Francisco del, ed. *Epistolario de Nueva España, 1505–1818.* 16 vols. Mexico City: Robredo y Porruá e Hijos, 1939–42.

————. *Papeles de Nueva España.* 9 vols. Madrid: Sucesores de Rivadeneyra and Hauser y Menet, 1905–36.

Pastor, Rodolfo. "El repartimiento de mercancías y los alcaldes mayores novohispanos: Un sistema de explotación, de sus origenes a la crisis de 1810," in *El gobierno provincial en la Nueva España, 1570–1787*, coord. Woodrow Borah, pp. 201–49. Mexico City: Universidad Autónoma de México, 1985.

————. *Campesinos y reformas: La Mixteca, 1700–1856.* Mexico City: El Colegio de Mexico, 1987.

Pérez García, Rosendo. *La Sierra Juárez.* 2 vols. Mexico City: Gráfica Cervantina, 1956.

Quinto censo de población, 1930, Oaxaca. Mexico City: Dirección General de Estadistica, 1935.

Reeck, Roger. "The Languages of the Sierra Zapoteca." Unpublished manuscript.

Romero Frizzi, María de los Angeles, *Economía y vida de los españoles en la Mixteca Alta, 1519–1720.* Ph.D. Dissertation, Universidad Iberoamericana, 1985.

Romero Frizzi, María de los Angeles, and Ronald M. Spores, comps. *Indice del Archivo del Juzgado de Teposcolula, Oaxaca: Epoca colonial.* Mexico City: Instituto Nacional de Antropología e Historia, 1976.

Romney, A. Kimball. "Kinship and Family," in *Handbook of Middle American Indians*, vol. 6, ed. Robert Wauchope and Manning Nash, pp. 207–37. Austin: University of Texas Press, 1967.

Roseberry, William. *Coffee and Capitalism in the Venezuelan Andes.* Austin: University of Texas Press, 1983.

Schmieder, Oscar. *The Settlements of the Tzapotec and Mije Indians.* University of California Publications in Geography 4 : 1–184. Berkeley, 1930.

Séptimo censo general de población, 6 de junio de 1950, Estado de Oaxaca. Mexico City: Dirección General de Estadística, 1953.

Sexto censo de población, 1940, Oaxaca. Mexico City: Dirección General de Estadística, 1948.

Spores, Ronald M. *The Mixtec Kings and Their People.* Norman: University of Oklahoma Press, 1967.

————. *The Mixtecs in Ancient and Colonial Times.* Norman: University of Oklahoma Press, 1984.

Spores, Ronald, and Miguel Saldaña, compilers. *Documentos para la etnohistoria del Estado de*

Oaxaca: Indice del Ramo de Indios del Archivo General de la Nación, México. Vanderbilt University Publications in Anthropology, no. 13. Nashville, Tenn., 1975.

————. *Documentos para la etnohistoria del Estado de Oaxaca: Indice del Ramo de Mercedes del Archivo General de la Nación, México.* Vanderbilt University Publications in Anthropology, no. 5. Nashville, Tenn., 1973.

————. *Documentos para la etnohistoria del Estado de Oaxaca: Indice del Ramo de Tributos del Archivo General de la Nación, México.* Vanderbilt University Publications in Anthropology, no. 17. Nashville, Tenn., 1976.

Stein, Stanley J. "Bureaucracy and Business in the Spanish Empire, 1759–1804: Failure of a Bourbon Reform in Mexico and Peru," *Hispanic American Historical Review* 61 (1981): 2–28.

Stern, Steve J. *Peru's Indian Peoples and the Challenge of Spanish Conquest.* Madison: University of Wisconsin Press, 1982.

Taylor, William B. *Drinking, Homicide and Rebellion in Colonial Mexican Villages.* Stanford: Stanford University Press, 1979.

————. "Landed Society in New Spain: A View from the South," *Hispanic American Historical Review* 54 (1974): 387–413.

————. *Landlord and Peasant in Colonial Oaxaca.* Stanford: Stanford University Press, 1972.

Van Young, Eric. "Conflict and Solidarity in Indian Village Life: The Guadalajara Region in the Late Colonial Period," *Hispanic American Historical Review* 64 (1984): 55–79.

Varner, John Grier, and Jeannette Johnson Varner. *Dogs of the Conquest.* Norman: University of Oklahoma Press, 1983.

Villa Rojas, Alfonso. "Notas introductorias sobre la condición cultural de los mijes," in *Cuentos mixes,* ed. Walter S. Miller, pp. 13–69. Mexico City: Instituto Nacional Indigenista, 1956.

Villaseñor y Sánchez, Joseph Antonio. *Theatro americano: Descripción general de los reynos, y provincias de la Nueva-España, y sus jurisdicciones.* 2 vols. Mexico City: Editora Nacional, 1952 (facsimile copy of 1746–48 ed.).

Wallerstein, Immanuel. *The Modern World-System: Capitalist Agriculture and the Origins of the European World-Economy in the Sixteenth Century.* New York: Academic Press, 1974.

Weber, Max. "Class, Status, Party," in *From Max Weber: Essays in Sociology,* ed. H. H. Gerth and C. Wright Mills, pp. 180–95. New York: Oxford University Press, 1958.

Weitlaner, Roberto J., and Howard F. Cline. "The Chinantec," in *Handbook of Middle American Indians,* vol. 7, ed. Robert Wauchope and Evon Z. Vogt, pp. 523–52. Austin: University of Texas Press, 1969.

Whitecotton, Joseph W. *The Zapotecs: Princes, Priests, and Peasants.* Norman: University of Oklahoma Press, 1977.

Wolf, Eric. *Sons of the Shaking Earth.* Chicago: University of Chicago Press, 1959.

Zavala, Silvio, and María Castelo, eds. *Fuentes para la historia del trabajo en Nueva España.* 8 vols. Mexico City: Fonda de Cultura Económica, 1939–46.

Zeitlin, Judith F. "Colonialism and the Political Transformation of Isthmus Zapotec Society," in *Five Centuries of Law and Politics in Central Mexico,* ed. Ronald Spores and Ross Hassig, pp. 68–85. Vanderbilt University Publications in Anthropology, no. 30. Nashville, Tenn., 1984.

Zilbermann, María Cristina. "Idolatrías de Oaxaca en el siglo XVIII," in XXXVI *Congreso Internacional de Americanistas: Actas y Memorias* 2:111–23. Seville, 1966.

INDEX